THE CASE MANAGEMENT SOURCEBOOK

A Guide to Designing and Implementing a Centralized Case Management System

CHERILYN G. MURER, J.D., C.R.A.
President, Murer Consultants, Inc.

LYNDEAN LENHOFF BRICK, J.D.
Senior Vice President, Murer Consultants, Inc.

HFMA® Healthcare Financial Management Association

McGraw-Hill
New York   San Francisco   Washington, D.C.   Auckland   Bogotá
Caracas   Lisbon   London   Madrid   Mexico City   Milan
Montreal   New Delhi   San Juan   Singapore
Sydney   Tokyo   Toronto

Library of Congress Cataloging–in–Publication Data

Murer, Cherilyn G.

    The case management sourcebook : a guide to designing and implementing a centralized case management system / by Cherilyn G. Murer and Lyndean Lenhoff Brick.

       p.   cm.

    Includes index.

    ISBN 0-7863-1221-1

    1. Hospitals--Case management services.   I. Brick, Lyndean Lenhoff.   II. Title.

    [DNLM: 1. Case Management.   2. Medical Informatics Applications.   3. Decision Making.   W 84.7 M975c 1997]

RA975.5.C36M87   1997

362.1'1'068--dc21

DNLM/DLC

for Library of Congress   97-12459

                                                                        CIP

McGraw-Hill

A Division of The **McGraw·Hill** Companies

2 3 4 5 6 7 8 9   BKM BKM   9 0 9 8 7 6 5 4 3 2 1 0 9

ISBN 0-7863-1000-6

Printed and bound by Book-mart Press, Inc.

This publication is designed to provide accurate and authoritative information in regard to the subject matter covered. It is sold with the understanding that neither the author nor the publisher is engaged in rendering legal, accounting, or other professional service. If legal advice or other expert assistance is required, the services of a competent professional person should be sought.

        —From a Declaration of Principles jointly adopted by a Committee of the American Bar Association and a Committee of Publishers.

McGraw-Hill books are available at special quantity discounts to use as premiums and sales promotions, or for use in corporate training programs. For more information, please write to the Director of Sales, McGraw-Hill, 11 West 19th Street, New York, NY 10011. Or contact your local bookstore.

ACKNOWLEDGEMENTS

The authors would like to express their gratitude to the tireless and dedicated staff of Murer Consultants, Inc., for their many contributions to the manuscript: Virginia Odegaard, Debra Frost, Andrea Figueroa, Janet Barile, and Lisa Furtak. Without their typing, graphic design, suggestions, camaraderie, and encouragement, the manuscript would never have taken shape.

Special thanks to our colleagues, Jayme Matchinski, J.D., and Deidre Donnellan, J.D., for their valuable input to and assistance with Chapters 6 and 8.

We are enormously grateful to John F. Haughton, M.D., M.S., FAAPMR, Vice President for Medical Affairs, Whittier Health Network, Haverhill, Massachusetts, for his significant contribution to Chapter 5. He is a leader in case management system technology, and we greatly benefited from his technical assistance and expertise.

Myron Brick is owed a deep gratitude for his copyediting, perspective suggestions, and thought-provoking dinner conversations.

Our partner, Michael Murer, J.D., provided unparalleled support and professional assistance. He is the consummate ally, and his astral insight foresaw the need for the book. He was also responsible for the context and content of Chapter 7.

And finally to a field of hard-working case managers, whose professionalism and vision make this book possible.

Cherilyn G. Murer, J.D., C.R.A.
President, Murer Consultants, Inc.
and
Lyndean Lenhoff Brick, J.D.
Senior Vice President, Murer Consultants, Inc.

F O R E W O R D

Although the concept of case management has been in existence since the early 1900s, becoming well known for its efforts in controlling worker's health care costs through the 1970s, case management today is being noticed as the most cost-effective approach to meeting the needs of managed care organizations in today's health care environment. This text addresses all aspects of case management, including its emergence, the systems of case management, how to implement a centralized case management model, legal responsibilities of case managers, and the future of case management.

Case management is a rapidly evolving profession demanding viable functional and financial outcomes in the management of episodes of illness through the complex healthcare system in existence today. As we all are aware, health care consumers are requiring cost-effective, quality healthcare services. Besides patients, these consumers include employer groups, and state and federal governments with expanded administration of Medicare and Medicaid managed care programs. Although many believe that case management is effective in controlling costs and providing co-ordinated, appropriate care, the efficacy of case management through outcomes and performance measures is yet to be defined. Outcome studies are currently underway to improve the credibility and document the value that case management brings to the healthcare arena.

Case management as a component of an integrated healthcare system is still in its infancy. Case management activities in today's integrated healthcare systems environment primarily focus on the acute segment of healthcare. An expanded focus must take priority to implement models that manage disease states across the healthcare continuum. Additionally, integration of levels of care is beginning to be developed. In most systems today, patients are transferred from levels of care in a coordinated manner. Many clinical pathways have been developed to manage patients through a particular level of care, but expansion to include a broader focus that addresses the various levels of care and a complete episode of illness is necessary. Case management systems in integrated health delivery systems must focus across the healthcare continuum to effectively lower costs and promote positive health outcomes.

The rapid increase in enrollment in entitlement programs such as Medicare and Medicaid managed care will be an important stimulus to the growth of case management in the future. Medicaid managed care is currently the fastest growing managed care program in the nation, and the fastest growing segment of case management. It is estimated that by the year 2001, over fifty percent of all Medicaid recipients nationwide will be enrolled in some form of managed care program. Medicare enrollment is also increasing with the number of risk contractors entering the market.

With the rapid growth of both Medicare and Medicaid managed care, there is a critical need to develop case management models that meet the needs of these high-risk populations. They represent significantly higher costs, many with disabilities and chronic and complex healthcare needs. Case management that is patient-focused, spans the continuum of care, and provides measurable outcomes is crucial to the success of these programs.

As Health Maintenance Organizations expand in the future, they will be required to demonstrate their ability to manage the wellness of their members in addition to management of disease programs. NCQA and HEDIS will continue to expand their indicators to measure quality of care in healthcare systems. Consumers of healthcare are also turning their attention to the results of this information which is beginning to be published in many markets.

With the evolution of integrated health care delivery systems, case management must evolve in consonance with the delivery systems to provide appropriate, high-quality care. Case managers are being held accountable for the measurement of functional and financial outcomes. Employers, payors, and patients are demanding this accountability.

Provider-based case management models where physicians function as the case manager are popular in many managed care systems. These models often compensate the physician for this service, and generally there are financial incentives for physicians to control costs. Patient outcome and satisfaction, in addition to other measures are used to evaluate the physician's performance under these models. Many large insurers like Mutual of Omaha Companies' Managed Health Care Operations are supportive of provider-based systems of case management for a number of reasons. First, under a capitated, shared-risk model, it is imperative that all parties focus on appropriate use of services. Although oversight and appropriate delegation of services are contractually arranged, integrated systems that provide case management can be effective in the management of healthcare for today's managed care patient. The payor-based case manager can effectively assist the physician with the coordination of plan benefits and the ability to be creative in the authorization of those benefits. Flexibility in plan design to meet patients' individual needs is imperative to successful case management services.

Secondly, provider-based systems of case management can be more effective and efficient in the delivery of case management services. Coordination of appropriate care is driven by the primary care physician as the case manager. Appropriate utilization of services and referral to specialty services by the primary care physician enhances the patient's health outcomes.

Lastly, physicians like to be in control of their patient's care and maintain coordination of their healthcare needs. In this provider-based model of case management, they remain in charge of their patient's care, which leads to greater autonomy and physician satisfaction with the managed care organization.

The future of healthcare depends upon quality, patient-centered case management. In *The Case Management Sourcebook,* you will acquire the information needed to successfully deliver efficient case management services that will offer a valuable service to the healthcare delivery team.

Marcia A. Friesen, R.N., B.S., C.C.M., ABQAURP
Plan Manager, Medicare/Medicaid Managed Care Programs
Mutual of Omaha

CONTENTS

1

The Case for Case Management

Virtually everyone has heard that the American system of healthcare is in crisis. Millions have limited access to care; we spend more per capita on healthcare than any other nation without demonstrably better outcomes; and the bureaucratic and exceedingly complex nature of the system equally frustrates the patient, the provider, and the payor.

In this complicated healthcare system, case management is the process by which care delivery is assessed and guided. It has become the primary tool to effectively serve patients with numerous and complex needs while simultaneously seeking to reduce utilization and costs. Case management has become all the more necessary as the development of nonacute hospital care providers have expanded the so-called healthcare "continuum." The sheer magnitude and diversity of healthcare options today, compounded by increasing reimbursement and regulatory complexity, has resulted in a fragmented healthcare delivery. Issues of access, government bureaucracy, and limited healthcare dollars compound the problems. Case management has emerged as the necessary link to piece together and navigate such a system.

These problems are not new. In the late 1960s and early 1970s, public activism seemed to advocate some form of comprehensive national healthcare program to address the inequities and inefficiencies of the American healthcare system. During this period, Congress enacted sweeping Medicaid and Medicare amendments to the Social Security Act of 1964, which provided significantly more coverage and services to a much larger segment of America. In 1970, Senator Edward Kennedy made the first of his many attempts over the next 20 years to enact a national healthcare plan. Subsequent proposals to cure the ills of healthcare were forthcoming from nearly all branches of government. This level of legislative activity regarding healthcare alarmed many business leaders. Although corporate America clearly understood that healthcare costs were out of control, they feared a national system of healthcare that would force businesses to pay an even larger portion of the country's healthcare costs. Moreover, they were deeply concerned that the government would continually seek to regulate more aspects of their relationships with employees. Rather than opting for a socialized system of healthcare, business leaders initiated a 25-year campaign to cut costs through the introduction of competition and accountability into the healthcare marketplace.

Indeed, the influence of corporate America is largely responsible for our present healthcare system of *managed competition*. That is, competition is implemented through the regulatory power of the State and it is this mandated competition that will address problems such as escalating costs, overutilization, inadequate access, and poor quality. To this end, corporate leaders pushed for legislation creating the first Health Maintenance Organizations (HMOs). These early HMOs offered promise of full coverage for employees at lower costs. Cost containment measures became an operational necessity for plans and insurers offering new managed products.

Today, managed competition is implemented through what has commonly become known as *managed care*. Gorski[1] describes the evolution of managed care as comprising five different phases: (1) carrying out utilization reviews and restricting access, (2) managing benefit use, (3) managing care with a primary emphasis on cost control, (4) managing outcomes, and

(5) integrating managed care systems horizontally and vertically. At each phase of managed care, the successful implementation of managed competition depends on a cohesive and centralized system of case management. Indeed, case management has become recognized as an essential component of managed care. The cornerstone proposed to contain costs through managed care is case management.

The concept focuses on a series of techniques that involve planning, care coordination, education, utilization review, and patient and family advocacy. Historically, case management has been defined as a process that assists in coordinating access to medically necessary care for individuals. *Mosby's Medical, Nursing, and Allied Health Dictionary,* 4th edition, refers to the process as "the assignment of a health care provider to assist a patient in assessing health and social service systems and to assure that all required services are obtained." The term has been applied to such disparate functions as referral source generation, prior authorization of service by the payor, service coordination, and even counseling. In its broadest context, case management has been applied to quasi-medical services in order to coordinate the involvement of entities such as local education authorities, vocational rehabilitation agencies, and custodial care providers to enable an individual to function at the highest attainable level within the least restrictive situs of care.

The underlying premise of case management is that active oversight of healthcare delivery will ensure that individuals receive appropriate and quality service in a cost-effective manner. Notwithstanding the relative simplicity of the concept of case management, its successful execution is exceedingly complex and widely misunderstood. Countless systems generically labeled "case management" seek to influence patient care and outcome. As many definitions of case management exist as practitioners. It is difficult to find consensus in the industry concerning even the basics of case management. Which patients ought to be managed? What is the role of the case manager? Is case management only episodic? Who ought to pay for case management? For whom does the case manager work? And, even, does case management work? About the only point of agreement is that case management is a prerequisite to the ongoing successful reform of the healthcare system.

Since the early 1990s, targeted healthcare reform has been on the national agenda. Escalating costs specific to the healthcare industry, coupled with an increase in the volume and complexity of service delivery, have largely accounted for the rise in healthcare spending since 1980.[2] In fact, the United States spent significantly more per capita on healthcare in 1994 than the other 26 richest nations, according to the Organization for Economic Cooperation and Development, Paris. U.S. per capita healthcare spending was $3,516, or 14.3 percent of the gross domestic product (GDP). As a point of reference, Switzerland was the second highest spender, paying $2,294 per capita, or 9.6 percent of its GDP.[3] Given the escalating costs of healthcare, it's not surprising that healthcare reform was a major 1992 campaign promise of President Clinton, whose plan took its legislative form as the Health Care Security Act, introduced during the first session of the 103rd Congress. The bill proposed universal coverage for every person in the United States. Had it been enacted, the legislation would have surely restructured both the commercial insurance industry and the provider delivery network. Although subsequent legislation[4] passed in 1996 guarantees the portability of health insurance, it falls far short of the reform initiatives required to control costs and simultaneously provide access to quality care. Historically in the United States, reform has been and remains largely in the hands of the industry itself.

Given that the industry is composed of numerous players motivated by many different kinds of ideological, political, and economic considerations, comprehensive national healthcare reform is a complex and yet unrealized objective. Cost control has been the mantra of the payor, quality has been the theme of the provider, and the government and public call for equal access. By design or default, case management must be recognized today as the best tool to both achieve and reconcile the often conflicting goals of healthcare reform.

It is generally agreed that the roots of case management can be traced to the institutions and notion of public health.[5] Early practitioners of case management were public health nurses and social workers. Generally regarded as the first public healthcare nurse,[6] Lillian Wald was also the country's first case manager. A social reformer by philosophy and a nurse by training, this daughter of the upper class founded the Henry Street Nurses Settlement in 1895. By 1910 the organization had a staff of 54 nurses who were dedicated to caring for the needs of the poor while confronting a larger set of social problems, including crowded tenement homes, disease, and unemployment. Wald envisioned that the public healthcare nurse should provide more than episodic treatment. The nurse should be the link between a family's social, economic, and health needs and the services the individual needs to become or stay healthy. Wald believed she was the public healthcare manager for these families in order to forward the interests of the community at large.

Like the modern-day case manager, Wald's nurses created cooperative relationships with hospitals, employers, and other diverse organizations that enabled patients to receive ice, pasteurized milk, medicine, food, and even employment. Wald's unique vision of management as related to these patients went beyond simply caring for individuals during illness but encompassed an agenda of industry-wide reform in healthcare. In fact, as early as 1909, Wald advocated that home care could be a cost-effective investment for insurance companies. As the prototype case manager, Wald convinced Metropolitan Life that it could reduce the number of death benefits it paid if home visiting nurses cared for policyholders during illness. The experiment proved successful and by 1914 the company proudly claimed that the program had contributed to a 12.8% decline in deaths of its insured. Moreover, by 1925, Metropolitan declared that 240,744 lives had been saved and that the company had saved $43,000,000.[6]

The forerunner of the contemporary case manager emerged as the United States entered World War II, with the Public Health Service Act of 1944. Realizing that the country owed its soldiers assistance in resolving problems attributable to war injuries, and understanding that the cost of care to these individuals would be great, the government, as well as insurance companies, began to employ nurses and social workers to assist with the coordination of care for returning soldiers who had suffered serious injuries requiring multidisciplinary intervention. The Surgeon General, Thomas Parran, spoke about the importance of managing the risks of catastrophic diseases in words that still ring hauntingly true: "The heavy cost of catastrophic disease falls unpredictably and unevenly upon the population. For the individual family, I believe that these risks should be met on a national basis, either through insurance, or through public taxes, or preferably through a combination of both."[7] Against the backdrop of war and a public and government struggling to revitalize and protect the nation's health, the case manager functioned both as client advocate and societal resource manager. This dual-purpose role for case management continues to this day and remains a source of conceptual confusion to many as client-focused and cost-containment objectives are simultaneously advanced.[8]

Contemporary case management was also fueled by some of the major ideological movements of the 1960s and 1970s. For instance, the deinstitutionalization of the developmentally disabled and chronically mentally ill underscored the need for intervention if these individuals were to have access to even a fragmented set of services. Formalized systems of case management emerged as a response to ensure that these individuals received help in defining their service needs and locating and arranging for that service. Although altruistic in aim, many of these programs were federally funded. In fact, since the early 1970s the Health Care Financing Administration (HCFA) has provided financing for demonstration projects for case management. Most of the demonstration projects were targeted at the low-income frail elderly to provide alternative solutions to meeting long-term care needs. Rather than nursing home placement, case managers sought to utilize home and community-based services. These programs met with resounding success and were particularly important to the growth of case management. This was the first time that the value of case management was officially proven and documented.

Recognizing the utility of case management services, Congress in 1981 amended the Social Security Act to authorize Medicaid coverage of case management services.[9] States were now authorized to furnish case management as a distinct service under home and community-based service and develop general systems of case management in order to direct patients to appropriate services. Subsequent legislation[10] required states to target case management service to preidentified groups such as developmentally disabled persons, children with developmental delays, individuals with AIDS or HIV-related dis-orders, individuals with hemophilia, and pregnant women and infants. Although there was no limit to the number or size of the target groups to whom the state could provide case management services, HCFA was creating legislative restraints to ensure that those in most need of case management had access to it. In fact, numerous laws mandate case management services to specific groups of people with health-related disabilities or disorders in-cluding all individuals with serious emotional illness who re-ceive substantial public funds, children with special needs, chil-dren in foster care, and the homeless.[11] Historically, federal support has been critical to the nationwide growth and accep-tance of case management. The formalization of approaches and practices in the field of case management first occurred in the public sphere. However, it wasn't until the privatization of case management that its full potential was understood.

In response to the harsh reality of the escalating costs of worker disability, during the late 1970s and throughout the 1980s, Worker's Compensation insurance carriers began hiring large numbers of nurses. These nurses were assigned to assist insured employees with work-related disabilities to return to work and to take an active role in seeking to lessen the ongoing treatment costs of the disability. By 1980 Worker's Compen-sation benefits totaled $13.6 billion, a 453% increase over 1970. Private case management companies proliferated across the country.

The initial focus of case management in the worker's com-pensation setting was to reduce costs associated with both the short-term and long-term effects of occupational injury and dis-ability. Instead of arbitrarily funding endless medical treatment and disability compensation, controlled spending became the new objective that was to be implemented through private case management. Litigation costs, suspected fraud, and reimburse-ment for loss of wages as well as medical care payments were all burdening the system. Accordingly, case managers were charged with the task of maximizing patient outcomes while controlling rapidly growing workers' compensation costs. Vocational spe-cialists, rehabilitation-trained nurses, claims examiners, indus-trial psychologists, and other specialists comprised the staff of these new private case management firms. These specialists were generally charged with cross-line accountability to ensure effective care coordination, early intervention, and development of a structured rehabilitation program to facilitate the employee's return to the work force. These programs produced significant results and all reports indicated that case managers saved money in the worker's compensation arena.

In 1986, the Health Insurance Association of America (HIAA) sought to document the value of coordinated case management. This report found an $11 savings in paid out costs associated with disability for every $1 spent on case management.[12] In 1994 HIAA conducted a similar survey demonstrating an even more consequential impact as the result of case management. The study focused on insurance companies offering group and individual disability plans and medical lines of business. From 1991 to 1993, group disability lines with case management programs reported savings of approximately $30 for every $1 invested. This not only further validated the worth of case management, but it underscored the improvement in case management techniques from the earlier survey. This is an almost three-fold increase from the cost/savings ratios of $1 to $11 shown less than 10 years earlier. The report also showed that case management not only saves money but that it influences outcomes. Nearly 40% of individuals in rehabilitation case management programs returned to work and more than 10% accepted a lump sum settlement from their insurer. The report concluded that this high percentage of cases successfully closed and served—nearly 50%—is largely attributable to the active intervention of case management. News of the remarkable impact of worker disability case management spread quickly in the early 1990s throughout the growing managed care industry.

Throughout this century, various forms of case management have been used with differing degrees of success to address the key issues of our healthcare system—cost, access, and quality. In one way or another, the key players of the healthcare industry—the government, the employer, and the provider—have sought to achieve their respective goals through the use of a prototype of case management. Until the advent of managed care, however, no significant alignment of incentives existed among these healthcare players for case management services to produce much change in the system. Although case management has been a feature of the United States' health system for decades, it wasn't until the 1990s, when a substantial segment of the population was enrolled in managed care plans, that case management became a key tool of reform.

Today, contemporary case management is nurtured by the realities of managed care. Insurance companies, HMOs, PPOs, and healthcare providers can all look to case management to both control individual case costs and to stimulate the growth of the entire continuum of care while maintaining a fiduciary focus on the patient. To accomplish this heady task, case management must be both a centralized and a systematized core component of the healthcare system. This book is intended to be a comprehensive guide to understanding, developing, and implementing centralized case management. The role of managed care and capitation in relation to case management is a central theme; the post–acute care continuum will be detailed; and the importance of distinguishing the regulatory, clinical, and financial factors of each venue is discussed in relationship to service utilization options. The prevailing systems of case management are explored and critiqued, and Chapter 4 provides a step-by-step guide to the design and implementation of a venue-based system of case management. Additionally, the book seeks to delineate the role of the case manager and provide some specific guidance to conflict resolution in care decisions faced daily by the case manager. Worksheets, case studies, and other management tools have been included to provide the healthcare manager with practical assistance in the development and operation of a centralized case management system.

REFERENCES

1. Gorski T. The evolution of managed care practices. *Treatment Today* Spring:10–12, 1995.
2. ProPAC Report on Secretary's Proposal for PPS for Hospital Outpatient Services, Prospective Payment Assessment Commission Congressional Report, No. C-95-01, July 1, 1995.
3. Montague J. Hey, Big Spender. *Hospitals* 70:12, 1996.
4. HR3103, Health Insurance Portability and Accountability Act of 1996.

5. Case Management Society of America (CMSA) Standards of Practice for Case Management, 1995, p. 1; Severson M. Survival strategies for independents. *Continuing Care* 15:17, 1996.

6. Buhler-Wikerson RN. Public health then and now. Bringing care to the people: Lillian Wald's legacy to public health nursing. *Am J Public Health* 83:1778, 1993.

7. Lee PR. The evolution of Public Health. *JAMA* 272:1315, 1994.

8. Raiff NR. *Advanced case management: New strategies for the nineties.* Newbury Park: Sage, p. 5.

9. §1915(b) and 1915(c) of the Social Security Act.

10. Consolidated Omnibus Budget Reconciliation Act (P.L. 99-272, COBRA).

11. Developmental Disabilities Act of 1970, P.L. 91-517, Education for All Handicapped Children Act of 1975, P.L. 94-142, federal Adoption Assistance and Child Welfare Act of 1980, P.L. 96-272, and Homeless Assistance Act of 1987, P.L. 95-478.

12. Gradison B. Management programs serve customers and insurers. *Best's Review, Life-Health Insurance Edition* 96:64, 1996.

13. P.L. 93-222, 87 Stat. 914 (codified at 42 USCC §300e et seq.)

2

CHAPTER

Case Management
in the Continuum

The Health Maintenance Organization Act of 1973[1] did more than facilitate the arrival of HMOs. It heralded the first formalized, albeit rudimentary, alignment of payor and provider incentives within the healthcare industry. This same legislation instilled the dual choice provision obligating employers with more than 25 workers to offer their employees the opportunity to enroll in a federally qualified HMO if one was available in their region. Subsequent to this Act, Blue Cross and Blue Shield plans and commercial insurers began to organize Health Maintenance Organizations (HMO), Preferred Provider Organizations (PPO), and other Alternative Delivery Systems (ADS) as distinct lines of business. Each ADS was dependent upon its own network of contracting service providers, who would agree to be paid under the ADS's fee structure and to comply with cost containment measures in exchange for the promise of increased patient volume. Case managers became the implementers of such cost containment measures as preadmission certification, concurrent review of nonemergency hospital admissions, and coordination of benefits for patients with more than one insurer. Throughout the 1980s, federal commitment to the HMO/managed care concept increased as coverage restrictions that had previously imposed considerable barriers to their growth were lifted. The Reagan administration viewed HMOs as a means to encourage competition in the industry while reducing government involvement in healthcare.

By 1990, about 40 million Americans were enrolled in a variety of managed care arrangements, up from 10 million in 1980. Since then, Americans have been enrolling in managed care plans in record numbers, through their employers and through Medicaid and Medicare. Today, more than half of all insured Americans receive healthcare under some form of managed care. In fact, HMO enrollment grew 14% to 58.2 million in 1995, from 51.1 million in 1994, and is expected to increase to about 70 million in 1996, according to the American Association of Health Plans. Likewise, PPO enrollment increased 15% to 91 million in 1995 from 79.2 million in 1994.

The phenomenal growth of managed care has fueled the tandem importance of centralized case management. Managed care principles encourage the growth of a continuum of care with a broad array of services, especially less expensive venue options. Profit to the managed care company is largely dependent on controlling utilization of service. Managed care also depends on service that is provided efficiently and cost effectively. Without a mechanism to ensure quality and efficiency, the consumer/patient will likely disenroll and switch to a competing managed care plan. These dictums of managed care require a system of centralized case management to enhance service coordination among the varying venues and providers, to ensure quality and appropriateness of service and to contain costs by controlling client access to services. This is not to suggest that client advocacy should be overlooked, but that centralized case management is a complex administrative system serving multiple functions. Case management not only involves client advocacy and service coordination, but also financial, clinical, regulatory, and gatekeeping functions.

The task of the case manager is further complicated by the fact that historical fee-for-service financial mechanisms, particularly those of the country's largest insurer, Medicare, have encouraged system fragmentation and episodic care. A single patient suffering from a disease or disorder will conventionally be moved from provider to provider without any real care coordination or planning for the patient's long-term needs. For example, a stroke patient primarily insured by Medicare may be seen first in the emergency room of the hospital, followed by admission to an acute hospital for a four- or five-day stay. At this point, Medicare will be billed separately by several physician providers as well as the hospital. Following the short acute care stay, the patient will likely be transferred to a rehabilitation facility or skilled nursing unit for rehabilitation, where a new physician, often a rehabilitation specialist, may enter the picture. Following rehabilitation discharge, the patient could receive home care under the Medicare system or be transferred to a nursing facility. If the patient ceased to be homebound, therapy could be delivered by a Comprehensive Outpatient Rehabilitation Facility (CORF), rehabilitation agency, hospital outpatient department, or an independent practicing therapist. All the while, the patient will likely be seeing his or her family physician as well as neurological and perhaps cardiac specialists. Each provider in this care continuum has differing financial incentives to treat or not treat the same stroke patient. Moreover, because our present healthcare delivery approach lacks systematic design, each venue is in fact governed by strikingly different regulations, and providers tend to limit their thinking to specific intervention strategies that meet the patient's immediate needs. Clearly the resulting fragmentation within this delivery system of multiple venues of care, loosely coined *the continuum of care,* may not best meet the long-term or overall needs of the patient. It also seems apparent that this system on its own may not be the most cost-effective means of addressing the problem.

Since the advent of the Diagnosis-Related Group (DRG) payment system, in the mid 1980s, hospitals have been financially encouraged to discharge patients from acute care as soon as medically possible. Under this system, which still governs hospital inpatient Medicare payment, Medicare pays hospitals a fixed amount per diagnosis or disease regardless of the patient's length of stay or acuity level. Rehabilitation units and hospitals, long-term care hospitals, psychiatric units and hospitals, as well as a smaller number of cancer and children's hospitals, are not subject to the DRG payment system, but essentially remain cost-based.* Consequently, acute hospitals under both traditional Medicare and managed care have incentives to manage their patients in the most cost-effective manner since they receive the same payment for that patient's illness regardless of the resources used. Accordingly, the need for the post-acute care continuum is evident. Hospitals and other healthcare organizations in the 1990s have developed, acquired, or affiliated with providers such as home health agencies, skilled nursing facilities, and specialty hospitals, including long-term care, comprehensive outpatient rehabilitation facilities, day hospitals, and partial-day psychiatric programs, just to name a few.

The goal is for the hospital and/or healthcare system to judiciously allocate its resources by consistently discharging the patient to the least costly and restrictive venue of care that still appropriately serves the needs of the patient. Case management is a prerequisite to integrating successfully these often disjointed venues of care while simultaneously ensuring quality and desired outcome. In large part, the post-acute care continuum has emerged to allow for acute care discharge options given that the patient's hospital stay is now carefully managed to ensure that its length is minimized. Therefore, one key function of case management is to reduce inpatient hospital stays through active discharge placement within the continuum. Although certainly a true statement, it is nonetheless misleading in its simplicity.

Case management requires careful consideration of the financial, regulatory, and clinical factors unique to each venue within the continuum. The case manager must be aware of the multiple components of the post-acute care continuum and the attendant factors of each venue. Without fully understanding

---

*These exempted providers today receive Medicare reimbursement in the form of a TEFRA payment. TEFRA payments are typically established in the provider's "base year" which is generally the first full year of operations. The payment reflects the cost of caring for the average patient in the base year and thereafter serves as a limit or cap to individual patient reimbursement. The limit is updated annually for inflation. TEFRA caps vary significantly from institution to institution as they are set based on costs in each provider's base year.

the continuum and the interplay of payment and venue ownership incentives with cost and quality issues, the case manager may make inappropriate decisions that nevertheless seem in keeping with the goals of shortening an inpatient stay and reducing costs. For instance, if a Medicare patient was ventilator dependent and medically stable, the case manager might consider several discharge options. Inpatient rehabilitation programs, specialty or long-term care hospitals, and skilled or subacute programs could all theoretically provide the same service and obtain equally desirable outcomes. If it is determined that the patient has the potential to be weaned from the ventilator, significant resources will be expended on his care. If the hospital has a rehabilitation unit, the hospital case manager might opt to place the patient in this venue thinking that this will provide significant revenue to her employer while ensuring that the patient receives quality care. Moreover, the physicians involved are supportive of this decision and will continue to attend the patient daily on this unit and be paid for such care under Medicare. This decision, however, may not be either in the hospital's financial interest nor provide the patient with the best care possible. If the hospital has a rehabilitation unit with a lower TEFRA cap (e.g., less than $20,000), the program might suffer a net loss as a result of admitting the patient. The costs of caring for a ventilator-dependent patient and weaning him or her can often exceed $20,000. Because the TEFRA cap provides a ceiling or cap to payment, the hospital would not generally be reimbursed for any of its costs exceeding this limit. Moreover, other venues of care such as long-term care hospitals, may actually provide specialized treatment to ventilator patients and will likely be positioned to receive much better Medicare reimbursement than a rehabilitation program.

In addition, the case manager, to make an informed decision, must also understand all the rules and regulations relating to each venue (for additional listing of the various federal regulations affecting placement decisions by venue of care, see Appendix 2, "Venue Utilization by Federal Regulation"). For example, patients admitted to a Medicare-certified rehabilitation unit must be able to tolerate at least three hours of therapy daily.* A patient admitted to a long-term care hospital must be expected to have a relatively long length of stay, as the federal rules require that all long-term care hospitals have patients whose stays on average aggregate 25 days or longer.** In some circumstances, rules that apply to Medicare patients may be waived or are not applicable to managed care patients. For example, Medicare benefits provide for inpatient skilled nursing services if a patient has had a previous three-day hospital stay for the same condition or illness that will be treated in the skilled program.[1] In other words, a Medicare patient cannot be

---

*§211(D)(3) The Three Hour Rule for Inpatient Hospital Rehabilitation Services: The general threshold for establishing the need for inpatient hospital rehabilitation services is that the patient must require and receive at least 3 hours per day of physical and/or occupation therapy. (The furnishing of services no less than 5 days per week satisfies the requirement for "daily" services). Although most patients requiring an inpatient stay for rehabilitation need and receive at least 3 hours per day of physical and/or occupational therapy, there can be exceptions because individual patients' needs vary. In some cases patients who require inpatient hospital rehabilitation services may need, on a priority basis, other skilled rehabilitative modalities such as speech-language pathology services, or prosthetic-orthotic services and their stage of recovery makes the concurrent receipt of intensive physical therapy or occupational therapy services inappropriate. In such cases, the 3 hour per day requirement can be met by a combination of these other therapeutic services instead of or in addition to physical therapy and/or occupational therapy. An inpatient stay for rehabilitation care can also be covered even though the patient has a secondary diagnosis or medical complication that prevents him from participating in a program consisting of 3 hours of therapy per day. Inpatient hospital care in these cases may be the only reasonable means by which even a low intensity rehabilitation program may be carried out. Document the existence and extent of complicating conditions affecting the carrying out of a rehabilitation program to ensure that inpatient hospital care for less than intensive rehabilitation care is actually needed.

**Under §412.23 a long term care hospital must have a provider agreement under Part 489 to participate as a hospital. It must have an average length of inpatient stay greater than 25 days:

(i) As computed by dividing the number of total inpatient days (less leave or pass days) by the number of total discharges for the hospital's most recent complete cost reporting period;

(ii) If a change in the hospital's average length of stay is indicated, as computed by the same method for the immediately preceding 6 month period; or

(iii) If a hospital has undergone a change of ownership (as described in §489.18) at the start of a cost reporting period or at any time within the preceding 6 months, the hospital may be excluded from the prospective payment system as a long term care hospital for a cost reporting period if, for the 6 months immediately preceding the start of the period (including time before the change of ownership), the hospital has the required average length of stay, continuously operated as a hospital, and continuously participated as a hospital in Medicare.

admitted to a skilled program unless the patient has recently had an inpatient acute-care hospital stay.

Depending on the managed care provider or capitation plan, it is sometimes possible to admit a patient for skilled care without meeting this requirement. For instance, if an elderly patient is seen in the emergency room for a severe urinary tract infection, the best course of action may be direct admission to the skilled unit. The acute hospital level of care may be more intensive in scope of service and cost than is necessary. If the patient is a traditional Medicare patient, this option is not possible. However, if the patient is enrolled in a Medicare risk or other capitated or managed care plan, such an alternative should be encouraged.

It is within the province of case management to be able to utilize this intricate continuum of care appropriately. This task is complicated by the fact that today, and for the foreseeable future, the delivery system must simultaneously address the often conflicting demands and requirements of at least three different payment systems—fee-for-service (indemnity insurance and Medicare primarily), per diems and discounts (managed care organizations such as HMOs and PPOs), and capitation (large managed-care organizations, Medicaid and Medicare). Fee-for-service, which was routine until the mid-1980s, meant that hospitals and other providers were paid their billed charges for services rendered. As HMOs and PPOs began to proliferate, they sought discounts from providers, or, alternatively, introduced other payment mechanisms such as per diem payments to hospitals—fixed amounts per day, per patient. With a per diem payment, all the varied costs associated with the stay in a hospital or other facility, including emergency room use, surgery, nursing care, room and board, supplies, and other costs would be included in the payment. In a capitated situation, a provider or health system is paid a fixed amount per member per month for all agreed-on services that might be needed by an HMO's enrollees. With the advent of capitated contracting, centralized case management takes on a larger meaning.

CAPITATION, THE CONTINUUM, AND THE CASE MANAGER

Strictly speaking, capitation refers only to a payment mechanism—a specific sum of money paid to a provider(s) for ongoing care of an individual or group of people for a set period of time. The payment amount is set in advance of the actual period of service, and it therefore represents a prediction, or a reasonable estimate, of the amount of money that will be required to provide that care. Accordingly, profit to the provider becomes dependent on decreased utilization of the medical system across the board. Decreased utilization in turn will depend on a number of factors including promotion of wellness and use of less costly venues of care. For patients covered by capitation contracts, case managers will be especially concerned about managing treatment so that the fewest expenditures are incurred and the most appropriate resources are provided. With respect to capitation contracts, case management can be a mechanism for assuring that providers remain attractive to capitated payors and that providers retain or increase market share as well as revenue. Moreover, a system of centralized case management can help networks identify areas of overutilization, which reduces the amount in their capitation risk pools.

Technically, a contract based on capitation can include or exclude almost any medical service. Payment on a capitated basis can be provided for only primary care, primary care plus diagnostics, or for referrals to specialists. Capitation can also cover the gamut of the medical system, including mental health care. By its nature, a capitated contract creates some degree of risk to the provider. Utilization beyond the anticipated level could result in net financial loss to the provider. Therefore, critics of capitation worry that capitation might negatively affect the quality of care to the individual patient. In today's healthcare system, it is naive to assert that all care decisions should be made in a vacuum insulated from their financial effects. A more enlightened view would assert that capitation affects individual care decisions through intermediate filters of group process, clinical pathways, consensus among peers, and policy formation. These intermediate filters specify correct clinical practice and attempt to establish rules concerning resource utilization. The rules are prescribed both with respect to the clinical considerations and financial ramifications involved. In part, it is the role of case management to intervene when standard rule-based care is not the correct course to take regardless of the economic considerations involved. Although most of the controversy surrounding capitation deals with the potential for denying needed care to patients who are in capitated plans, it is possible that capitation can favorably influence the design of the delivery system.

Perhaps no problem besieges the American healthcare system more than its fragmented delivery system. The causes of this fragmentation are numerous and complex. However, prominent among these causes is the American system of financing care, which both mirrors and perpetuates the problems that plague medical care. Less expensive venues can often provide the most appropriate care to patients, but the Medicare system often encourages use of other, more costly, venues. Physicians and organizations who want to integrate often find that the payment system is their biggest obstacle. Complementary medicine and wellness programs, which have achieved remarkable outcomes around the world, are usually not developed because there is no payor source. Presently, doing the right thing for a patient can even prove financially disadvantageous. For example, a hospital in Twin Falls, Idaho, recently spearheaded a campaign to reduce bicycle injuries in its pediatric population; the hospital experienced a direct $150,000 decrease in emergency room revenues.

Truly integrated care has enormous potential both to reduce cost and improve quality and access. Capitation removes the root cause of fragmented healthcare and provides the prerequisite foundation to integration. Aggregating payment for all medical care of a defined population makes integration and innovation much more readily achievable. It encourages the development of alternative sites and approaches to care delivery. Resources can be transferred and shared without reference to only "bottom-line" thinking. Capitation can simultaneously foster provider independence and encourage cooperation among all parties to the healthcare system. In order for capitation to be a positive force in the redesign of the healthcare system, the provider who is being paid under capitation must be capable of achieving such redesign. A centralized system of case management will be a primary tool of the redesign. With the development of a capitated network, case management should deal with an entire episode of illness or injury and include the coordination and integration of direct clinical and supportive services in various healthcare settings. If massage therapy is warranted, the case manager should advocate its use. Under capitation, there is no worry about what is or is not reimbursable. Case managers should be responsible for developing gatekeeping screens for guiding admission to the most appropriate venue; they should have a key role in assuring that critical pathways and practice parameter standards are followed and are clinically appropriate; a centralized system of case management must conduct variation analysis for addressing the needs of patients who do not easily fit within standard practice. Case managers should participate in the formation of capitated contracts and in the re-negotiation of these agreements. Case managers can document and report important information to this process such as cost of care and outcome achieved. Not only should case managers redesign the care to capitated patients from a corporate perspective, but they should be active at the facility level. Case managers must continue to be patients' advocates under capitation. This function will be particularly important under newly capitated systems because referring physicians will want to protect their capitated risk pools by bypassing some costly care. Properly designed, a system of capitated care not only aligns financial incentives for the delivery network, but can also improve care of patients. Centralized case management will be the primary architect in this redesign.

Clearly, capitation has become a preferred payment methodology by a number of managed care organizations. Not only are employers advocating implementation of the capitated coverage model, but both HCFA and Congress have been supporters of a full-risk contracting program for Medicare beneficiaries. Additionally, many states have recently initiated full capitated contracts for Medicaid recipients. The Medicare risk contracting program, authorized by the Tax Equity and Fiscal Responsibility Act (TEFRA) of 1982, began operation in 1985. This program offers the option of HMO enrollment for beneficiaries who are Medicare-eligible, because of either age or disability. The intent of the risk program was to reduce cost to the government while increasing the Medicare beneficiaries' choices and coverage for care. Presently, Medicare pays participating plans a capitated rate set at 95 percent of what Medicare is expected to spend in the county on coverage under the fee-for-service (or traditional

Medicare) program. This is called the adjusted average per capita costs (AAPCCs)* payment methodology and is intended to achieve at least 5 percent savings to Medicare. By setting risk payments at 95 percent of fee-for-service levels, the Medicare program should save 5 percent of what it would have spent if enrollees remained under traditional Medicare coverage. Plans that choose to participate in the risk-contracting program anticipate their costs for providing Medicare-covered services to be less than or equal to their capitated payments. Medicare does not share in any additional savings if a plan's costs are lower than Medicare payments.

Like capitation growth in general, enrollment in risk-based Medicare plans has grown substantially. In June of 1995, 2.7 million beneficiaries participated in Medicare's risk-contracting program. Between 1987 and 1995, the number of Medicare beneficiaries whose healthcare was paid for by capitation almost tripled. Despite this increase in the number of covered individuals, present Medicare risk enrollment is still believed to be less than 15 percent of Medicare's total population.** As Medicare risk programs establish more significant track records and as Congress modifies its policies to be more supportive of Medicare capitated models, it is reasonable to expect continued growth in enrollment. Indeed, capitation in both the public and private sectors of healthcare will continue to be a preferred model of managed care payment for the future.

---

*The AAPCCs are determined on a county-specific basis across the country and vary significantly. In 1995, the published AAPCCs ranged from $177 to $679 monthly. AAPCCs for urban counties are higher on average, and they vary more than those for rural counties.

**A number of shortcomings are likely to be causes of the low level of overall beneficiary participation including the range of HMO choices available to beneficiaries. A number of plans have not established Medicare risk HMOs because of wide geographic variations in payment rates, volatility of payment rates over time, and inclusion of certain fee-for-service payments in the capitation amount. It is not likely, however, that payment rates will be increased as the risk plans may actually be costing Medicare more overall. Either by design or default, Medicare risk HMOs seem to be enrolling healthier individuals. The present Medicare payment formula for HMOs does not adjust adequately for the better health and consequent lower expected costs of HMO enrollees. The findings of the HCFA Office of Research and Demonstrations indicated that the cost of caring for HMO enrollees was 11.3 percent lower than for the fee-for-service population. Therefore, Medicare is actually losing money on every beneficiary who moves into the risk products.

Given the growing application of capitation models to all of America's healthcare system, it is vital that case managers understand how best to function in this risk-laden arena. Patient education and disease prevention emphasizing high-risk patients will assume increased importance. Of course, cost of product and services will be key factors in any matrix of treatment options. However, it has become alarmingly commonplace for some within the healthcare industry to declare that case management's function is to ensure that patients keep moving to the lowest cost venue of care. Such an approach not only ignores the extremely regulatory nature of the continuum, but it assumes that all players within the industry are capitated. This is simply not the case. Very few systems are 100% capitated. Although capitation surely seems a trend in the future of managed care payment schemes, we remain in a significant transitional period. For example, Medicare reimbursement remains the primary revenue source for most hospitals. In fact, in 1994 spending on Medicare rose by more than 11%, compared with only a 4% increase in the private sector (Table 2–1).[2] Total hospital spending during this time period was $338.5 billion. It is likely that this growth in spending will be tempered throughout the coming years, but traditional Medicare, as well as forms of managed care payment in addition to capitation, will remain dominant reimbursement sources for the foreseeable future. Therefore, it is incumbent on the case manager to recognize the interplay of the financial, clinical, and regulatory issues inherent in utilization of the post-acute care continuum.

DEFINING THE CONTINUUM

At any one time, the case manager today addresses treatment and placement options for patients who have the same clinical needs but different forms of reimbursement. Consequently, these patients may have very different placement results. A detailed understanding of the components of the full care continuum is a prerequisite to successful implementation of centralized case management. The case manager must first identify what components can be included in the community's healthcare continuum. Depending on the market, a number of alternative sites of care and programs should be considered as components of this

TABLE 2–1

Medicare Spending Growth
National health expenditures by category for selected years (in billions)

Spending Category	1970	1980	1990	1992	1993	1994
Hospital Care	$28.0	$102.7	$256.4	$305.3	$324.2	$338.5
Physician Services	13.6	45.2	146.3	174.7	181.1	189.4
Dental Services	4.7	13.3	31.6	37.0	39.2	42.2
Other Professional	1.4	6.4	34.7	42.1	46.3	49.6
Home Care	0.2	2.4	13.1	19.6	23.0	26.2
Drugs	8.8	21.6	59.9	71.3	75.2	78.6
Vision Products	1.6	3.8	10.5	11.9	12.6	13.1
Nursing Home	4.2	17.6	50.9	62.3	67.0	72.3
Other Personal Healthcare	1.3	4.0	11.2	15.6	17.8	21.8
Administrative Costs	2.7	11.8	38.6	42.8	51.0	58.7
Government Public Health	1.5	6.7	19.6	23.4	25.7	28.8
Research and Construction	5.3	11.6	24.5	27.6	29.2	30.2

Sources: HCFA, Office of National Health Statistics

continuum. Some of these venues of care have developed in response to reimbursement rules and regulations, whereas others have been created to address historical patterns of practice outside of the hospital setting. The following are some of the key components of a full continuum of care:

Alternative Birthing Centers (ABCs) are special facilities where women can deliver babies in a homelike environment using natural childbirth techniques. As a result of physicians' greater confidence in identifying uncomplicated pregnancies, the increased use of nurse-midwives, and the trend away from the routine use of anesthetics, ABCs have gained increased acceptance as a safe, low-cost alternative to a hospital delivery. ABCs have also been encouraged by managed care providers seeking to reduce the costs of uncomplicated births.

Ambulatory Surgical Centers (ASCs) have shifted a great number of patients from hospital beds to outpatient settings. For years, the principal danger of surgery has been the side effects of anesthesia, not the operation itself. New short-acting anesthetics are much safer for patients, resulting in fewer complications. Combined with less-invasive surgical techniques and technology such as fiberoptic scopes and lasers, many patients can undergo a surgical procedure without being admitted to the hospital and leave soon after the procedure to recover at home. Both Medicare and managed care plans generally provide coverage for procedures conducted in an ambulatory surgery setting. Medicare specifically recognizes the existence of ambulatory surgical centers (ASCs) in C.F.R. §416.61.

Payment by Medicare for facility services in freestanding ASCs is on the basis of a prospectively determined rate. The rate for each procedure takes into account the special costs incurred in providing services appropriate for the surgical procedures, but is established in such a manner to ensure that the amount paid to an ASC is substantially less than if the procedure had been performed on an inpatient basis. Payment to hospital-affiliated ambulatory surgical centers is based on the lesser of (1) reasonable cost or (2) a blended amount, which in general averages the provider's reasonable costs with the payment for freestanding ASCs. Case managers must know which specific procedures Medicare authorizes for ASC reimbursement. Moreover, it is critical that there is a strategically developed policy as to the appropriate utilization of the ASC given its potential impact on inpatient revenue.

Complementary Medicine Clinic is a freestanding facility or a program of a larger facility offering diagnosis, treatment, and therapy outside of conventional medicine. Under such a model, patients take primary responsibility for their own health and wellness. A multitude of resources, including physicians who are supportive of nontraditional medicine and healing are readily available in this setting. The clinic can offer a wide range of services including such diverse treatments and products as acupuncture, aromatherapy, biofeedback, massage, diet and nutrition counseling and supplements, herbal medicine, chiropractic care, and meditation. Because capitated patients are not tied to the traditional fee-for-service system, a case manager has more flexibility in deciding if complementary medicine would be a viable option. Moreover, these options may prove also to be more cost effective, particularly for chronic problems, than some conventional treatments. In fact, many managed care organizations are offering to cover this care just as they cover standard medical practitioners such as cardiologists and allergists. Some states have also mandated that to operate as an HMO, the insurer must provide coverage for certain alternative medicine. It is incumbent upon the case manager to know what alternative therapies are readily and reputably available for inclusion into the continuum. Once this has been determined, the case manager must identify which plans provide coverage for which services.

Comprehensive Outpatient Rehabilitation Facility (CORF) is either a freestanding or hospital or skilled nursing-based center that is exclusively engaged in providing, under a physician's direction, diagnostic, therapeutic, and restorative services to outpatients for the rehabilitation of injured, disabled, or sick persons. CORFs are legislatively recognized by forty-two C.F.R. §485.50 and provide for cost-based care to Medicare patients. CORFs, however, can treat both Medicare and non-Medicare patients. The CORF, at a minimum, must provide the following services: (1) physician's services (rendered by physicians who are available at the facility on a full or part-time basis); (2) physical therapy; and (3) social or psychological services. The following CORF services are reimbursed by Medicare: physician services, nursing services, psychological services, social services, respiratory services, physical therapy, occupational therapy, speech therapy, prosthetic/orthotic services, durable medical equipment and drugs and biologicals (which are not self administered). Patients admitted to a CORF can be referred for service without the requirement of an inpatient stay. Moreover, there is no per patient visit limit or limit to the length of stay if the service is medically appropriate. Because the CORF generally provides comprehensive and consolidated services, it can often serve as a cost-effective alternative to hospital-based care for both managed care and capitated patients as well as Medicare beneficiaries. To the case manager, the CORF should be an important component of a full continuum of care.

Day Hospital is a freestanding or hospital-based program designed to provide a structured comprehensive rehabilitation and/or medical program for individuals with acute and chronic disorders, including postsurgical, respiratory, neurological, pain, and oncological conditions. Hospital-type services are provided, including assessment, diagnostic evaluation, treatment, and management and monitoring of patients. This structured out-patient program usually consists of 4 to 6 hours of treatment designed to provide multidisciplinary services to enhance the functionality of the individual. Day hospitals typically offer lower charges than comparable hospital services and routinely package-price their services. Depending on the organization of the day hospital, its overhead costs can be substantially lower than an acute care hospital. Emergency room services, intensive care units, surgery suites, and so forth are not components of the day hospital. A day hospital is not presently a specifically recognized Medicare venue of care. However, Medicare patients can be treated in a day hospital and reimbursement is generally available under Part B or hospital outpatient routes.

Day hospitals have primarily emerged in response to man-aged care's need to have bundled payment schemes for outpa-tient services. The case manager must first determine the avail-ability of day hospital services and subsequently analyze the cases of patients most appropriate for admission. Moreover, a network having access to a day hospital may be able to secure additional managed care contracts because of the availability of these bundled services.

Home Healthcare permits many patients to be discharged from the hospital sooner, to recover from an illness at home. HMOs pro-vide a variety of services in the home, including skilled nursing, rehabilitation therapy, and sometimes homemaker assistance. Likewise, coverage is provided for home healthcare services prescribed by a physician for treatment and/or rehabilitation of homebound patients, including part-time or intermittent nursing services. Under Medicare regulations,[3] home health services can be covered under both Part A or Part B, although the services will always be covered under Part A when an individual is eligible for both programs. In general, the following services are covered under the Medicare program:

1. Part-time or intermittent skilled nursing care provided by or under the supervision of a registered professional nurse.
2. Physical, occupational, or speech therapy.
3. Medical social services under the direction of a physician.

4. Part-time or intermittent services of a home health aide who has successfully completed an approved training program.
5. Medical supplies (but not drugs and biologicals, except for osteoporosis drugs) and durable medical equipment.
6. Medical services of interns and residents-in-training under an approved teaching program of a hospital with which the agency is affiliated.
7. Any of the foregoing items and services that (a) are provided on an outpatient basis under arrangements made by the home health agency at a hospital or skilled nursing facility, or at a rehabilitation center, and (b) involve the use of equipment that cannot readily be made available to the patient in his or her place of residence, or which are furnished at the facility while he or she is there to receive items or services involving the use of such equipment (but transportation to the facility is excluded).
8. Reasonable and necessary homemaker services, without regard to whether there is someone available in the home to furnish the required assistance, where the Medicare criteria of home health services are met. However, if a family member or other individual is or will be or wants to provide services, it is not reasonable and necessary for the case manager to have the home health agency furnish such services.

Home health is arguably the fastest-growing component of the full healthcare continuum. Patients generally are supportive of early discharge from facilities given the availability of home healthcare. Despite the convenience of home health, several issues may sometimes influence the case manager to choose other options. The first is cost. For capitated patients, home health may actually cost the network more than other venues of care. If a patient requires daily or twice-daily visits by home health personnel, these costs could exceed the costs of the same service in a subacute or skilled nursing unit or possibly a CORF if transportation is available. Additionally, another venue may be able to provide care that is more intensive in scope and thus achieves better overall health outcome. Case managers must be judicious about always advocating home healthcare. A second issue to consider is meeting the "homebound" test. All too often, the home health agencies and physicians seemingly inappropriately apply the homebound test in order to obtain reimbursement for services that might not otherwise be covered. Homebound does not mean lack of transportation. Rather, homebound denotes a physical inability to leave home, that is, leaving the homes would require a considerable and taxing effort, and could even be dangerous to the patient's health. The case manager must understand the interplay of cost, regulation, and payor source when considering home healthcare.

Hospice Care   was first recognized by Medicare under the Tax Equity and Fiscal Responsibility Act of 1982. Hospice care is a method of caring for the terminally ill that helps them approach the end of their lives with as little disruption as possible. Hospice care usually provides supportive services such as pain control, home nursing, and homemaker assistance rather than curative-based care. A patient may opt to have hospice care for two periods of 90 days, a subsequent period of 30 days, and a final period of unlimited duration. If Medicare patients opt for hospice care, they must give up their right to other program coverage. Reimbursement for hospice providers for Medicare patients is based on a cost-related principle subject to a cap amount. HCFA annually sets daily payment amounts, which are adjusted to reflect local differences in wages to reimburse four categories of covered hospice care, including routine home care, continuous home care, inpatient respite care, and general home care.

Hospice care may or may not be a carve-out service under managed care contracts. It seems likely that providers in capitated contracts will seek to offer hospice care either directly or through arrangements. In making referrals to hospice care, the case manager, who will likely be acting directly in contact with a physician, must pay particular attention to the legal issues involved in death, dying, and medically necessary care.

Long Term Care Hospital   generally provides diagnostic and medical treatment or rehabilitation to patients with chronic disease or complex medical conditions whose average length of stay exceeds 25 days. It is a specifically recognized medical venue of care as per

42 C.F.R. §412.23(e). A long term care hospital is exempted from the Prospective Payment System (PPS) and thus receives Medicare reimbursement on the basis of reasonable costs subject to a TEFRA limit, as established during the provider's base year. A long term care hospital, with its TEFRA form of Medicare reimbursement, is an ideal vehicle to stem losses resulting from extended lengths of stay and increased patient acuity. Notwithstanding the existence of outlier payments, the Prospective Payment System (PPS) will typically not account for extraordinary costs of chronically ill or devastatingly ill Medicare patients. Therefore, the long term care hospital can serve as an ideal venue to accept patients from an acute care venue.

By its design and with its reimbursement parameters, most long-term care hospitals will serve primarily Medicare patients. However, managed care, Medicaid, and capitated patients can be wholly appropriate for admission if their medical needs are complex and it is expected that they will require a lengthy stay in the hospital. It is incumbent upon the case manager to note that the cost of care in long-term care hospitals can be quite high and yet the outcomes are often excellent. Cases generally considered appropriate for admission include medically complex respiratory infections and disorders, ventilator dependence, antibiotic therapy, cardiac, oncology, wound care, rehabilitation-related diagnoses with complex or tertiary needs, general debilitation, and post-surgical. Placement in a long term care hospital will require thorough understanding of how the long term care hospital is presently being reimbursed, the expected length of stay of the patient to be admitted, and the net financial impact to the referring provider.

Mental Health Services (and Partial Hospitalization Coverage) is generally a key component of the full care continuum. These services are available on an outpatient basis. For Medicare patients, Part B pays 62.5 percent of expenses incurred in any calendar year in connection with the treatment of mental, psycho-neurotic, or personality disorders of patients who are not, at the same time, patients of a hospital. If the patient is treated in a Medicare-certified partial hospitalization program, the 62.5 percent payment limit does not apply. This program must be hospital-based or affiliated and must be organized as a distinct ambulatory treatment service. The case manager must determine for Medicare patients which venue of care is the most appropriate and balance this with applicable payment limits.

For capitation and managed care patients, a number of venues including physician offices, hospitals, and other ambulatory clinics will offer mental health services. Such services may include psychiatry, drugs and biologicals, social work, psychology, family counseling, group treatment and therapy, as well as individual therapy.

Psychiatric Hospitals and Units provide inpatient psychiatric and medical care to patients who require 24-hour care and treatment and who have a specific psychiatric principal diagnosis that is listed in the third edition of the American Psychiatric Association's *Diagnostic and Statistical Manual,* or under Mental Disorders in the *International Classification of Diseases, Ninth Revision, Clinical Modification.* Typically, medical services, psychological services, social work, psychiatric nursing, occupational therapy, and recreational therapy are included in these programs. Additionally, programs will specialize in the treatment of geriatric patients with age-associated problems, including complex medical conditions, adolescent programs, and specialized substance abuse programs.

Providers of services to managed care patients usually offer package-priced programs. Medicaid, which is not capitated, may provide fee-for-service at predetermined rates. Medicare providers of inpatient care are usually exempted from the prospective payment system and are consequently reimbursed under the aforementioned TEFRA system. Depending on the precise TEFRA limit, a provider may have differing financial incentives that could influence a case manager's referral.

Rehabilitation Hospitals and Units, which are PPS-exempted regardless of the payor source, must admit an inpatient population of whom at least 75 percent require intensive rehabilitation services for the treatment of one or more of the following conditions:

- Stroke
- Spinal cord injury
- Congenital deformity

- Amputation
- Major multiple trauma
- Fracture of femur (hip fracture)
- Brain injury
- Polyarthritis, including rheumatoid arthritis
- Neurological disorders, including multiple sclerosis, motor neuron diseases, polyneuropathy, muscular dystrophy, and Parkinson's disease
- Burns

Additionally, the rehabilitation hospital or unit can admit another 25 percent of its patients who would be deemed likely to benefit from a comprehensive program of rehabilitation without regard to a specific diagnosis (C.F.R. §412.23). Patients admitted to these inpatient programs must be able to tolerate at least 3 hours of therapy daily and have a functional need that can benefit from at least two types of therapy. For patients who have less intense rehabilitation needs, federal regulations require that they be treated at a venue other than an exempted rehabilitation hospital or unit. The case manager must pay particular attention to the numerous admitting restrictions of these exempted PPS providers. Like all PPS-exempted providers, rehabilitation inpatient programs are paid under the TEFRA scheme of reimbursement. Hospitals and units with higher TEFRA caps are also often the programs best equipped to provide tertiary rehabilitation care. Such care is more complex in nature and is often most appropriate for patients with head injuries, spinal cord disorders, burns, major multiple trauma, and other neurological and muscular-skeletal diseases and disorders that require a specialized level of care. As a number of new venues that offer rehabilitation and related services have emerged, it is particularly important that the case manager evaluate the patient's precise needs and balance those needs with outcomes achievable in each venue as well as cost of care. These factors coupled with the general regulatory parameters of each venue will be decisive in issues of patient placement.

Subacute Care is commonly used and widely understood to be care provided to patients who do not meet the established criteria for medically necessary acute care. Subacute care includes patients with a range of intensity of needs from those in the immediate postacute period through those with minimal nursing and therapy needs. Medical regulations do not recognize a distinct reimbursement or venue category for subacute care. Rather, subacute care was spawned as a result of demand by managed care for a lower-cost venue of care.

Designed to be both comprehensive and intensive, subacute care offers a high-quality, yet cost-effective alternative to a lengthy stay in an acute care hospital. The basic philosophy behind the subacute approach to treatment is to provide services that are not generally available in a traditional nursing home, but do not require the expensive technology inherent to an acute care hospital setting.

The goal of the subacute unit is to provide care to medically stable patients who require specialized inpatient care as dictated by the diagnosis. A care plan is developed for each patient according to identified treatment goals, following completion of evaluation and assessment by appropriate team members, thereby providing a transitional level of care before discharge to home or a comprehensive outpatient rehabilitation facility. The desired average length of stay for the subacute unit will vary depending on product line distinction, acuity level, and discharge prognosis.

The patient mix in a subacute unit is significantly different from a community nursing facility. Focus in a subacute unit is goal-oriented restorative care rather than maintenance or custodial care. Subacute care should be considered an essential component of the continuum of care. A patient should be able to make the transition from the most restrictive to least restrictive care delivery mode in an expeditious and cost-effective manner, if subacute care is judiciously used at the most appropriate time.

Although subacute care units were originally designed to respond to the needs of capitated and managed care patients, many subacute programs are also licensed and certified as skilled nursing programs under both state law and applicable Medicare regulations. Therefore, medical patients can receive a program of subacute care provided there is an underlying certification, such as skilled nursing, that will allow for participation in the Medicare program and thus the resulting billing.

Skilled Nursing Programs furnish extended care services to inpatients in freestanding and hospital-based programs. These services typically involve skilled nursing or rehabilitation and are similar to the services provided in a hospital, but at a lower level of care. Medicare provides coverage for these services under Part A. For each spell of illness, payment may be made for the reasonable cost of up to 100 days of posthospital care.[4] To qualify for Medicare reimbursement, the case manager must determine if the patient can meet all of the following conditions simultaneously:

- Patient is otherwise eligible for Medicare Part A benefits
- Patient's stay in skilled care is pursuant to physician's certification of need
- Patient was a hospital inpatient for at least 3 days within the last 30 days
- Patient requires and receives skilled nursing care on a daily basis
- Patient's stay in a skilled program is necessitated by the same condition that caused hospital stay
- Services provided to patient will not be custodial in nature

These conditions are relevant only to Medicare patients and payment rules. Certified skilled nursing programs can, and often do, provide care to patients who have Medicare or managed care forms of payment. In these cases, it is critical to note which regulations have relevance. For example, to receive Medicare payment on one's behalf for posthospital extended care services, an individual must have been an inpatient of a hospital for at least three consecutive calendar days and have been transferred to a participating skilled facility usually within 30 days after discharge from the hospital. This is certainly not the case with patients who have capitated forms of coverage. In many instances, this will be an arbitrary requirement that has no clinical significance and only interferes with appropriate utilization of the care continuum. The case manager must again carefully study the interplay of the financial, regulatory, and clinical framework of placement decisions.

SUMMARY

Case management is the vehicle of patient flow in the care continuum. It is the means by which provider, payor, and consumer are assured that the most appropriate services are provided at the most appropriate time. In part, the function of the case manager is to be the guide through the maze (illustrated in Figure 2–1) of healthcare options and resources. Indeed, case management is the means by which a continuum of care can be effected.

For the past thirty years, it was presumed that the best bed was an acute bed and that the best environment for healthcare

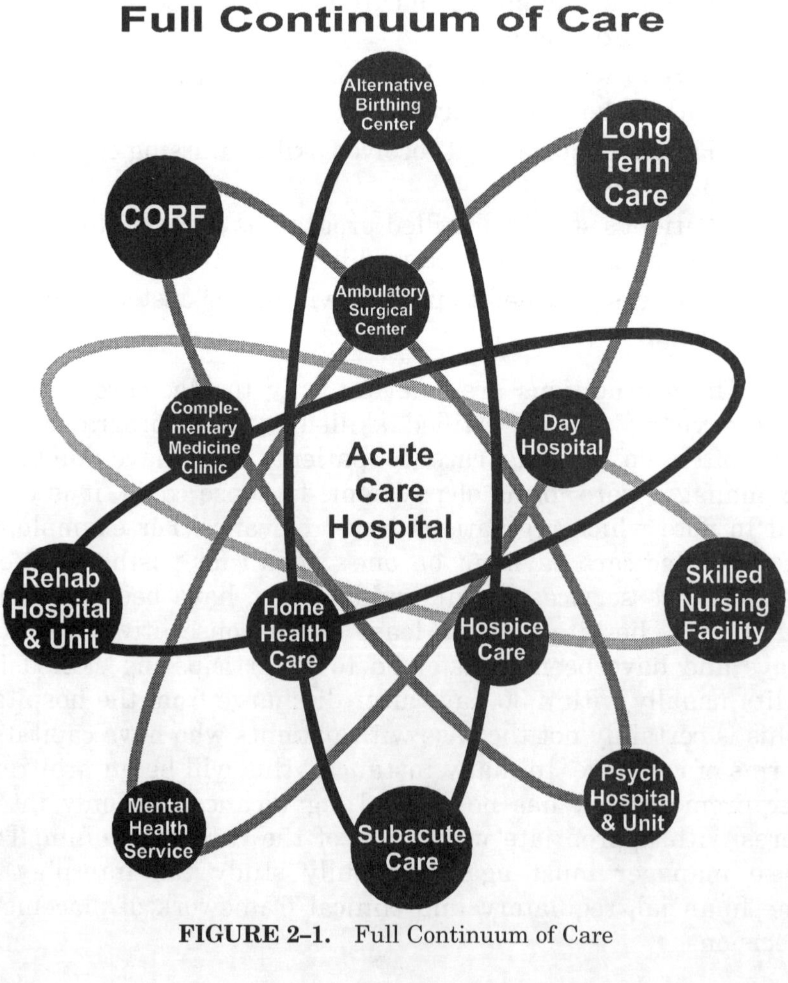

Full Continuum of Care

FIGURE 2–1.   Full Continuum of Care

delivery was the hospital. To limit the patient's length of stay in the hospital has been and even today remains a philosophical and financial struggle among physicians as well as patients and families. Our healthcare system comprises a multitude of players with often conflicting incentives and game plans. Medicare is the predominant payor source for most of the country's healthcare. This fact alone accounts for many of the incongruities in practice patterns and placement decisions.

Interests among the key parties involved in venue placement options are both overlapping and divergent. If a case manager is employed by a hospital owning several post-acute venues, the case manager must recognize that the physician may have conflicting financial interests to that of the institution. These differences will likely influence the length of stay and date of discharge from the acute bed. Although physician practice patterns are influenced by utilization review and peer relationships, the ability to continue billing in a specific venue has historically affected the timing of discharge from that venue. Likewise, a physician may express hesitation in the transfer of a patient to a more appropriate venue, preferring to retain the patient in the acute bed, primarily because of personal convenience and accessibility. At this point, it is often the role of the case manager to ensure that patient care issues are not being used as a subterfuge for personal financial gain. Clearly, this is not to suggest that many or even a significant number of practitioners operate in this manner. Rather, case managers must clearly justify use of the full continuum of care in keeping with the best interests of the patient and ever mindful of their job as stewards of scarce healthcare resources. The challenge of case management is to coordinate all necessary services across the continuum despite a myriad of conflicts that can interfere with the process.

REFERENCES

1. §212.1 Three-day prior hospitalization, skilled nursing facility manual (HCFA Pub. 12).
2. HCFA, Office of National Health Statistics.
3. Social Security Act §1883, §1861.
4. Social Security Act §1814, §1819.

3

CHAPTER

Organizational Models of Case Management and Their Effectiveness

Today case management has become recognized as a powerful approach to managing the care of patients over their continuum. At the individual patient level, case management is both a role and a predetermined process. As a system, case management must be developed and managed. Accordingly, many models for case management have emerged. Disease Management, Primary Care, Community-Based, and Episode-Based are several of the models currently in use. The most useful case management system for an organization will incorporate several models or approaches. The overwhelming consideration is to establish a system that addresses the varied needs and characteristics of a patient population as well as the organization. Despite the several approaches to case management, common features or functions of these different models have emerged. Case management is a system that:

1. Assesses need for medical/social intervention
2. Coordinates, processes, and negotiates services required by individuals and their families
3. Advocates for clients
4. Ensures appropriate utilization of limited resources over a predetermined time frame

These functions of case management are the core common elements of most system models. Assessment is generally understood as the very first step in the service allocation process. Many models of case management broadly define the assessment to include a screening, and the related function of intake, assessment, and goal establishment. Moreover, the assessment lays the groundwork to establish the relationship between the case manager and the provider, may allow for expression of the client's opinion of need, and contrasts the requirements of gatekeeping with the patient's opinion of necessary service. The assessment may be as brief as a data transfer and review of a medical chart or it may be a complete exploration of a patient's physical, psychological, and social status, and development of a goal statement for each area where there is dissatisfaction and recognition of a problem. In-depth assessments will also attempt to describe the individual's current and premorbid level of functioning and determine the likely prognosis for functioning or problem control. In sum, the assessment includes an identification of goals, resources, and limitations. Goals are negotiated based on input from the patient, provider, and payor. A plan, including a timeline, for reaching the goal is established. The assessment collects the requisite data to allow for service planning to begin.

Service planning or service coordination is widely believed to be the chief function of case management at this phase. The case manager implements the plan, employing a number of strategies. He or she may make specific recommendations as to appropriate venues of care and services provided or may arrange for others to directly negotiate for this care. It is critical that the case manager have access to a network of providers and venues capable of offering the requisite care at the right price. At this juncture, the case manager must ensure that the patient has met all admission criteria and that there are no impediments, regulatory or otherwise, that would prevent the patient from receiving the appropriate service. As care progresses, the case manager should closely monitor timeliness and effectiveness of the planned interventions to assure relevancy of the treatment vis-à-vis goal attainment. Revisions to the plan can be made when the desired outcomes do not seem likely. Again, the case manager will negotiate these changes with the patient, provider, and family. This process will continue until either the individual goals are attained or the patient's situation has become so routine that case management services are no longer warranted. Sometimes, a patient can be transferred to an inactive status until new needs emerge. Each of these phases of the case management process is documented in a record, according to the specifications established by the organization responsible for oversight of the system of case management.

In addition to the functions of assessment and service coordination, most models of case management share common concepts of the need for client advocacy. Case managers, more than any other professional in the field of managed healthcare, can and must support the involvement of consumers in the development, implementation, and monitoring of care. Thus client advocacy has taken on significant meaning in the field of case management. In the transition to managed care in the United States, consumers have generally had little to say. Case management is a mechanism to reverse this trend. Yet, consumers can be justifiably confused by the language of the system. Words such as *care maps, gatekeeping, carve outs, clinical indicators, outcomes,* and *capitation* are common banter among healthcare professionals, yet when used by case managers, they create even more frustration for a public already struggling with case management as a concept. Many individual patients genuinely express strong reservations about formalized systems of case management. It is not uncommon to hear a patient who is offered case management services respond, "I am not a case and I do not want to be managed." What is not understood is that the philosophy of case management also includes client advocacy.

Client advocacy assumes many forms in case management. Anecdotes about case managers intervening to ensure that patients obtain the requisite services are refreshingly common. A patient's leg is saved from amputation because a case manager insisted on a course of therapy. A long-term care hospital was able to wean a patient from a ventilator because of the intervention of case management. A dying patient was able to spend the last several weeks of her life at home with hospice care rather than in intensive care because a case manager spoke up. These stories attest to the vital function of client advocacy in the process of case management. Indeed, case managers are often the personnel most instrumental in determining how patients report their satisfaction with the care delivered. The level of client advocacy employed will vary depending on the role of case management within the sponsoring organization. The case manager may explore the client's (and caregiver's) understanding of the situation and preferred solutions to the health/social issues raised by the situation. Moreover, the case manager or the system itself will be responsible for service evaluation and monitoring. Did the patient receive the right service, was it a quality service delivered at the correct time, and for the appropriate duration? This evaluation process can be both qualitative, relying on staff judgment, and quantitative, using standardized scales or performance-based criteria. This type of advocacy is particularly important to certain populations such as the elderly or those with chronic illness who may be more vulnerable to fraud, abuse, and substandard treatment. Effective advocacy demands a careful balance between the client's ethical and legal rights and the need to allocate healthcare resources carefully. Complex issues arise when the case manager advocates for the patient against the direction or position of other parties to the care process. Because many case managers work for either the payor or the healthcare provider, a significant conflict exists when staff wants to advocate for a client against the employer. It is vital that the case management system adequately protect the rights of the patient yet balance them with the often competing priorities of the payor and provider. As will be detailed in Chapter 7, a system of case management must be developed with complete knowledge of the legal and ethical duties of all parties involved as well as the rights of the consumer. There must be an acknowledged need to establish and implement consistent policies and procedures to address these conflicts when they arise. Only in this way can the function of client advocacy be simultaneously conducted with case management's other function, appropriate utilization of limited resources.

In order to reduce costs, improve quality, and protect revenues, case management is charged with the responsibility of ensuring efficient utilization of services across the continuum. The extent or parameters of the continuum will be dependent on the specifics of the case management model employed. However, all systems share a common focus in providing for cost efficiency coupled with positive patient outcomes. The need for the re-source management function is undeniable. A case manager should ask the question, "How can the patient receive the requisite care in the most cost-effective manner?" Understanding how to access and utilize the various nonhospital venues of care is an important first step in this process.

Case management at this level is also a chief collaborator in the design and use of critical paths or care maps. In essence, critical paths and care maps are specific tools to achieve what the industry refers to as collaborative care. In collaborative care, a diverse group of healthcare players, representing the interests of provider(s), payor, and patient, collaborate to offer quality patient care capable of achieving measurable outcomes within a cost-effective framework. Collaborative care's primary implementation mechanism is the critical path or care map. These tools serve as a guideline to standardize treatment with related costs per outcome rather than per task. Moreover, critical paths serve to link cost, process, and outcome within a predetermined time frame. The map specifies the preferred treatment or intervention, the venue of service, the duration of the care, and projects both the cost and the likely outcome of the service. Care maps have initially developed across specific DRGs or procedures that are most amenable to standardization such as total knee replacements and cardiac catheterization. Care maps have been subsequently developed for chronic conditions such as chronic obstructive pulmonary disease (COPD) or diabetes. The use of these tools by the case manager is, however, only one method to assume appropriate monitoring of resource utilization. Critical paths usually function best to move homogeneous, uncomplicated groups of patients quickly and cost effectively through the healthcare delivery system. Other case management strategies will be needed to control resource consumption by atypical patients. Atypical patients include those patients who have complicated health problems or whose response to care is unusual and departs from what had been predicted.

Assessment, service planning, client advocacy, and resource utilization monitoring viewed together as integrated functions comprise the common role of case management in today's healthcare delivery system. Despite the fact that all models of case management share these universal attributes, systems of case management are varied and diverse in philosophy and organizational structure. Competition between alternative models is clearly an indicator of the field's significance, but it also creates confusion for the healthcare manager seeking to establish a system of case management. Although some models are relatively rudimentary, they all identify a target client group, a system level goal, and several preferred methods of intervention by case management. Different dimensions of and strategies for care coordination are combined to create a variety of case management models. A well-integrated process includes multiple strategies, including those outlined in Figure 3–1. Each strategy has a specific role within the delivery organization. To fully realize the multiple goals of a centralized system of case management, it will be important to link strategies to the appropriate patient population and the right circumstances.

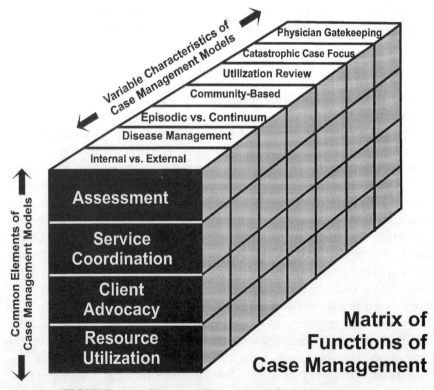

FIGURE 3–1. Matrix of Functions of Case Management

INTERNAL VERSUS EXTERNAL SYSTEMS OF CASE MANAGEMENT

Case management has become a required service of the health-care industry. As such, it can be provided internally by an organization or it can be purchased from external, independent firms. Internal case management programs are usually sponsored by care providers such as healthcare systems, hospitals, home health agencies, rehabilitation programs, and nursing facilities. External case management firms typically service self-insured employers and other third-party payors such as commercial insurers or HMOs as clients. Outside case management firms have traditionally been hired to follow catastrophic cases in which healthcare expenses are likely to be significant or in worker disability situations. Independent case management firms are finding that their market is shrinking. Most healthcare organizations today are opting to provide case management from a primarily internal perspective. As risk sharing and capitation become more prominent, healthcare providers are understanding the need to manage all patients. Given this potential case load, organizations are finding internal case management more cost effective. While the pendulum is swinging toward the internalization of these functions, independent case management firms that respond to the changing marketplace can still retain market share.

DISEASE MANAGEMENT

An organization can design a case management model that only follows the care of patients falling within specific disease or diagnostic categories. It is common for large hospitals to select diagnoses such as coronary bypass, joint replacement, or COPD on which to focus case management efforts. The determination as to which diagnoses to follow is usually based on several factors. First, which diagnoses are the most costly to treat? Second, which patients have the longest lengths of stay in an acute bed despite the existence of alternative nonacute hospital venues of care? Third, which diagnoses are historically associated with readmission to the hospital for the same condition? HMOs and other third-party payors, including capitated healthcare providers who use disease management models, often employ slightly different criteria in selecting which diagnostic group to follow. Although costs of individual care is an important consideration, potential overall savings to the organization is the significant goal of case management for the payor. Therefore, a case management system for a payor may follow a larger number of patients with a common disease, such as diabetes. The intervention may be as simple as making yearly appointments with a general practitioner or requesting the patient's attendance at an educational session. Often, the goal of case management under this disease management model will be prevention of exacerbation of the underlying condition. Although the scope of service delivery to the individual patient by case management can be minimal, the potential savings to the organization can be significant. Alternatively, disease state case management can be critical for both the payor and provider, and for the patient when complex circumstances arise. For instance, with active case management a woman referred to a health center for a breast lump could be counseled about the risks of breast cancer and the need for a diagnostic evaluation, obtain a mammogram, have the mammogram read, have the results sent to a case manager, have the case manager schedule a needle biopsy and provide preoperative testing. The integration of case management with this specific disease minimizes the risks of the initial mammogram being overlooked, reduces waiting time for results, and eliminates some of the problems of the primary practitioner not receiving the results in a timely manner. For the patient, case management enables all the elements of the care delivery process to function as a collaborative, actively communicating team. The case manager ensures this integration despite the existence of a fragmented delivery system.

EPISODIC VERSUS CONTINUUM CASE MANAGEMENT

Case management that is episode based begins with an event or illness that triggers a need and continues until the individual no longer requires care for that specific condition or phase of illness. In this circumstance case management is time limited. Usually the duration of case management becomes analogous to the time period of care delivery at a specific venue. That is, case management that begins with admission to a hospital continues until the patient is discharged from the hospital to a new venue of care or home. This model of case management will work with the patient and staff within each area of the hospital in which the patient receives care and will identify the patient's appropriate placement postdischarge. For instance, case management will follow a stroke patient through all the venues of the hospital—from the emergency room to acute care to a rehabilitation unit. The case manager will, in an episodic model, identify an appropriate discharge option, but will usually terminate services at this point. In some episodic models, especially those that follow a significant number of capitated clients, case managers may track the patient after discharge from a specific venue. For the stroke patient, the case manager may arrange to conduct posthospitalization phone calls to ascertain health status or arrange for follow-up physician visits.

In a true continuum-based model, case management begins with the identification of the need for enhanced coordination of services and resources for individuals and continues indefinitely until the issues are resolved or until the patient dies. While the patient is managed indefinitely if there exists an ongoing health issue, the intensity of service delivery will certainly fluctuate. A continuum-based model not only coordinates healthcare delivery across all venues and places of care, but it can follow a patient throughout a lifespan. In a capitated marketplace, continuum models will eventually proliferate as willingness and prevention become essential components to maintaining health.

COMMUNITY-BASED CASE MANAGEMENT

This model of case management is often sponsored by social service or community organizations. The case management agency can serve both a coordinating function and also may be a service provider, such as a home health agency or independent living center. Usually, clients of the community-based models are functionally impaired or have long term chronic disease or health problems. Recently, many community-based programs have identified a need to target their services to such diverse groups as HIV-positive or AIDS patients or those with severe mental illness. For HIV-positive and AIDS patients, community-based models perform such activities as provide education and information, arrange access to needed services, assist with realistic future planning, monitor disease status, deliver primary nursing care, monitor medication, and facilitate continuity of care with other healthcare providers. In this model, case management seeks to enhance the quality of life of persons infected with HIV, increase patient and family understanding of the disease and disease process, prevent further disease and disease processes, and prevent further disease transmission. At the same time, the goal is to decrease the overall cost of care through collaboration and delivery of services designed to reduce the frequency of hospitalization and emergency room visits. Community models that address the issues of persons with severe mental illness will often employ social workers as well as other professions to deliver case management services. The programs may be concerned not only with the patient's mental health status, but with social implications caused by the underlying disease or disorder. In such a model, case management may address concerns ranging from housing and employment to substance abuse and dysfunctional families while simultaneously coordinating more traditional medical care.

UTILIZATION REVIEW

A utilization review model of case management is often sponsored by managed care organizations such as HMOs. In such a system, case management is the tool to determine the necessity, appropriateness, and efficiency of the use of medical services, procedures, and facilities. Some of these systems control utilization before it occurs, as with authorization systems. A utilization review model also provides for concurrent review. That is, services are monitored as they are provided. The majority of utilization review programs focus on inpatient service, such as acute hospitalization, because these services are the most expensive. An effective utilization review model relies on case managers, operating as a team, to carry out all the diverse functions of the system in an efficient and cost-effective manner. Accordingly, many different personnel with diverse areas of specialty will serve as case managers in this context. They include the attending physician, the review coordinator, the physician reviewer, the discharge planner, the facility utilization review committee, and the facility quality assurance committee. Under the scenario of case management, utilization review can work like this: At regular intervals, case managers from the third-party payor assess the progress of each of the payor's hospitalized clients through review of medical charts and records and interview with attending physicians as well as hospital staff. The third-party payor staff will work with the hospital's case manager to facilitate this status evaluation and review. In many instances, the third-party payor will visit each hospital to conduct an on-site review. This involves a combination of telephone conversations (usually between payor case manager and facility case manager) and facsimile or E-mail transmissions. Some patients may be reviewed on a daily basis if their condition warrants it, whereas more stable, less serious patients are reviewed every few days. Through a utilization review focus, a case manager will evaluate each case according to standard utilization criteria, such as:

- Is the venue of care (ICU, surgical ward, rehab unit, etc.) appropriate to the patient's condition?
- Is ongoing hospitalization still necessary?
- Is the patient receiving treatment that is appropriate and likely to bring about the desired outcome?

Utilization-based models of case management are usually also designed to encourage a specific payor's standards of care. With a case manager from an HMO actively in place, physicians and other healthcare professionals are less inclined to practice in a vacuum or outside of customary community practice. In this way, case management becomes the mechanism for the payor to involve itself in the clinical decisions affecting its enrollees and can ensure that its standards of care are being maintained.

CATASTROPHIC CARE

One of the most popular and oldest models of case management is principally designed to follow catastrophic cases. These models have their roots in the worker's compensation insurance industry. Unlike some models of case management emerging in capitated markets, programs of catastrophic case management are responsive rather than preventive in focus. Until wellness programs and changes in lifestyle have an even greater impact on the health of the American worker, it remains critical to manage disabled employee's needs. In this scenario, case management becomes tantamount to disability management. As such, these programs have several major goals, including:

- Assuring access to requisite service in situations of complex and multiple need
- Seeking to prevent long-term institutionalization of persons suffering from severe accidents or illnesses
- Identifying cases where a return to work is possible and therefore facilitating such return through medical and other support services

For the case manager to be successful in accomplishing these goals, particularly re-employment, in such a model, early intervention is critical. It is also important to focus on some additional factors. These include a cooperative effort or partnership with the employer, and the continuation of the employee's income at a reasonable level during a period of rehabilitation. Under this model, the case manager may also be directly addressing the vocational as well as medical and rehabilitation needs of the disabled individual. If return to work with the former employer is not an option, then other employment alternatives, including retraining and job search assistance, must be part of the services available to be recommended by case management. Likewise, if a disabled patient is not secure in the knowledge that his or her income will be sufficient to meet basic needs, then the focus and attitude required for successful rehabilitation will not be present. Clearly, in the catastrophic case, unlike most other models of case management, cost control and decreased utilization may not be key features of the system. In fact, short term cost control may be counterproductive to the goals of re-employment for many of these patients. Indeed, in the area of disability case management, many expensive services, such as rehabilitation, will be necessary if long-term savings are to be achieved. Therefore, it is critical for the case manager to ensure that there is value (which should be expressed through positive patient outcomes) from the providers of these services. Indeed, case management in this model involves the process of medically, scientifically, and economically analyzing issues such as the need for long-term care in an institutional setting, maximum medical recovery, and return-to-work potential. Moreover, this model is also influenced by players outside of the normal healthcare arena, including those from the worker's compensation system.

GATEKEEPING

In this model, physicians are performing some aspects of case management in their gatekeeping role under managed care programs. As the trend toward managed care continues, more and more physicians are assuming the function of case management for HMOs. The physician gatekeeping focus is on coordinating medical care, and matching patient needs and preferences with the judicious use of healthcare resources. Gatekeeping, however, is a loaded word. Like traditional case managers, physicians acting in this capacity usually do an excellent job at client advocacy. Recent studies have indicated that HMO primary physicians serve their patients' advocacy needs very well as navigators in an increasingly complex medical world.[1] This seems contrary to the popular belief that gatekeepers only exist to limit the use of specialists, expensive tests, and costly high-tech treatments. To be an effective case manager, the physician must know how to refer efficiently within a network and how to communicate to patients what is being done and why. These are the same skills that all good case managers cultivate and presumably develop. It seems prudent to suggest therefore, that when physicians function in the role of gatekeeper they be trained as per the requirements of case management. In fact, they should be trained along with case managers. Only in this way will the aim of an integrated care delivery system, with case management assured a pivotal place, be realized.

SUMMARY

The various paradigms of case management have been detailed and are summarized in Table 3–1. In practice, systems of case management will typically embrace features of several of these models in order to best meet their organization's needs. When

T A B L E   3–1

Models of Case Management
A Comparison

Dimensions	Internal/External	Disease Management	Episodic/Continuum	Community Based	Utilization Review	Catastrophic Care	Gatekeeping
Goals							
Minimize inpatient hospitalization	✓	✓	✓		✓		✓
Minimize cost of long term care and disability	✓		✓	✓		✓	
Maximize health organization profits and revenues	✓	✓	✓		✓		✓
Primary Care Management Personnel							
Nurses	✓	✓	✓	✓	✓	✓	
Social workers	✓			✓	✓		
Physicians	✓				✓		✓
Reimbursement Mechanisms							
Fixed budget			✓	✓			
Annual capitation							✓
Administrative cost	✓	✓	✓		✓		
Fee-for-service and billable hours	✓						

designing a system of centralized case management, the health-care manager will benefit from an understanding of these different approaches.

To have an effective system of case management, an organization cannot simply select a single model and duplicate it. Rather, the best systems of case management are developed in an individual context that takes into account the particular circumstances and needs of all involved players. Of course, the level of usefulness of case management will depend on a host of factors. Patient-to-staff ratios, type of patients managed, available budgets for case management, extent of authority vested with case managers, are a few of the most determinative factors. Notwithstanding the individuality of case management systems, case management is working. Statistics tell an impressive part of the story: Almost 80 percent of American's largest companies and 30 percent of companies with fewer than 500 employees use case management services.[2] The Health Insurance Association of America, which is based in Washington, D.C., routinely affirms that insurance companies save $30 for every dollar spent on case management programs. That is an impressive return on investment in any market.

Anecdotal reports also attest to the effectiveness of case management. Hospitals and case management organizations generally believe that readmissions drop, reimbursement for charges increases, and patients are significantly benefited through the intervention of case management. Firms such as Honeywell, United Parcel Service, and General Motors all can tell how case management has improved clinical care and lowered costs for its employees. Despite the popularity of case management, few randomized clinical trials have examined its true efficacy for such indicators as reducing hospitalizations, improving clinical outcomes, and decreasing dependency on the healthcare system. Although several studies have been conducted, their results are seemingly contradictory.

In a study conducted at a university-affiliated Veterans Affairs Medical Center, it was concluded that "frequent contacts for education, care, and accessibility by case managers using protocols were ineffective in reducing nonelective readmissions."[3] The study was conducted with 668 patients aged

45 years or older who were discharged from the general medical inpatient service of the program, who had access to a phone, and who received primary care at the hospital's clinics. The patients were evenly randomized to a case management intervention group and control group. Within 24 hours of discharge, the first intervention was employed by case management. Educational materials as well as information on obtaining access to additional service was mailed. Within 5 days, patients were called to review and resolve unmet needs, detect early warning signs, and discuss any barriers to keeping appointments. If the patient made no visit to the outpatient clinic within 30 days, the case manager again contacted the patient. Patients were followed up for 12 months. The study sought to clinically prove what descriptive studies have indicated regarding the idea that readmissions of high-risk patients are potentially preventable. The study cited noncompliance, unmet social needs, unrecognized clinical deterioration, and inadequate patient education as likely causes of these preventable admissions. As such, the interventions employed were targeted at several of the likely contributing factors. Approximately 49 percent of patients in each group were readmitted to the hospital during the follow-up period. Patients in the intervention group made 15 percent more outpatient visits to their primary care physicians than their counterparts in the control groups. Accordingly, the intermediate goal of the case management intervention, to increase outpatient care, was achieved. Unfortunately, in this setting case management seemed to have little effect in reducing readmissions for medical inpatients during a one-year follow-up.

However, certain limits of the study should be understood. The type and extent of training, if any, for the nurses functioning as case managers was not identified. The only intervention used was the telephone. Case management might have been enhanced by making home visits, which would likely have required lower caseloads. Moreover, it is not known what venues of care other than primary care were available to the case managers for referral. The results of this study underscore the need for formalized evaluation of the various methods of intervention that are at the disposal of case management. In this scenario, telephone intervention did not produce the desired outcome of a decrease in hospital read-missions. Moreover, these findings point out the importance of ensuring that each system of case management is designed to have an internal system of ongoing program evaluation. Although the Veterans Administration study did not yield demonstrable proof of the usefulness of a telephonic approach to case management, other studies have documented more suc-cessful approaches to case management.

A recent study from Stanford University of 585 patients, who were all insured by the same HMO, produced favorable re-sults. In this study patients were less than 70 years old and had been recently hospitalized for a heart attack.[4] They all received the HMO's usual care, including physician counseling on smok-ing cessation, nutritionist counseling on dietary change, and physician-managed lipid-lowering drug therapy. Half of the pa-tients were offered an additional intervention of case manage-ment, including significant telephonic intervention. Additionally, these patients visited the nurse up to four times per year for ex-ercise testing or counseling. The patients also completed ques-tionnaires and were monitored for specific indicators rather than just general well being. Activities such as losing weight, lower-ing cholesterol, and increasing exercise were monitored. Overall, the case managers spent an average of approximately nine hours per year on each patient. At the end of the first year, death rates between the control group and the group receiving case manage-ment intervention were no different. However, those assigned to the case management group were faring much better in attain-ing goals with respect to risk-factor modification. Low-density lipoprotein (LDL) cholesterol levels averaged 132 in the usual-care patients versus 107 in the patients who had received case management. Similarly, smoking cessation rates were also bet-ter in the group receiving intervention. In this study, case man-agement proved a valuable contribution in an agenda to improve care and lower costs. The nine hours of nursing time per patient cost an estimated $500. In contrast, cardiac rehabilitation could have cost $2,500.

Additional studies and research are needed to document the most effective case management strategies. Case manage-ment is being practiced in an age of evidence-based medicine without the benefit of scientific analysis. For case management to continue to flourish; for the effectiveness of the various models of case management to be known; for case management to become more than just an intervention, but rather a health-care policy, there must be continuous and systematic evaluation of its efficacy.

REFERENCES

1. Franks P, Clancy CM, Gatekeeping revisited: Protecting patients from over treatment. *N Engl J Med* 6:424–429, 1992.
2. Hurley ML. Case management—Communicating real savings. *Business and Health* 14:29–36, 1996.
3. Fitzgerald JF, Smith DM, Martin DK, Freedman JA, Katz BP. A case manager intervention to reduce readmissions. *Arch Intern Med* 154:1721, 1994.
4. Case management and lowered heart risk. *Harvard Heart Letter* 5:4, 1995.

4

Designing a System of Centralized Case Management

These are trying times for the healthcare executive. As our elected officials put forward bold initiatives to reshape care delivery, the support for change gains ever more momentum. It is, however, the individual providers, payors, and patients who ultimately must make the restructured delivery system work. The collaboration of healthcare organizations representing the varied interests of all players is certainly a first step in this process. Integrated delivery systems that span multiple venues of care are being organized to address the problems of fragmentation and complex payment systems. These integrated systems, notwithstanding their potential to address many of the problems of present healthcare delivery, are creating a different set of issues. Compounding the difficulty of accessing and navigating integrated systems is the vexing challenge of matching client need with services in the expanding but loosely organized continuum. Integrated delivery systems have also resulted in increased reimbursement complexity. The act of integration may have enabled the provider to manage capitated forms of reimbursement for the first time. Unless the system is fully capitated, which would be very unlikely, handling multiple systems of payment as diverse as Medicare and capitation takes particular expertise.

Centralized case management is quickly emerging as the necessary link in the chain that holds together the integrated delivery systems. As integrated delivery systems are formed by parties with varying incentives and areas of expertise, it becomes even more critical to bridge these differences through case management, as depicted in Figure 4–1. The sheer magnitude and diversity of the healthcare market demands a centralized means to ensure the desired integration of the delivery system. To be successful, the case management system must address the agendas of multiple and diverse audiences. The best way to accomplish that is to design and develop a centralized system of case management based on clear identification of need and delineation of accountability.

Initiating and designing an effective case management system involves the implementation of five steps or phases.

1. The situational audit
2. Goal/role identification
3. Organizational structuring

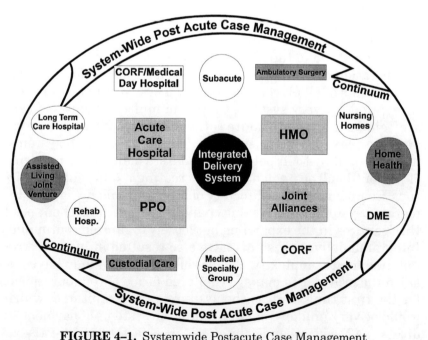

FIGURE 4–1. Systemwide Postacute Case Management

4. Service delivery design

5. Program evaluation implementation

In the first phase, the organization seeking to establish a case management system must conduct an internal audit of the environment and circumstances in which the system is to function. The audit underscores issues and problems that in theory may be resolved or diminished through the use of case management. In phase two, the organization must define the purposes and goals of the system. Moreover, as a system is being developed, it will be important to distinguish differences in role and function between case management and case manager. In the third phase, decisions as to how this system is to be structured are made and lines of authority are drawn. The next phase articulates the service delivery design and establishes parameters for integration throughout the continuum. The final phase evaluates the performance of the system against predetermined objectives. Please see Figure 4–2 for a reference of these phases. The following is a sample timeline and significant activity list for a case management design project for a hospital. At the outset of the system design, a detailed timetable such as the one in Table 4–1 should be developed to ensure a consistency of expectations among the teams and management of the sponsoring organization.

Before outlining these phases of centralized case management development in detail, it is important to explore further the conceptual framework of centralized case management as a

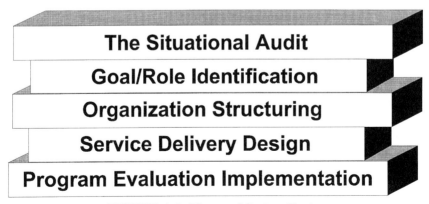

FIGURE 4–2. Phases of System Design

T A B L E   4 – 1

Project Time Line
Centralized Case Management

Month 1	Month 2	Month 3	Month 4	Month 5	Month 6
Orient senior administrative staff to the concept of case management	Present results of ■ Analysis of patient case mix ■ DRG revenue loss analysis ■ Need analysis for designated post acute venues	Present findings of situational audit and recommendations for program/service enhancement	Education and training of case managers ■ Session II	Confirm postacute venues' availability during an 18-month window	Strategic work session ■ Formal presentation of final document
Identify project liaison(s)					
Initiate situational audit		Conduct medical roundtable to orient physicians to purpose, objectives and means of centralized case management	Identify discharge triggers per venue as a key to the outcome indicator system	Identify future postacute venue capabilities within a 36-month window	Begin implementation of centralized case management system
Identify existing postacute venues for targeted analysis including:	Enroll case managers for training				Establish accountability measures and time frames for status review
■ CIR			Complete model for functional outcome by venue of care	Conduct second medical roundtable	
■ Subacute	Complete pretraining skills assessment evaluation of case managers	Consensus as to scope of case management for disease, venue, and payor arrangement	Confirm organizational structure for system	Review strategic opportunities for expansion sensitive to political, environmental, and clinical capabilities	
■ Home health					
■ Ambulatory surgery					
■ Outpatient services					
Complete venue inventory	Conduct initial training session ■ Session I	Prepare profile of case manager ■ Develop job description ■ Identify staffing complement		Discuss marketing strategies to enhance managed care market	
Complete physician specialty analysis					
Complete human resource inventory	Complete situational audit				
Complete financial information worksheets					
Initiate DRG analysis		Confirm status and terms of existing managed care contracts			
Initiate need analysis for:					
■ CIR					
■ Subacute					
■ Long term care hospital					
■ Medical day hospital					
Review procedures for use of ambulatory surgery					

starting point for any design process. A system of centralized case management is premised on its relationship to a provider organization, which is usually either a healthcare service provider or a managed care organization. Therefore, the design of a centralized case management system will be largely dependent on the needs and wants of the organization to be benefited by its creation. Although individual patient need is taken into account through the delivery of service by the case manager, the centralized system and its structure should reflect the priorities and characteristics of the sponsoring organization. At the outset of the design process, it is common for organizational leadership and managers to have fundamental questions concerning the startup of the system. Of course, many questions cannot be answered until the system has been completely designed, but there will be many questions, some of which can be anticipated. Change has been so rapid and momentous of late that any new system, regardless of its function or purpose, may be met with suspicion and distrust. Sometimes, factions within an organization will seek to sabotage the development of a centralized system of case management out of fear of the unknown. Therefore, even before any initial design phase, it is important to address individuals' questions about case management in order to reduce the likelihood of proliferating misinformation and rumor. Box 4–1 will serve as both a rehearsal for the manager who will be faced with startup questions and as an ongoing resource tool.

CONDUCTING THE SITUATIONAL AUDIT

Step one for successful design of a system of centralized case management is to conduct an organization situational audit. The purpose of the audit is to specifically identify the environment in which the system is to be implemented and to determine the needs and problems of that specific organization that must be addressed through the establishment of such a system. At the conclusion of the audit, management should be able to answer two fundamental questions: Which patients should be followed and what venues are preferred discharge options?

The audit allows the design team to assemble information on cost of care in each venue within the organization. The financial incentives for preferring one venue of care over another will be

---

B O X   4 – 1

COMMON STARTUP QUESTIONS AND SHORT ANSWERS FOR DEVELOPMENT OF A SYSTEM OF CASE MANAGEMENT

COMMON STARTUP QUESTIONS	THE SHORT ANSWER
How do we decide which patients to follow with a system of case management?	Ideally, all patients should be followed. Initially, start with a list of 15 diagnoses for which you believe case management will make the largest impact.
Can only nurses be case managers?	No. Look for individuals who combine clinical, negotiation, and financial skills.
To whom should case managers report?	It doesn't matter, provided it is a centralized system and its leadership has clear authority within the larger organization.
Should each venue or unit have a case manager?	No, this is counterproductive to a system of case management that places patients across the continuum.
Do clinical pathways eliminate the need for case management?	No, they are just one of a case manager's tools in assuring cost-effective, outcome-based care across a number of diverse venues.
Do we document the intervention and activities of case management?	Yes, often it is appropriate for inclusion into the case record.
What is an appropriate patient load for an individual case manager?	It depends on a number of factors, including severity of illness of patients, number of venues in continuum, availability of computerization of the system, etc. Typical patient loads range from 1 to 25 up to 1 to 100.

Do standard Medicare patients require case management services?	Most definitely, to assure appropriate venue utilization given the diverse financial, regulatory, and clinical issues involved for each individual. Moreover healthcare providers have a duty to treat Medicare patients in the same manner as other patients.
Is case management a directly reimbursable service?	Not usually, with some limited exceptions. However, case management saves money and ensures appropriate utilization of resources. Under appropriate circumstances, case management services may be an allowable cost if reasonable and related to patient care for Medicare purposes.
How do case managers deal with physicians who "are not with the program"?	As with everything, relationship building is an important and necessary skill for case managers. When that doesn't work, the case manager must have strong administrative backup and support to take further action.
At what point should case management become involved?	This will depend on the model. However, a case manager ideally should monitor the patient from the very first contact with the organization. In fact, in some models of case management, case managers conduct preoperative educational services.

Who should be responsible for designing a system of centralized case management?	It doesn't matter, as long as the individual or team given such responsibility have actual authority to proceed within a predetermined timetable.
Does the system have to be computerized?	Clearly not. Yet, an effective system will be even more productive if it incorporates some of the emerging software programs for case management.
How long does it take to develop a system of case management?	For a provider-based network in a medium-sized urban area, such a system could reasonably be expected to be developed within four to six months.

determined through this process. Moreover, the audit analyzes patients by diagnosis, payor source, and referral, with respect to issues of uncompensated care, length of stay, readmission to an acute care venue, and the reasons for hospital admission of nursing home and home health patients. Compliance with care plans throughout the organization should be reviewed to determine the need for case management oversight in areas where care plans are not meeting intended objectives and where care plans do not exist as a primary focus of case management. The quarterly reports of the utilization review committees in each venue should be examined for trends relating to discharge problems, length of stay, or appropriateness of service issues, which will influence the design of a case management system.

The audit itself is an intense project that should be conducted within a relatively short time frame. For a multivenue healthcare provider, the audit should take approximately four to six weeks to accomplish. Devoting an inordinate amount of time to this phase of the system design could inappropriately shift the focus from targeted analysis to reengineering. Designing a system of case management clearly cannot solve all issues facing a healthcare organization. Although case management may address some of the most vexing ones, it is not the panacea for all of an organization's ills. Centralized case management must be integrated with other clinical and administrative systems to ensure effective and well-run delivery of healthcare. The initial steps in the audit will be determining what information can be acquired, who has the primary responsibility for obtaining it, and what is the purpose of analyzing this particular data. Box 4–2 identifies some key pieces of information that the manager of a hospital-based network may find useful. Moreover, the chart is based on the assumption that a team has been assembled to collect and review the data within a given time frame.

DATA COLLECTION TOOLS

A number of tools and methodologies exist to collect and analyze the requisite information. There is no one approach to conducting the situational audit. The situational audit allows the design of the system to see the terrain before painting the landscape. It is the foundation for ongoing development of the case management system. Data is collected about clinical, financial, and organization issues that are germane to the effective functioning of the system.

Six sample data collection tools are included, which can assist the manager in the information gathering stage. Each tool is represented by one or more worksheets.

Tool #1 DRG Analysis

The first tool is a DRG analysis. The data collected reviews all acute care discharges for a specific period to reveal patterns of significant overutilization of acute care beds. The DRGs are grouped by diagnostic category to identify what types of diagnoses have the most significant uncompensated care, and the most need for an alternative venue of care.

For the purposes of this analytical tool, uncompensated care is defined as the amount that exceeds capitation under the PPS System. As such, it represents the amount of nonreimbursed care by Medicare. Furthermore, along with experience and customary usage, the DRG system may be used as a benchmark. It has been determined that managed care, through its negotiations with the provider, generally will not exceed the per

BOX 4-2

REQUIRED INFORMATION FOR SITUATIONAL AUDIT OF A HEALTHCARE NETWORK OR HOSPITAL PROVIDER

INFO/ACTIVITY	PRIMARY RESPONSIBILITY	COMPLETED ✓WHEN DONE
▪ Payor mix in aggregate		
▪ Payor mix by diagnosis		
▪ DRG analysis for hospital inpatients (Box 4–3)		
▪ Identify by diagnosis, payor, and physician of patients with more than one admission within last twelve months		
▪ Venue inventory (Box 4–4)		
▪ Referral mix		
▪ Cost of care by venue		
▪ Critical path existence		
▪ Success/compliance rate of critical paths presently in use		
▪ Admission criteria by venue of care		
▪ Determination of Medicare reimbursement status for nonacute venues (CORF, LTCH, Psych Unit, Rehab, etc.) (Box 4–9)		
▪ Analysis of all referrals from skilled nursing units and other nursing homes to acute care by payor, diagnosis, and physician		
▪ Review of each venue's last four quarters of utilization review reports		
▪ Analysis of hospital readmissions by patients receiving home health services		

diem or other rate paid by Medicare and therefore will not compensate for any days past the DRG length of stay.

To ascertain the actual average length of stay per DRG, the actual lengths of stay per patient per DRG that exceeded the DRG length of stay are totaled and are divided by the total number of patients. Next, the actual average length of stay is compared to the DRG average length of stay computed by HCFA (based on analysis of national data). The total payment received per case is identified for each DRG using the average national payment determined by HCFA using a base rate of $4,000. The payment per diem is computed by dividing the total payment received per case by the DRG specified average length of stay. The per diem amount is then used to calculate the amount of uncompensated care per case; it denotes an amount that the facility is potentially forfeiting due to excessive lengths of stay in acute care. Ultimately, the amount of uncompensated care per DRG is calculated by multiplying the loss per case by the total number of patients discharged within a given DRG.

A facility must assume that nearly all patients who exceed the DRG designated length of stay will cause the hospital to incur significant losses. This assumption is based on the fact that Medicare reimbursement guidelines are an adequate gauge of appropriate utilization of, and reimbursement for, acute care.

When examining revenue losses by DRG, it is helpful to group the DRGs into related diagnostic categories, such as cardiac care, respiratory care, rehabilitation, postsurgical, etc. In reviewing and analyzing the DRG data the manager may note particularly significant trends of overutilization of acute care in groupings of related diagnoses, which may be better served in another venue of care.

The breakdown of revenue losses is significant because it readily targets those specializations that could be developed in alternative postacute venues of care. Additionally, it provides further insight into the order of patient/DRG priority for inclusion into the case management system, all in relation to the magnitude of the amount of uncompensated care. In other words, this is a key tool in determining which patients should be followed by the case management program to be developed. In Box 4–3, all columns for DRGs 1–130 have been completed to assist in understanding this format. In order to utilize the DRG

B O X   4 – 3

SAMPLE: UNCOMPENSATED CARE BY DRG

DRG	DEFINITION	# OF PTS.	ACT. ALOS	DRG LOS	DIFF.	PAYMENT PER CASE	PAYMENT PER DIEM	AVG. LOSS PER CASE	TOTAL LOSS PER DRG
1	Craniotomy, Age over 17, Except for Trauma	101	22.4	13.5	8.9	$12,626.00	$935.26	$8,323.81	$840,704.55
2	Craniotomy for Trauma, Age over 17	23	27.3	13.9	13.4	12,387.20	891.17	11,941.62	274,657.20
3	Craniotomy, Age 0–17	36	24.8	12.7	12.1	12,158.40	957.35	11,583.99	417,023.55
4	Spinal Procedures	18	17.0	11.0	6.0	9,316.80	846.98	5,081.89	91,474.04
5	Extracranial Vascular Procedures	13	10.8	5.6	5.2	6,240.40	1,114.36	5,794.66	75,330.54
6	Carpal Tunnel Release	1	15.0	3.2	11.8	2,535.60	792.38	9,350.03	9,350.03
7	Peripheral and Cranial Nerve and Other Nervous System Procedures with CC	3	24.3	17.4	6.9	10,002.00	574.83	3,966.31	11,898.93
8	Peripheral and Cranial Nerve and Other Nervous System Procedures without CC	3	6.7	4.7	2.0	3,674.00	781.70	1,563.40	4,690.21
9	Spinal Disorders and Injuries	7	12.0	8.8	3.2	5,021.20	570.59	1,825.89	12,781.24
10	Nervous System Neoplasm with CC	8	14.8	9.7	5.1	5,047.20	520.33	2,653.68	21,229.46
11	Nervous System Neoplasm without CC	1	7.0	5.5	1.5	3,093.60	562.47	843.71	843.71
12	Degenerative Nervous System Disorders	11	16.4	9.0	7.4	3,829.60	425.51	3,148.78	34,636.60
13	Multiple Sclerosis and Cerebellar Ataxia	7	15.1	7.2	7.9	3,125.20	434.06	3,429.04	24,003.27
14	Specific Cerebrovascular Disorders Except Transient Ischemic Attacks	148	15.8	8.7	7.1	4,782.40	549.70	3,902.88	577,625.97
15	Transient Ischemic Attacks and Precerebral Occlusions	28	6.9	4.9	2.0	2,763.60	564.00	1,128.00	31,584.00
16	Nonspecific Cerebrovascular Disorders with CC	6	10.5	7.8	2.7	4,195.20	537.85	1,452.18	8,713.11
17	Nonspecific Cerebrovascular Disorders without CC	1	7.0	4.6	2.4	2,478.00	538.70	1,292.87	1,292.87

18	Cranial and Peripheral Nerve Disorders with CC	8	10.0	7.2	2.8	$3,650.40	$507.00	$1,419.60	$11,356.80
19	Cranial and Peripheral Nerve Disorders without CC	6	7.0	4.8	2.2	2,370.00	493.75	1,086.25	6,517.50
20	Nervous System Infection Except Viral Meningitis	17	18.1	11.7	6.4	8,331.20	712.07	4,557.24	77,473.04
21	Viral Meningitis	5	9.8	8.6	1.2	5,736.80	667.07	800.48	4,002.42
22	Hypertensive Encephalopathy	1	13.0	5.4	7.6	3,122.40	578.22	4,394.49	4,394.49
23	Nontraumatic Stupor and Coma	2	8.0	5.6	2.4	3,201.60	571.71	1,372.11	2,744.23
24	Seizure and Headache, Age Greater than 17 with CC	26	10.4	6.6	3.8	3,858.80	584.67	2,221.73	57,765.07
25	Seizure and Headache, Age Greater than 17 without CC	69	7.0	4.1	2.9	2,206.00	538.05	1,560.34	107,663.56
26	Seizure and Headache, Age 0–17	40	6.4	4.3	2.1	2,508.00	583.26	1,224.84	48,993.49
27	Traumatic Stupor and Coma, Coma Greater than 1 hour	16	16.3	7.4	8.9	5,382.80	727.41	6,473.91	103,582.53
28	Traumatic Stupor and Coma, Coma Less than 1 hour, Age over 17 with CC	18	14.2	8.3	5.9	4,868.00	586.51	3,460.39	62,286.94
29	Traumatic Stupor and Coma, Coma Less than 1 Hour, Age Greater than 17 without CC	10	8.0	4.6	3.4	2,480.00	539.13	1,833.04	18,330.43
30	Traumatic Stupor and Coma, Coma Less than 1 Hour, Age 0–17	35	5.5	2.0	3.5	1,474.80	737.40	2,580.90	90,331.50
31	Concussion, Age Greater than 17 with CC	0	0.0	5.6	—	3,050.80	544.79	—	—
32	Concussion, Age Greater than 17 without CC	0	0.0	3.4	—	1,854.00	545.29	—	—
33	Concussion, Age 0–17	1	3.0	1.6	1.4	1,023.60	639.75	895.65	895.65
34	Other Disorders of Nervous System with CC	17	16.4	7.5	8.9	4,344.80	579.31	5,155.83	87,649.10
35	Other Disorders of Nervous System without CC	2	7.5	4.9	2.6	2,346.40	478.86	1,245.03	2,490.06
36	Retinal Procedures	4	4.8	1.8	3.0	2,395.60	1,330.89	3,992.67	15,970.67
37	Orbital Procedures	11	7.2	3.9	3.3	3,235.60	829.64	2,737.82	30,115.97

DRG	DEFINITION	# OF PTS.	ACT. ALOS	DRG LOS	DIFF.	PAYMENT PER CASE	PAYMENT PER DIEM	AVG. LOSS PER CASE	TOTAL LOSS PER DRG
38	Primary Iris Procedures	0	0.0	2.7	—	$1,602.00	$593.33	—	—
39	Lens Procedures with or without Vitrectomy	1	3.0	1.9	1.1	2,022.00	1,064.21	$1,170.63	$1,170.63
40	Extraocular Procedures Except Orbit, Age Greater than 17	3	7.7	3.6	4.1	2,496.40	693.44	2,843.12	8,529.37
41	Extraocular Procedures Except Orbit, Age 0–17	1	3.0	1.6	1.4	1,524.00	952.50	1,333.50	1,333.50
42	Intraocular Procedures Except Retina, Iris and Lens	10	5.9	2.2	3.7	2,274.80	1,034.00	3,825.80	38,258.00
43	Hyphema	0	0.0	3.6	—	1,360.00	377.78	—	—
44	Acute Major Eye Infections	2	8.5	6.0	2.5	2,302.00	383.67	959.17	1,918.33
45	Neurological Eye Disorders	3	7.3	4.3	3.0	2,484.40	577.77	1,733.30	5,199.91
46	Other Disorders of the Eye, Age Greater than 17 with CC	1	10.0	6.1	3.9	3,021.20	495.28	1,931.59	1,931.59
47	Other Disorders of the Eye, Age Greater than 17 without CC	1	4.0	3.9	0.1	1,732.40	444.21	44.42	44.42
48	Other Disorders of the Eye, Age 0–17	2	3.5	2.9	0.6	1,674.40	577.38	346.43	692.86
49	Major Head and Neck Procedures	1	45.0	6.8	38.2	6,842.40	1,006.24	38,438.19	38,438.19
50	Sialoadenectomy	1	8.0	2.3	5.7	2,852.40	1,240.17	7,068.99	7,068.99
51	Salivary Gland Procedures Except Sialoadenectomy	0	0.0	3.0	—	2,735.20	911.73	—	—
52	Cleft Lip and Palate Repair	5	5.6	3.0	2.6	3,660.80	1,220.27	3,172.69	15,863.47
53	Sinus and Mastoid Procedures, Age Greater than 17	3	7.3	3.4	3.9	3,458.80	1,017.29	3,967.45	11,902.34
54	Sinus and Mastoid Procedures, Age 0–17	0	0.0	3.2	—	2,870.40	897.00	—	—
55	Miscellaneous Ear, Nose, Mouth, and Throat Procedures	15	7.9	2.8	5.1	2,582.00	922.14	4,702.93	70,543.93
56	Rhinoplasty	0	0.0	3.1	—	3,073.00	991.29	—	—
57	Tonsillectomy and Adenoidectomy Procedures Except Tonsillectomy and/or Adenoidectomy Only, Age Greater than 17	0	0.0	5.2	—	4,069.60	782.62	—	—

58	Tonsillectomy and Adenoidectomy Procedures Except Tonsillectomy and/or Adenoidectomy Only, Age 0–17	9	4.3	1.5	2.8	$1,290.80	$860.53	$2,409.49	$21,685.44
59	Tonsillectomy and/or Adenoidectomy Only, Age Greater than 17	0	0.0	1.9	—	1,840.80	968.84	—	—
60	Tonsillectomy and/or Adenoidectomy Only, Age 0–17	4	2.8	1.5	1.3	1,089.60	726.40	944.32	3,777.28
61	Myringotomy with Tube Insertion, Age Greater than 17	0	0.0	5.1	—	4,007.60	785.80	—	—
62	Myringotomy with Tube Insertion, Age 0–17	5	5.0	1.3	3.7	1,286.80	989.85	3,662.43	18,312.15
63	Other Ear, Nose, Mouth, and Throat OR Procedures	27	8.8	5.0	3.8	4,418.80	883.76	3,358.29	90,673.78
64	Ear, Nose, Mouth, and Throat Malignancy	0	0.0	8.4	—	4,567.60	543.76	—	—
65	Dysequilibrium	7	8.0	3.8	4.2	2,026.80	533.37	2,240.15	15,681.03
66	Epistaxis	2	5.0	3.9	1.1	2,030.40	520.62	572.68	1,145.35
67	Epiglottitis	0	0.0	4.7	—	3,352.40	713.28	—	—
68	Otitis Media and URI, Age Greater than 17 with CC	3	8.3	5.4	2.9	2,840.00	525.93	1,525.19	4,575.56
69	Otitis Media and URI, Age Greater than 17 without CC	1	6.0	4.2	1.8	2,053.20	488.86	879.94	879.94
70	Otitis Media and URI, Age 0–17	4	5.8	4.4	1.4	2,324.80	528.36	739.71	2,958.84
71	Laryngotracheitis	0	0.0	4.2	—	2,603.20	619.81	—	—
72	Nasal Trauma and Deformity	0	0.0	4.4	—	2,464.00	560.00	—	—
73	Other Ear, Nose, Mouth, and Throat Diagnoses, Age Greater than 17	2	8.0	5.5	2.5	3,046.40	553.89	1,384.73	2,769.45
74	Other Ear, Nose, Mouth and Throat Diagnoses, Age 0–17	10	7.7	2.1	5.6	1,428.40	680.19	3,809.07	38,090.67
75	Major Chest Procedures	22	21.9	12.4	9.5	12,220.40	985.52	9,362.40	205,972.87
76	Other Respiratory System OR Procedures with CC	10	33.1	13.9	19.2	10,050.40	723.05	13,882.57	138,825.67
77	Other Respiratory System OR Procedures without CC	3	13.0	6.0	7.0	4,252.00	708.67	4,960.67	14,882.00
78	Pulmonary Embolism	6	18.3	9.2	9.1	5,684.40	617.87	5,622.61	33,735.68

DRG	DEFINITION	# OF PTS.	ACT. ALOS	DRG LOS	DIFF.	PAYMENT PER CASE	PAYMENT PER DIEM	AVG. LOSS PER CASE	TOTAL LOSS PER DRG
79	Respiratory Infections and Inflammations, Age over 17 with CC	20	15.8	10.7	5.1	$6,782.00	$633.83	$3,232.54	$64,650.84
80	Respiratory Infections and Inflammations, Age over 17	1	9.0	7.4	1.6	3,703.60	500.49	800.78	800.78
81	Respiratory Infections and Inflammations, Age 0–17	6	13.2	7.1	6.1	5,729.20	806.93	4,922.27	29,533.62
82	Respiratory Neoplasms	17	16.4	8.9	7.5	5,294.80	594.92	4,461.91	75,852.47
83	Major Chest Trauma with CC	2	11.5	7.2	4.3	3,812.00	529.44	2,276.61	4,553.22
84	Major Chest Trauma without CC	0	0.0	4.3	—	1,998.40	464.74	—	—
85	Pleural Effusion with CC	5	10.0	8.2	1.8	4,756.00	580.00	1,044.00	5,220.00
86	Pleural Effusion without CC	1	5.0	4.9	0.0	2,701.20	551.27	55.13	55.13
87	Pulmonary Edema and Respiratory Failure	3	8.7	7.5	1.2	5,322.40	709.65	851.58	2,554.75
88	Chronic Obstructive Pulmonary Disease	35	13.2	6.9	6.3	4,021.20	582.78	3,671.53	128,503.57
89	Simple Pneumonia and Pleurisy, Age over 17 with CC	45	14.5	8.0	6.5	4,526.80	565.85	3,678.03	165,511.13
90	Simple Pneumonia and Pleurisy, Age over 17 without CC	6	7.8	5.7	2.1	2,769.60	485.89	1,020.38	6,122.27
91	Simple Pneumonia and Pleurisy, Age 0–17	58	7.9	4.4	3.5	2,733.60	621.27	2,174.45	126,118.36
92	Interstitial Lung Disease with CC	1	12.0	8.1	3.9	4,833.60	596.74	2,327.29	2,327.29
93	Interstitial Lung Disease without CC	0	0.0	5.7	—	3,080.00	540.35	—	—
94	Pneumothorax with CC	5	11.0	8.5	2.5	4,970.80	584.80	1,462.00	7,310.00
95	Pneumothorax without CC	4	5.8	4.9	0.9	2,458.40	501.71	451.54	1,806.17
96	Bronchitis and Asthma, Age Greater than 17 with CC	8	9.6	6.2	3.4	3,395.20	547.61	1,861.88	14,895.07
97	Bronchitis and Asthma, Age Greater than 17 without CC	4	9.5	4.9	4.6	2,448.80	499.76	2,298.87	9,195.49
98	Bronchitis and Asthma, Age 0–17	43	7.7	4.1	3.6	2,142.40	522.54	1,881.13	80,888.66
99	Respiratory Signs and Symptoms with CC	3	5.0	4.1	0.9	2,807.60	684.78	616.30	1,848.91
100	Respiratory Signs and Symptoms without CC	6	3.0	2.8	0.2	2,020.40	721.57	144.31	865.89
101	Other Respiratory System Diagnoses with CC	7	8.8	6.2	2.6	3,622.00	584.19	1,518.90	10,632.32

102	Other Respiratory System Diagnoses without CC	2	11.0	4.0	7.0	$2,135.60	$533.90	$3,737.30	$7,474.60
103	Heart Transplant	0	0.0	35.8	—	54,198.00	1,513.91	—	—
104	Cardiac Valve Procedures with Cardiac Catheterization	12	29.8	18.0	11.8	30,430.40	1,690.58	19,948.82	239,385.81
105	Cardiac Valve Procedures without Cardiac Catheterization	7	18.3	13.0	5.3	23,062.40	1,774.03	9,402.36	65,816.54
106	Coronary Bypass with Cardiac Catheterization	34	19.7	13.6	6.1	22,673.20	1,667.15	10,169.60	345,766.30
107	Coronary Bypass without Cardiac Catheterization	32	16.9	10.4	6.5	16,789.60	1,614.38	10,493.50	335,792.00
108	Other Cardiothoracic Procedures	4	33.5	14.7	18.8	24,432.40	1,662.07	31,246.88	124,987.52
110	Major Cardiovascular Procedures with CC	32	19.3	12.2	7.1	16,318.40	1,337.57	9,496.77	303,896.76
111	Major Cardiovascular Procedures without CC	3	8.3	7.5	0.8	9,209.60	1,227.95	982.36	2,947.07
112	Percutaneous Cardiovascular Procedures	148	9.0	5.3	3.7	7,952.40	1,500.45	5,551.68	821,647.97
113	Amputation for Circulatory System Disorders Except Upper Limb and Toe	10	23.5	17.2	6.3	11,106.00	645.70	4,067.90	40,678.95
114	Upper Limb and Toe Amputation for Circulatory Disorders	7	15.3	10.9	4.4	6,154.00	564.59	2,484.18	17,389.28
115	Permanent Cardiac Pacemaker Implant with Acute Myocardial Infarction, Heart Failure or Shock	1	13.0	12.7	0.3	14,374.40	1,131.84	339.55	339.55
116	Other Permanent Cardiac Pacemaker Implant or AICD Lead or Generator Procedure	18	11.1	6.5	4.6	9,805.60	1,508.55	6,939.35	124,908.26
117	Cardiac Pacemaker Revision Except Device Replacement	3	8.0	4.9	3.1	4,668.40	952.73	2,953.48	8,860.43
118	Cardiac Pacemaker Device Replacement	1	5.0	3.5	1.5	6,232.80	1,780.80	2,671.20	2,671.20
119	Vein Ligation and Stripping	2	8.0	5.6	2.4	3,979.60	710.64	1,705.54	3,411.09
120	Other Circulatory System OR Procedures	19	16.1	10.7	5.4	7,846.40	733.31	3,959.87	75,237.44
121	Circulatory Disorders with Acute Myocardial Infarction and Cardiovascular Complication, Discharged Alive	54	8.6	8.6	—	6,408.80	745.21	—	—

DRG	DEFINITION	# OF PTS.	ACT. ALOS	DRG LOS	DIFF.	PAYMENT PER CASE	PAYMENT PER DIEM	AVG. LOSS PER CASE	TOTAL LOSS PER DRG
122	Circulatory Disorders with Acute Myocardial Infarction without Cardiovascular Complication, Discharged Alive	8	7.5	6.0	1.5	$4,516.80	$752.80	$1,129.20	$9,033.60
123	Circulatory Disorders with Acute Myocardial Infarction, Expired	3	15.0	5.1	9.9	5,714.40	1,120.47	11,092.66	33,277.98
124	Circulatory Disorders Except Acute Myocardial Infarction with Cardiac Catheter and Complex Diagnosis	54	8.6	5.5	3.1	5,062.80	920.51	2,853.58	154,093.22
125	Circulatory Disorders Except Acute Myocardial Infarction with Cardiac Catheter without Complex Diagnosis	44	6.3	3.2	3.1	3,380.40	1,056.38	3,274.76	144,089.55
126	Acute and Subacute Endocarditis	3	32.7	18.4	14.3	11,089.60	602.70	8,618.55	25,855.64
127	Heart Failure and Shock	60	13.2	7.1	6.1	4,095.60	576.85	3,518.75	211,125.30
128	Deep Vein Thrombophlebitis	0	0.0	7.5	—	3,128.00	417.07	—	—
129	Cardiac Arrest, Unexplained	2	6.5	3.8	2.7	4,523.20	1190.32	3,213.85	6,427.71
130	Peripheral Vascular Disorders with CC	39	14.6	7.4	7.2	3,670.80	496.05	3,571.59	139,291.98
131	Peripheral Vascular Disorders without CC	—	—	5.6	—	2,355.60	420.64	—	—
132	Atherosclerosis with CC	—	—	4.7	—	2,918.40	620.94	—	—
133	Atherosclerosis without CC	—	—	3.5	—	2,139.20	611.20	—	—
134	Hypertension	—	—	4.4	—	2,304.40	523.73	—	—
135	Cardiac Congenital, and Valvular Disorders, Age over 17 with CC	—	—	5.8	—	3,402.80	586.69	—	—
136	Cardiac Congenital and Valvular Disorders, Age Greater than 17 without CC	—	—	3.7	—	2,240.00	605.41	—	—
137	Cardiac Congenital, and Valvular Disorders, Age 0–17	—	—	3.3	—	2,631.20	797.33	—	—
138	Cardiac Arrhythmia and Conduction Disorders with CC	—	—	5.2	—	3,185.60	612.62	—	—
139	Cardiac Arrhythmia and Conduction Disorders without CC	—	—	3.3	—	1,975.60	598.67	—	—

140	Angina Pectoris	—	4.0	—	$2,503.20	$625.80	—	—
141	Syncope and Collapse with CC	—	5.1	—	2,810.00	550.98	—	—
142	Syncope and Collapse without CC	—	3.6	—	2,069.60	574.89	—	—
143	Chest Pain	—	3.0	—	2,067.67	689.22	—	—
144	Other Circulatory System Diagnoses with CC	—	6.4	—	4,232.00	661.25	—	—
145	Other Circulatory System Diagnoses without CC	—	3.7	—	2,462.00	665.41	—	—
146	Rectal Resection with CC	—	12.2	—	10,146.80	831.70	—	—
147	Rectal Resection without CC	—	8.0	—	6,187.60	773.45	—	—
148	Major Small and Large Bowel Procedures with CC	—	14.7	—	12,888.00	876.73	—	—
149	Major Small and Large Bowel Procedures without CC	—	8.2	—	6,008.80	732.78	—	—
150	Peritoneal Adhesiolysis with CC	—	12.8	—	10,260.80	801.63	—	—
151	Peritoneal Adhesiolysis without CC	—	6.8	—	4,725.60	694.94	—	—
152	Minor Small and Large Bowel Procedures with CC	—	9.7	—	7,131.60	735.22	—	—
153	Minor Small and Large Bowel Procedures without CC	—	6.7	—	4,460.40	665.73	—	—
154	Stomach, Esophageal and Duodenal Procedures, Age Greater than 17 with CC	—	17.0	—	16,696.00	982.12	—	—
155	Stomach, Esophageal, and Duodenal Procedures, Age Greater than 17 without CC	—	7.2	—	5,559.20	772.11	—	—
156	Stomach, Esophageal, and Duodenal Procedures, Age 0–17	—	6.0	—	3,492.80	582.13	—	—
157	Anal and Stomal Procedures with CC	—	6.1	—	4,128.00	676.72	—	—
158	Anal and Stomal Procedures without CC	—	3.0	—	2,178.00	726.00	—	—
159	Hernia Procedures Except Inguinal and Femoral, Age Greater than 17 with CC	—	5.6	—	4,426.40	790.43	—	—
160	Hernia Procedures Except Inguinal and Femoral, Age Greater than 17 without CC	—	3.1	—	2,629.60	848.26	—	—
161	Inguinal and Femoral Hernia Procedures, Age Greater than 17 with CC	—	4.6	—	3,621.20	787.22	—	—

DRG	DEFINITION	# OF PTS.	ACT. ALOS	DRG LOS	DIFF.	PAYMENT PER CASE	PAYMENT PER DIEM	AVG. LOSS PER CASE	TOTAL LOSS PER DRG
162	Inguinal and Femoral Hernia Procedures, Age Greater than 17 without CC	—	—	2.2	—	$2,062.40	$937.45	—	—
163	Hernia Procedures, Age 0–17	—	—	4.8	—	2,910.00	606.25	—	—
164	Appendectomy with Complicated Principal Diagnosis with CC	—	—	10.2	—	8,658.00	848.82	—	—
165	Appendectomy with Complicated Principal Diagnosis without CC	—	—	6.3	—	4,790.40	760.38	—	—
166	Appendectomy without Complicated Principal Diagnosis with CC	—	—	6.3	—	5,386.00	854.92	—	—
167	Appendectomy without Complicated Principal Diagnosis without CC	—	—	3.7	—	3,131.20	846.27	—	—
168	Mouth Procedures with CC	—	—	5.4	—	4,342.40	804.15	—	—
169	Mouth Procedures without CC	—	—	2.7	—	2,459.60	910.96	—	—
170	Other Digestive System OR procedures with CC	—	—	14.6	—	11,125.20	762.00	—	—
171	Other Digestive System OR Procedures without CC	—	—	5.9	—	4,255.20	721.22	—	—
172	Digestive Malignancy with CC	—	—	9.4	—	5,196.00	552.77	—	—
173	Digestive Malignancy without CC	—	—	4.6	—	2,504.80	544.52	—	—
174	GI Hemorrhage with CC	—	—	6.2	—	3,890.40	627.48	—	—
175	GI Hemorrhage without CC	—	—	3.9	—	2,143.60	549.64	—	—
176	Complicated Peptic Ulcer	—	—	6.9	—	4,174.40	604.99	—	—
177	Uncomplicated Peptic Ulcer with CC	—	—	5.6	—	3,224.80	575.86	—	—
178	Uncomplicated Peptic Ulcer without CC	—	—	3.9	—	2,322.80	595.59	—	—
179	Inflammatory Bowel Disease	—	—	8.2	—	4,457.20	543.56	—	—
180	GI Obstruction with CC	—	—	6.8	—	3,655.60	537.59	—	—
181	GI Obstruction without CC	—	—	4.2	—	1,990.00	473.81	—	—
182	Esophagitis, Gastroenteritis, and Miscellaneous Digestive Disorders, Age Greater than 17 with CC	—	—	5.6	—	3,074.00	548.93	—	—

183	Esophagitis, Gastroenteritis, and Miscellaneous Digestive Disorders, Age Greater than 17 without CC	—	3.8	—	$2,142.40	$563.79	—	—
184	Esophagitis, Gastroenteritis, and Miscellaneous Digestive Disorders, Age 0–17	—	3.4	—	1,696.00	498.82	—	—
185	Dental and Oral Diseases Except Extractions and Restorations, Age Greater than 17	—	5.7	—	3,324.80	583.30	—	—
186	Dental and Oral Diseases Except Extractions and Restorations, Age 0–17	—	2.9	—	1,712.80	590.62	—	—
187	Dental Extractions and Restorations	—	3.8	—	2,540.00	668.42	—	—
188	Other Digestive System Diagnoses, Age Greater than 17 with CC	—	6.8	—	4,080.40	600.06	—	—
189	Other Digestive System Diagnoses, Age Greater than 17 without CC	—	3.7	—	2,010.80	543.46	—	—
190	Other Digestive System Diagnoses, Age 0–17	—	4.5	—	2,682.80	596.18	—	—
191	Pancreas, Liver, and Shunt Procedures with CC	—	18.2	—	17,670.40	970.90	—	—
192	Pancreas, Liver, and Shunt Procedures without CC	—	8.9	—	7,043.60	791.42	—	—
193	Biliary Tract Procedures Except only Cholecystectomy with or without Common Duct Exploration with CC	—	15.7	—	12,598.80	802.47	—	—
194	Biliary Tract Procedures Except Only Cholecystectomy with or without Common Duct Exploration without CC	—	9.2	—	6,624.80	720.09	—	—
195	Cholecystectomy with Common Duct Exploration with CC	—	11.4	—	9,830.40	862.32	—	—
196	Cholecystectomy with Common Duct Exploration without CC	—	7.5	—	5,944.40	792.59	—	—
197	Cholecystectomy Except by Laparoscope without Common Duct Exploration with CC	—	9.7	—	8,318.40	857.57	—	—
198	Cholecystectomy Except by Laparoscope without Common Duct Exploration without CC	—	5.3	—	4,372.00	824.91	—	—

DRG	DEFINITION	# OF PTS.	ACT. ALOS	DRG LOS	DIFF.	PAYMENT PER CASE	PAYMENT PER DIEM	AVG. LOSS PER CASE	TOTAL LOSS PER DRG
199	Hepatobiliary Diagnostic Procedure for Malignancy	—	—	13.2	—	$9,441.20	$715.24	—	—
200	Hepatobiliary Diagnostic Procedure for Nonmalignancy	—	—	13.1	—	11,879.20	906.81	—	—
201	Other Hepatobiliary or Pancreas OR Procedures	—	—	17.0	—	12,928.80	760.52	—	—
202	Cirrhosis and Alcoholic Hepatitis	—	—	8.7	—	5,234.80	601.70	—	—
203	Malignancy of Hepatobiliary System or Pancreas	—	—	8.9	—	4,953.60	556.58	—	—
204	Disorders of Pancreas Except Malignancy	—	—	7.3	—	4,550.40	623.34	—	—
205	Disorders of Liver Except Malignancy, Cirrhosis, and Alcoholic Hepatitis with CC	—	—	8.4	—	4,913.60	584.95	—	—
206	Disorders of Liver Except Malignancy, Cirrhosis, and Alcoholic Hepatitis without CC	—	—	4.7	—	2,488.00	529.36	—	—
207	Disorders of the Biliary Tract with CC	—	—	6.4	—	4,025.20	628.94	—	—
208	Disorders of the Biliary Tract without CC	—	—	3.7	—	2,264.40	612.00	—	—
209	Major Joint and Limb Reattachment Procedures of Lower Extremity	—	—	8.6	—	9,269.20	1,077.81	—	—
210	Hip and Femur Procedures Except Major Joint Procedures, Age Greater than 17 with CC	—	—	10.6	—	7,370.80	695.36	—	—
211	Hip and Femur Procedures Except Major Joint Procedures, Age Greater than 17 without CC	—	—	7.9	—	5,196.00	657.72	—	—
212	Hip and Femur Procedures, Except Major Joint Procedures, Age 0–17	—	—	4.1	—	3,633.60	886.24	—	—
213	Amputation for Musculoskeletal System and Connective Tissue Disorders	—	—	11.3	—	6,893.60	610.05	—	—
214	Back and Neck Procedures with CC	—	—	8.2	—	7,694.80	938.39	—	—

215	Back and Neck Procedures without CC	—	—	—	4.8	—	—	$4,390.80	$914.75	—	—	—
216	Biopsies of Musculoskeletal System and Connective Tissue	—	—	—	13.3	—	—	8,418.40	632.96	—	—	—
217	Wound Debridement and Skin Graft Except Hand for Musculoskeletal and Connective Tissue Disorders	—	—	—	18.9	—	—	12,033.60	636.70	—	—	—
218	Lower Extremity and Humerus Procedures Except Hip, Foot and Femur, Age Greater than 17 with CC	—	—	—	7.4	—	—	5,611.20	758.27	—	—	—
219	Lower Extremity and Humerus Procedures Except Hip, Foot and Femur, Age Greater than 17 without CC	—	—	—	4.4	—	—	2,794.65	635.15	—	—	—
220	Lower Extremity and Humerus Procedures Except Hip, Foot, and Femur, Age 0–17	—	—	—	5.3	—	—	3,850.40	726.49	—	—	—
221	Knee Procedures with CC	—	—	—	9.3	—	—	7,164.40	770.37	—	—	—
222	Knee Procedures without CC	—	—	—	4.7	—	—	3,940.80	838.47	—	—	—
223	Major Shoulder/Elbow Procedures or Other Upper Extremity Procedures with CC	—	—	—	3.2	—	—	3,264.80	1,020.25	—	—	—
224	Shoulder, Elbow, and Forearm Procedures Except Major Joint Procedures without CC	—	—	—	2.7	—	—	2,772.80	1,026.96	—	—	—
225	Foot Procedures	—	—	—	5.1	—	—	3,602.40	706.35	—	—	—
226	Soft Tissue Procedures with CC	—	—	—	7.7	—	—	5,352.40	695.12	—	—	—
227	Soft Tissue Procedures without CC	—	—	—	3.2	—	—	2,799.60	874.88	—	—	—
228	Major Thumb of Joint Procedures of Other Hand of Wrist Procedures with CC	—	—	—	3.5	—	—	3,363.60	961.03	—	—	—
229	Hand or Wrist Procedures Except Major Joint Procedures without CC	—	—	—	2.5	—	—	2,385.60	954.24	—	—	—
230	Local Excision and Removal of Internal Fixation Devices of Hip and Femur	—	—	—	5.5	—	—	3,658.00	665.09	—	—	—
231	Local Excision and Removal of Internal Fixation Devices Except Hip and Femur	—	—	—	5.4	—	—	4,510.00	835.19	—	—	—
232	Arthroscopy	—	—	—	5.8	—	—	4,624.00	797.24	—	—	—

DRG	DEFINITION	# OF PTS.	ACT. ALOS	DRG LOS	DIFF.	PAYMENT PER CASE	PAYMENT PER DIEM	AVG. LOSS PER CASE	TOTAL LOSS PER DRG
233	Other Musculoskeletal System and Connective Tissue OR Procedures with CC	—	—	10.6	—	$7,620.40	$718.91	—	—
234	Other Musculoskeletal System and Connective Tissue OR Procedures without CC	—	—	4.8	—	3,811.60	794.08	—	—
235	Fractures of Femur	—	—	8.8	—	3,585.60	407.45	—	—
236	Fractures of Hip and Pelvis	—	—	7.6	—	3,108.80	409.05	—	—
237	Sprains, Strains, and Dislocation of Hip, Pelvis, and Thigh	—	—	5.0	—	2,214.00	442.80	—	—
238	Osteomyelitis	—	—	12.3	—	5,975.60	485.82	—	—
239	Pathological Fractures and Musculoskeletal and Connective Tissue Malignancy	—	—	9.0	—	4,135.20	459.47	—	—
240	Connective Tissue Disorders with CC	—	—	8.7	—	4,755.60	546.62	—	—
241	Connective Tissue Disorders without CC	—	—	5.2	—	2,334.00	448.85	—	—
242	Septic Arthritis	—	—	9.3	—	4,576.00	492.04	—	—
243	Medical Back Problems	—	—	6.4	—	2,848.80	445.13	—	—
244	Bone Diseases and Specific Arthropathies with CC	—	—	6.6	—	2,938.40	445.21	—	—
245	Bone Diseases and Specific Arthropathies without CC	—	—	4.7	—	1,925.20	409.62	—	—
246	Nonspecific Arthropathies	—	—	4.8	—	2,211.60	460.75	—	—
247	Signs and Symptoms of Musculoskeletal and Connective Tissue	—	—	4.5	—	2,212.80	491.73	—	—
248	Tendonitis, Myositis, and Bursitis	—	—	5.8	—	2,846.80	490.83	—	—
249	Aftercare, Musculoskeletal System and Connective Tissue	—	—	5.0	—	2,594.40	518.88	—	—
250	Fractures, Sprains, Strains, and Dislocations of Forearm, Hand, and Foot, Age Greater than 17 with CC	—	—	5.7	—	2,780.00	487.72	—	—

251	Fractures, Sprains, Strains, and Dislocations of Forearm, Hand, and Foot, Age Greater than 17 without CC	—	—	—	$1,804.00	$530.59	—	3.4	—
252	Fractures, Sprains, Strains, and Dislocations of Forearm, Hand, and Foot, Age 0–17	—	—	—	1,456.80	809.33	—	1.8	—
253	Fractures, Sprains, Strains, and Dislocations of Upper Arm and Lower Leg Except Foot, Age Greater than 17 with CC	—	—	—	3,046.80	435.26	—	7.0	—
254	Fractures, Sprains, Strains, and Dislocations of Upper Arm and Lower Leg Except Foot, Age Greater than 17 without CC	—	—	—	1,729.60	402.23	—	4.3	—
255	Fractures, Sprains, Strains, and Dislocations of Upper Arm and Lower Leg Except Foot, Age 0–17	—	—	—	1,932.40	666.34	—	2.9	—
256	Other Musculoskeletal System and Connective Tissue Disorders	—	—	—	2,558.80	544.43	—	4.7	—
257	Total Mastectomy for Malignancy with CC	—	—	—	3,537.20	842.19	—	4.2	—
258	Total Mastectomy for Malignancy without CC	—	—	—	2,795.60	901.81	—	3.1	—
259	Subtotal Mastectomy for Malignancy with CC	—	—	—	3,316.40	808.88	—	4.1	—
260	Subtotal Mastectomy for Malignancy without CC	—	—	—	2,336.00	1,061.82	—	2.2	—
261	Breast Procedure for Nonmalignancy Except Biopsy and Local Excision	—	—	—	2,972.80	1,189.12	—	2.5	—
262	Breast Biopsy and Local Excision for Nonmalignancy	—	—	—	2,596.40	665.74	—	3.9	—
263	Skin Grafts and/or Debridement for Skin Ulcers or Cellulitis with CC	—	—	—	9,416.00	535.00	—	17.6	—
264	Skin Grafts and/or Debridement for Skin Ulcers or Cellulitis without CC	—	—	—	4,665.20	485.96	—	9.6	—
265	Skin Grafts and/or Debridement Except for Skin Ulcers of Cellulitis with CC	—	—	—	5,581.20	672.43	—	8.3	—

DRG	DEFINITION	# OF PTS.	ACT. ALOS	DRG LOS	DIFF.	PAYMENT PER CASE	PAYMENT PER DIEM	AVG. LOSS PER CASE	TOTAL LOSS PER DRG
266	Skin Grafts and/or Debridement Except for Skin Ulcers of Cellulitis without CC	—	—	4.0	—	$2,943.20	$735.80	—	—
267	Perianal and Polonisal Procedures	—	—	4.2	—	2,774.00	660.48	—	—
268	Skin, Subcutaneous Tissue, and Breast Plastic Procedures	—	—	3.9	—	3,342.40	857.03	—	—
269	Other Skin, Subcutaneous Tissue, and Breast Procedures with CC	—	—	10.9	—	6,810.00	624.77	—	—
270	Other Skin, Subcutaneous Tissue, and Breast Procedures without CC	—	—	3.6	—	2,644.00	734.44	—	—
271	Skin Ulcers	—	—	10.0	—	4,537.20	453.72	—	—
272	Major Skin Disorders with CC	—	—	8.2	—	4,028.80	491.32	—	—
273	Major Skin Disorders without CC	—	—	6.1	—	2,535.60	415.67	—	—
274	Malignant Breast Disorders with CC	—	—	9.2	—	4,433.60	481.91	—	—
275	Malignant Breast Disorders without CC	—	—	4.1	—	2,052.80	500.68	—	—
276	Nonmalignant Breast Disorders	—	—	5.4	—	2,454.80	454.59	—	—
277	Cellulitis, Age Greater than 17 with CC	—	—	7.6	—	3,521.60	463.37	—	—
278	Cellulitis, Age Greater than 17 without CC	—	—	5.7	—	2,340.00	410.53	—	—
279	Cellulitis, Age 0–17	—	—	4.3	—	2,683.20	624.00	—	—
280	Trauma to Skin, Subcutaneous Tissue and Breast, Age Greater than 17 with CC	—	—	5.7	—	2,691.60	472.21	—	—
281	Trauma to Skin, Subcutaneous Tissue and Breast, Age Greater than 17 without CC	—	—	3.9	—	1,737.60	445.54	—	—
282	Trauma to Skin, Subcutaneous Tissue, and Breast, Age 0–17	—	—	2.2	—	1,426.40	648.36	—	—
283	Minor Skin Disorders with CC	—	—	6.3	—	2,862.00	454.29	—	—
284	Minor Skin Disorders without CC	—	—	4.3	—	1,736.80	403.91	—	—
285	Amputation of Lower Limb for Endocrine, Nutritional and Metabolic Disorders	—	—	17.5	—	10,108.00	577.60	—	—
286	Adrenal and Pituitary Procedures	—	—	9.3	—	9,048.40	972.95	—	—

287	Skin Grafts and Wound Debridement for Endocrine, Nutritional, and Metabolic Disorders	—	16.4	—	$8,414.00	$513.05	—	—
288	OR Procedures for Obesity	—	8.0	—	7,612.00	951.50	—	—
289	Parathyroid Procedures	—	4.6	—	4,025.20	875.04	—	—
290	Thyroid Procedures	—	3.0	—	3,172.40	1,057.47	—	—
291	Thyroglossal Procedures	—	2.0	—	2,040.80	1,020.40	—	—
292	Other Endocrine, Nutritional, and Metabolic OR Procedures with CC	—	15.0	—	10,878.80	725.25	—	—
293	Other Endocrine, Nutritional, and Metabolic OR Procedures without CC	—	6.6	—	4,641.60	703.27	—	—
294	Diabetes, Age over 35	—	6.5	—	2,985.20	459.26	—	—
295	Diabetes, Age 0–35	—	5.1	—	2,973.20	582.98	—	—
296	Nutritional and Miscellaneous Metabolic Disorders, Age Greater than 17 with CC	—	7.4	—	3,671.60	496.16	—	—
297	Nutritional and Miscellaneous Metabolic Disorders, Age Greater than 17 without CC	—	4.7	—	2,122.00	451.49	—	—
298	Nutritional and Miscellaneous Metabolic Disorders, Age 0–17	—	4.3	—	2,168.40	504.28	—	—
299	Inborn Errors of Metabolism	—	6.1	—	3,247.20	532.33	—	—
300	Endocrine Disorders with CC	—	8.3	—	4,392.80	529.25	—	—
301	Endocrine Disorders without CC	—	4.9	—	2,401.20	490.04	—	—
302	Kidney Transplant	—	14.6	—	16,557.60	1,134.08	—	—
303	Kidney, Ureter, and Major Bladder Procedures for Neoplasm	—	11.6	—	10,295.60	887.55	—	—
304	Kidney, Ureter, and Major Bladder Procedures for Nonneoplasm with CC	—	11.7	—	9,325.20	797.03	—	—
305	Kidney, Ureter, and Major Bladder Procedures for Nonneoplasm without CC	—	5.6	—	4,546.40	811.86	—	—
306	Prostatectomy with CC	—	7.3	—	4,840.40	663.07	—	—
307	Prostatectomy without CC	—	3.6	—	2,647.60	735.44	—	—
308	Minor Bladder Procedures with CC	—	8.1	—	5,786.00	714.32	—	—
309	Minor Bladder Procedures without CC	—	3.4	—	3,188.40	937.76	—	—

DRG	DEFINITION	# OF PTS.	ACT. ALOS	DRG LOS	DIFF.	PAYMENT PER CASE	PAYMENT PER DIEM	AVG. LOSS PER CASE	TOTAL LOSS PER DRG
310	Transurethral Procedures with CC	—	—	5.0	—	$3,663.60	$732.72	—	—
311	Transurethral Procedures without CC	—	—	2.5	—	2,158.00	863.20	—	—
312	Urethral Procedures, Age Greater than 17 with CC	—	—	5.3	—	3,383.20	638.34	—	—
313	Urethral Procedures, Age Greater than 17 without CC	—	—	2.6	—	1,909.60	734.46	—	—
314	Urethral Procedures, Age 0–17	—	—	2.3	—	1,801.20	783.13	—	—
315	Other Kidney and Urinary Tract OR Procedures	—	—	10.7	—	8,129.20	759.74	—	—
316	Renal failure	—	—	8.4	—	5,136.00	611.43	—	—
317	Admission for Renal Dialysis	—	—	3.9	—	2,059.60	528.10	—	—
318	Kidney and Urinary Tract Neoplasms with CC	—	—	8.1	—	4,478.40	552.89	—	—
319	Kidney and Urinary Tract Neoplasms without CC	—	—	3.3	—	2,212.00	670.30	—	—
320	Kidney and Urinary Tract Infections, Age Greater than 17 with CC	—	—	7.4	—	3,780.40	510.86	—	—
321	Kidney and Urinary Tract Infections, Age Greater than 17 without CC	—	—	5.2	—	2,443.60	469.92	—	—
322	Kidney and Urinary Tract Infections, Age 0–17	—	—	4.7	—	2,185.60	456.02	—	—
323	Urinary Stones with CC and/or ESW Lithotripsy	—	—	3.9	—	2,888.40	740.62	—	—
324	Urinary Stones without CC	—	—	2.3	—	1,548.80	673.39	—	—
325	Kidney and Urinary Tract Signs and Symptoms, Age Greater than 17 with CC	—	—	5.2	—	2,590.40	498.15	—	—
326	Kidney and Urinary Tract Signs and Symptoms, Age Greater than 17 without CC	—	—	3.4	—	1,674.40	492.47	—	—
327	Kidney and Urinary Tract Signs and Symptoms, Age 0–17	—	—	3.1	—	2,888.80	931.87	—	—

328	—	—	Urethral Stricture, Age Greater than 17 with CC	4.8	—	—	$2,692.80	$561.00	—	—	—	—
329	—	—	Urethral Stricture, Age Greater than 17 without CC	2.5	—	—	1,716.40	686.56	—	—	—	—
330	—	—	Urethral Stricture, Age 0–17	1.6	—	—	1,161.20	725.75	—	—	—	—
331	—	—	Other Kidney and Urinary Tract Diagnoses, Age Greater than 17 with CC	7.0	—	—	3,977.20	568.17	—	—	—	—
332	—	—	Other Kidney and Urinary Tract Diagnoses, Age Greater than 17 without CC	4.3	—	—	2,407.60	559.91	—	—	—	—
333	—	—	Other Kidney and Urinary Tract Diagnoses, Age 0–17	7.2	—	—	4,150.80	576.50	—	—	—	—
334	—	—	Major Male Pelvic Procedures with CC	7.5	—	—	6,868.80	915.84	—	—	—	—
335	—	—	Major Male Pelvic Procedures without CC	6.1	—	—	5,378.80	881.77	—	—	—	—
336	—	—	Transurethral Prostatectomy with CC	4.8	—	—	3,409.20	710.25	—	—	—	—
337	—	—	Transurethral Prostatectomy without CC	3.3	—	—	2,452.00	743.03	—	—	—	—
338	—	—	Testes Procedures for Malignancy	5.7	—	—	3,895.20	683.37	—	—	—	—
339	—	—	Testes Procedures for Nonmalignancy, Age Greater than 17	4.4	—	—	3,306.00	751.36	—	—	—	—
340	—	—	Testes Procedures for Nonmalignancy, Age 0–17	2.4	—	—	1,806.40	752.67	—	—	—	—
341	—	—	Penis Procedures	3.8	—	—	4,076.80	1,072.84	—	—	—	—
342	—	—	Circumcision, Age Greater than 17	4.1	—	—	2,675.60	652.59	—	—	—	—
343	—	—	Circumcision, Age 0–17	1.7	—	—	1,578.00	928.24	—	—	—	—
344	—	—	Other Male Reproductive System OR Procedures for Malignancy	3.6	—	—	3,976.40	1,104.56	—	—	—	—
345	—	—	Other Male Reproductive System OR Procedures Except for Malignancy	4.5	—	—	3,008.40	668.53	—	—	—	—
346	—	—	Malignancy of Male Reproductive System with CC	7.7	—	—	3,839.20	498.60	—	—	—	—
347	—	—	Malignancy of Male Reproductive System without CC	3.7	—	—	1,959.60	529.62	—	—	—	—
348	—	—	Benign Prosthetic Hypertrophy with CC	5.1	—	—	2,689.60	527.37	—	—	—	—
349	—	—	Benign Prosthetic Hypertrophy without CC	3.2	—	—	1,637.60	511.75	—	—	—	—

DRG	DEFINITION	# OF PTS.	ACT. ALOS	DRG LOS	DIFF.	PAYMENT PER CASE	PAYMENT PER DIEM	AVG. LOSS PER CASE	TOTAL LOSS PER DRG
350	Inflammation of the Male Reproductive System	—	—	5.4	—	$2,714.80	$502.74	—	—
351	Sterilization, Male	—	—	1.3	—	1,388.80	1,068.31	—	—
352	Other Male Reproductive System Diagnoses	—	—	4.3	—	2,322.80	540.19	—	—
353	Pelvic Evisceration, Radical Hysterectomy, and Radical Vulvectomy	—	—	9.8	—	7,546.00	770.00	—	—
354	Uterine and Adnexa Procedures for Nonovarian/Adnexal Malignancy with CC	—	—	6.9	—	5,498.80	796.93	—	—
355	Uterine and Adnexa Procedures for Nonovarian/Adnexal Malignancy without CC	—	—	4.3	—	3,509.20	816.09	—	—
356	Female Reproductive System Reconstructive Procedures	—	—	3.6	—	2,864.80	795.78	—	—
357	Uterine and Adnexa Procedures for Ovarian or Adnexal Malignancy	—	—	10.9	—	9,133.60	837.94	—	—
358	Uterine and Adnexa Procedures for Nonmalignancy with CC	—	—	5.4	—	4,407.20	816.15	—	—
359	Uterine and Adnexa Procedures for Nonmalignancy without CC	—	—	3.8	—	3,194.80	840.74	—	—
360	Vagina, Cervix, and Vulva Procedures	—	—	4.3	—	3,274.40	761.49	—	—
361	Laparoscopy and Incisional Tubal Interruption	—	—	4.8	—	4,418.80	920.58	—	—
362	Endoscopic Tubal Interruption	—	—	1.4	—	2,075.60	1,482.57	—	—
363	D and C, Conization, and Redioimplant for Malignancy	—	—	3.7	—	2,588.00	699.46	—	—
364	D and C, Conization, and Redioimplant Except for Malignancy	—	—	3.7	—	2,495.00	674.32	—	—
365	Other Female Reproductive System OR Procedures	—	—	9.2	—	6,850.80	744.65	—	—
366	Malignancy of Female Reproductive System with CC	—	—	9.1	—	4,844.40	532.35	—	—

367	Malignancy of Female Reproductive System without CC	—	3.3	—	$1,794.40	$543.76	—	—
368	Infections of Female Reproductive System	—	7.3	—	3,881.60	531.73	—	—
369	Menstrual and Other Female Reproductive System Disorders	—	4.0	—	2,038.00	509.50	—	—
370	Cesarean Section with CC	—	5.9	—	3,590.40	608.54	—	—
371	Cesarean Section without CC	—	3.8	—	2,536.00	667.37	—	—
372	Vaginal Delivery with Complicating Diagnosis	—	3.4	—	1,960.80	576.71	—	—
373	Vaginal Delivery without Complicating Diagnosis	—	2.2	—	1,354.80	615.82	—	—
374	Vaginal Delivery with Sterilization and/or D and C	—	3.1	—	2,460.80	793.81	—	—
375	Vaginal Delivery with OR Procedure Except Sterilization and/or D and C	—	4.4	—	2,840.40	645.55	—	—
376	Postpartum and Postabortion Diagnoses without OR Procedure	—	3.4	—	1,405.20	413.29	—	—
377	Postpartum and Postabortion Diagnoses with OR Procedure	—	5.7	—	3,904.80	685.05	—	—
378	Ectopic Pregnancy	—	3.0	—	2,820.80	940.27	—	—
379	Threatened Abortion	—	2.8	—	1,281.60	457.71	—	—
380	Abortion without D and C	—	2.1	—	1,392.40	663.05	—	—
381	Abortion with D and C, Aspiration Curettage, or Hysterectomy	—	2.2	—	1,625.20	738.73	—	—
382	False Labor	—	1.5	—	742.40	494.93	—	—
383	Other Antepartum Diagnoses with Medical Complications	—	4.0	—	1,624.00	406.00	—	—
384	Other Antepartum Diagnoses without Medical Complications	—	2.5	—	1,163.60	465.44	—	—
385	Neonates, Died or Transferred to Another Acute Care Facility	—	1.8	—	5,096.40	2,831.33	—	—
386	Extreme Immaturity or Respiratory Distress Syndrome of Neonate	—	17.9	—	15,199.60	849.14	—	—

DRG	DEFINITION	# OF PTS.	ACT. ALOS	DRG LOS	DIFF.	PAYMENT PER CASE	PAYMENT PER DIEM	AVG. LOSS PER CASE	TOTAL LOSS PER DRG
387	Prematurity with Major Problems	—	—	13.3	—	$7,611.20	$572.27	—	—
388	Prematurity without Major Problems	—	—	8.6	—	4,821.20	560.60	—	—
389	Full Term Neonate with Major Problems	—	—	7.7	—	5,188.80	673.87	—	—
390	Neonate with Other Significant Problems	—	—	4.8	—	2,154.00	448.75	—	—
391	Normal Newborn	—	—	3.1	—	924.40	298.19	—	—
392	Splenectomy, Age Greater than 17	—	—	13.2	—	12,808.40	970.33	—	—
393	Splenectomy, Age 0–17	—	—	9.1	—	6,335.60	696.22	—	—
394	Other OR Procedures of the Blood and Blood-Forming Organs	—	—	8.5	—	6,285.20	739.44	—	—
395	Red Blood Cell Disorders, Age Greater than 17	—	—	6.0	—	3,247.20	541.20	—	—
396	Red Blood Cell Disorders, Age 0–17	—	—	2.1	—	1,143.60	544.57	—	—
397	Coagulation Disorders	—	—	6.9	—	1,996.00	289.28	—	—
398	Reticuloendothelial and Immunity Disorders with CC	—	—	7.4	—	4,855.60	656.16	—	—
399	Reticuloendothelial and Immunity Disorders without CC	—	—	4.8	—	2,689.20	560.25	—	—
400	Lymphoma and Leukemia with Major OR Procedures	—	—	11.8	—	10,269.60	870.31	—	—
401	Lymphoma and Nonacute Leukemia with Other OR Procedures with CC	—	—	13.7	—	9,617.20	701.99	—	—
402	Lymphoma and Nonacute Leukemia with Other OR Procedures without CC	—	—	4.8	—	3,684.80	767.67	—	—
403	Lymphoma and Nonacute Leukemia with CC	—	—	10.7	—	6,782.40	633.87	—	—
404	Lymphoma and Nonacute Leukemia without CC	—	—	5.2	—	3,028.40	582.38	—	—
405	Acute Leukemia with Major OR Procedure Age 0–17	—	—	4.9	—	4,336.00	884.90	—	—
406	Myeloproliferative Disorders or Poorly Differentiated Neoplasms with Major OR Procedure with CC	—	—	12.8	—	10,598.40	828.00	—	—

407	Myeloproliferative Disorders or Poorly Differentiated Neoplasms with Major OR Procedure without CC	—	—	5.3	—	4,504.80	$849.96	—	—
408	Myeloproliferative Disorders or Poorly Differentiated Neoplasms with Other OR Procedures	—	—	8.4	—	6,234.40	742.19	—	—
409	Radiotherapy	—	—	7.7	—	3,914.00	508.31	—	—
410	Chemotherapy without Leukemia as Secondary Diagnosis	—	—	3.3	—	2,699.60	818.06	—	—
411	History of Malignancy without Endoscopy	—	—	3.7	—	1,790.40	483.89	—	—
412	History of Malignancy with Endoscopy	—	—	3.0	—	1,806.00	602.00	—	—
413	Other Myeloproliferative Disorders or Poorly Differentiated Neoplasms with CC	—	—	9.9	—	5,438.00	549.29	—	—
414	Other Myeloproliferative Disorders or Poorly Differentiated Neoplasms without CC	—	—	5.4	—	2,681.60	496.59	—	—
415	OR Procedure for Infectious and Parasitic Diseases	—	—	18.7	—	14,054.40	751.57	—	—
416	Septicemia, Age Greater than 17	—	—	9.5	—	5,970.80	628.51	—	—
417	Septicemia, Age 0–17	—	—	7.5	—	5,700.00	760.00	—	—
418	Postoperative and Posttraumatic Infections	—	—	7.6	—	3,851.20	506.74	—	—
419	Fever of Unknown Origin, Age Greater than 17 with CC	—	—	6.6	—	3,717.20	563.21	—	—
420	Fever of Unknown Origin, Age Greater than 17 without CC	—	—	4.9	—	2,547.20	519.84	—	—
421	Viral Illness, Age Greater than 17	—	—	5.1	—	2,747.20	538.67	—	—
422	Viral Illness and Fever of Unknown Origin, Age 0–17	—	—	4.3	—	2,343.60	545.02	—	—
423	Other Infectious and Parasitic Diseases Diagnoses	—	—	10.0	—	6,338.40	633.84	—	—
424	OR Procedures with Principal Diagnosis of Mental Illness	—	—	22.6	—	10,229.20	452.62	—	—
425	Acute Adjustment Reactions and Disturbances of Psychosocial Dysfunction	—	—	5.7	—	2,831.60	496.77	—	—

DRG	DEFINITION	# OF PTS.	ACT. ALOS	DRG LOS	DIFF.	PAYMENT PER CASE	PAYMENT PER DIEM	AVG. LOSS PER CASE	TOTAL LOSS PER DRG
426	Depressive Neuroses	—	—	6.5	—	$2,384.00	$366.77	—	—
427	Neuroses Except Depressive	—	—	6.4	—	2,387.60	373.06	—	—
428	Disorders of Personality and Impulse Control	—	—	9.4	—	3,008.40	320.04	—	—
429	Organic Disturbances and Mental Retardation	—	—	10.4	—	3,707.60	356.50	—	—
430	Psychoses	—	—	11.5	—	3,592.00	312.35	—	—
431	Childhood Mental Disorders	—	—	7.6	—	2,526.40	332.42	—	—
432	Other Mental Disorder Diagnoses	—	—	7.2	—	3,015.20	418.78	—	—
433	Alcohol/Drug Abuse or Dependence, Left Against Medical Advice	—	—	4.1	—	1,342.40	327.41	—	—
434	Alcohol/Drug Abuse or Dependence, Detoxification or Other Symptomatic Treatment with CC	—	—	6.7	—	2,894.00	431.94	—	—
435	Alcohol/Drug Abuse or Dependence, Detoxification or Other Symptomatic Treatment without CC	—	—	5.5	—	1,748.80	317.96	—	—
436	Alcohol/Drug Dependence with Rehabilitation Therapy	—	—	17.2	—	3,662.40	212.93	—	—
437	Alcohol/Drug Dependence with Combined Rehabilitation and Detoxification Therapy	—	—	13.6	—	3,608.40	265.32	—	—
439	Skin Grafts for Injuries	—	—	8.9	—	5,318.00	597.53	—	—
440	Wound Debridements for Injuries	—	—	11.2	—	6,998.00	624.82	—	—
441	Hand Procedures for Injuries	—	—	3.5	—	3,136.00	896.00	—	—
442	Other OR Procedures for Injuries with CC	—	—	9.5	—	8,054.00	847.79	—	—
443	Other OR Procedures for Injuries without CC	—	—	3.3	—	3,018.80	914.79	—	—
444	Traumatic Injury, Age over 17 with CC	—	—	6.2	—	2,959.60	477.35	—	—
445	Traumatic Injury, Age over 17 without CC	—	—	4.0	—	1,856.00	464.00	—	—
446	Traumatic Injury, Age 0–17	—	—	2.4	—	1,998.00	832.50	—	—

447	Allergic Reactions, Age Greater than 17	—	3.1	—	$1,870.40	$603.35	—
448	Allergic Reactions, Age 0–17	—	2.9	—	1,445.60	498.48	—
449	Poisoning and Toxic Effects of Drugs, Age Greater than 17 with CC	—	5.1	—	3,120.40	611.84	—
450	Poisoning and Toxic Effects of Drugs, Age Greater than 17 without CC	—	2.7	—	1,667.20	617.48	—
451	Poisoning and Toxic Effects of Drugs, Age 0–17	—	2.1	—	4,136.40	1,969.71	—
452	Complications of Treatment with CC	—	5.6	—	3,430.80	612.64	—
453	Complications of Treatment without CC	—	3.4	—	1,742.00	512.35	—
454	Other Injury, Poisoning, and Toxic Effect Diagnoses with CC	—	6.4	—	3,545.60	554.00	—
455	Other Injury, Poisoning, and Toxic Effect Diagnoses without CC	—	3.2	—	1,751.60	547.38	—
456	Burns, Transferred to Another Acute Care Facility	—	10.2	—	8,688.40	851.80	—
457	Extensive Burns without OR Procedures	—	5.6	—	6,522.80	1,164.79	—
458	Nonextensive Burns with Skin Graft	—	19.8	—	14,035.60	708.87	—
459	Nonextensive Burns with Wound Debridement or Other OR Procedures	—	12.5	—	7,017.20	561.38	—
460	Nonextensive Burns without OR Procedure	—	8.0	—	4,009.20	501.15	—
461	OR Procedures with Diagnoses of Other Contact with Health Services	—	5.2	—	3,772.80	725.54	—
462	Rehabilitation	—	16.7	—	6,649.20	398.16	—
463	Signs and Symptoms with CC	—	6.0	—	2,868.00	478.00	—
464	Signs and Symptoms without CC	—	4.1	—	1,896.00	462.44	—
465	Aftercare with History of Malignancy as Secondary Diagnosis	—	3.2	—	1,785.60	558.00	—
466	Aftercare without History of Malignancy as Secondary Diagnosis	—	4.9	—	2,127.60	434.20	—
467	Other Factors Influencing Health Status	—	5.1	—	1,488.80	291.92	—
468	Extensive OR Procedure Unrelated to Principal Diagnosis	—	17.7	—	14,307.60	808.34	—

DRG	DEFINITION	# OF PTS.	ACT. ALOS	DRG LOS	DIFF.	PAYMENT PER CASE	PAYMENT PER DIEM	AVG. LOSS PER CASE	TOTAL LOSS PER DRG
469	Principal Diagnosis Invalid as Discharge Diagnosis	—	—	0.0	—	$0.00	—	—	—
470	Ungroupable	—	—	0.0	—	0.00	—	—	—
471	Bilateral or Multiple Major Joint Procedures of Lower Extremity	—	—	11.0	—	14,999.60	$1,363.60	—	—
472	Extensive Burns with OR Procedures	—	—	30.4	—	46,550.00	1,531.25	—	—
473	Acute Leukemia without Major OR Procedure, Age over 17	—	—	16.3	—	14,448.00	886.38	—	—
475	Respiratory System Diagnosis with Ventilator Support	—	—	13.7	—	14,802.00	1,080.44	—	—
476	Prosthetic OR Procedure Unrelated to Principal Diagnosis	—	—	15.6	—	8,930.80	572.49	—	—
477	Nonextensive OR Procedure Unrelated to Principal Diagnosis	—	—	9.5	—	6,088.40	640.88	—	—
478	Other Vascular Procedures with CC	—	—	9.5	—	8,890.80	935.87	—	—
479	Other Vascular Procedures without CC	—	—	5.1	—	5,401.20	1,059.05	—	—
480	Liver Transplant	—	—	34.7	—	73,032.40	2,104.68	—	—
481	Bone Marrow Transplant	—	—	39.4	—	61,230.40	1,554.07	—	—
482	Tracheostomy for Face, Mouth, and Neck Diagnoses	—	—	17.4	—	14,692.00	844.37	—	—
483	Tracheotomy Except for Face, Mouth, and Neck Diagnoses	—	—	54.1	—	67,508.80	1,247.85	—	—
484	Craniotomy for Multiple Significant Trauma	—	—	20.2	—	23,922.80	1,184.30	—	—
485	Limb Reattachment, Hip and Femur Procedures for Multiple Significant Trauma	—	—	14.4	—	12,616.00	876.11	—	—
486	Other OR Procedures for Multiple Significant Trauma	—	—	16.8	—	19,805.60	1,178.90	—	—
487	Other Multiple Significant Trauma	—	—	10.2	—	7,734.40	758.27	—	—

488	HIV with Extensive OR Procedures	—	—	—	21.5	—	$17,541.60	$815.89	—
489	HIV with Major Related Condition	—	—	—	12.5	—	7,263.20	581.06	—
490	HIV with or without Other Related Condition	—	—	—	8.0	—	4,252.00	531.50	—
491	Major Joint and Limb Reattachment Procedures of Upper Extremity	—	—	—	5.3	—	6,494.00	1,225.28	—
492	Chemotherapy with Acute Leukemia as Secondary Diagnosis	—	—	—	16.9	—	14,721.60	871.10	—
493	Laparoscopic Cholecystectomy without Common Duct Exploration with CC	—	—	—	6.1	—	6,325.20	1,036.92	—
494	Laparoscopic Cholecystectomy without Common Duct Exploration without CC	—	—	—	2.3	—	3,384.80	1,471.65	—
495	Lung Transplant	—	—	—	26.3	—	51,338.40	1,952.03	—

analysis as part of the situational audit for case management, it will be necessary to obtain data on all discharges by DRG with corresponding lengths of stay. The worksheets can then be completed and the organization will be able to determine which diagnoses have the longest lengths of stay as well as which ones receive the most uncompensated care. Accordingly, these diagnoses may be initially considered for inclusion into the case management system.

Tool #2 Venue Inventory

Box 4–4 helps the manager identify the various venue options that can be included in the case management system. It facilitates discussion about what the role of case management should be vis-à-vis the various venues. Should case management merely consider the venue a discharge option or should the patients from each of these venues be followed within a centralized system of case management? Also, the venue inventory chart identifies who controls and/or owns the specific sites of care. Is it affiliated or owned by the network sponsoring the case management system? If so, this venue may be considered a preferred venue option for discharge and the patients admitted to this venue may also be followed by a case manager of the central system.

BOX 4 – 4

CENTRALIZED CASE MANAGEMENT VENUE INVENTORY

OPTIONS	YES	NO	PRIMARY	SECONDARY	HOSPITAL	# BEDS OR SITES
Hospital-based skilled nursing unit						
Freestanding skilled nursing facility						

Hospital-based inpatient rehabilitation unit					
Long-term care hospital					
Rehabilitation hospital					
Ambulatory surgery					
Outpatient diagnostic center					
Oral surgery center					
Off-site or rural clinics					
Home health					
Medical day hospital (CORF)					
Outpatient physical/occupational therapy					
Sports medicine					
Cardiac outpatient rehabilitation					
Hospital-based inpatient psychiatric unit					
Psychiatric partial day hospital					
Geriatric/ psych unit					
Children's hospital					
Pediatric birth-to-three outpatient program					
Pediatric sub-acute					

Freestanding cancer clinic					
Women's health center					
Alternative medicine clinic					
Other specialty postacute clinics or venue (please list and identify on reverse side)					

PRIMARY—owned/controlled by hospital or health system or managed care organization
SECONDARY—preferred referral relationship, non-ownership or control by hospital or system, or managed care organization

An additional purpose of the venue inventory is to assist the case management design team in determining what sites of non-inpatient hospital care exist within a community and which should be included in the case management system. At the outset of a system design, there may not be consensus as to which venues are essential components of the continuum. This decision will depend on who is the sponsoring organization of the case management system and what are the goals to be addressed through implementation of the system. Notwithstanding the fact that the objectives of the system may not be finalized at this stage, all possible venues of care should be identified so that pertinent information will be available to future analysis.

Tool #3 Physician Specialty Analysis

The physician specialty analysis details the category of physicians who refer to a particular facility and the number of patients referred. This information has several purposes related to the design of the case management system. First, it identifies which physicians should be consulted regarding the design of the system of case management. Second, it is another method for assessing which groups of patients with which diagnoses will need to be followed. Moreover, a lack of certain specialties may also be revealed and may require assessment. For instance, if no obstetricians are included in the review, it will not be necessary to include a birthing center. Conversely, if pulmonologists are significant sources of referrals, then venues such as long term care hospitals and CORFs may need to be developed where they do not already exist. The worksheet in Box 4–5 or a similar version should be completed for each venue or organization participating in the case management system.

BOX 4 – 5

PHYSICIAN SPECIALTY ANALYSIS

MEDICAL SPECIALTY	# PHYSICIANS ON ACTIVE STAFF	ANNUAL # OF PATIENTS ADMITTED BY SPECIALTY
Allergy and immunology		
Anesthesiology		
Cardiac surgery		
Cardiology		
Cardiovascular surgery		
Dental/oral surgery		
Emergency medicine		
ENT		
Family practice		
General surgery		
Geriatric medicine		
Infectious disease		
Internal medicine		
Nephrology		
Neurology		
Obstetrics		
Occupational medicine		
Oncology		
Orthopedic		
Otolaryngology		
Pediatrics		

Physical medicine and rehabilitation		
Plastic surgery		
Psychiatry		
Pulmonary medicine		
Rheumatology		
Thoracic surgery		
Other		

Tool #4 Individual Venue Capabilities and Assessment

In order for the aim of centralized case management to be realized, the full healthcare continuum must comprise a number of venues of care. To be included within the continuum, the capabilities of each venue must be known and evaluated. Box 4–6 is a worksheet that can be used to collect the requisite information. When making the decision as to which sites of care are to serve as discharge options for the case management system, the design team must be able to answer at least the following questions about each venue:

1. What patients are appropriate for admission?
2. What services are available?
3. Who will be treating the patients?
4. What is the cost of care? How is that determined?
5. What is the quality of care?
6. What outcomes does the venue achieve?

The information collected will not only assist the design team in determining which patients to send where, but it will help serve to compare similar venues. For example, it may not be necessary to include more than one ambulatory surgery center, rehabilitation hospital, or home health agency in the continuum as developed by the case management design team. The following worksheet allows the team to compare the facilities with respect to available services, cost of care, and outcome. Therefore, a review of this information will enable facilities to be included in or excluded from the continuum.

BOX 4-6

INDIVIDUAL VENUE CAPABILITIES ASSESSMENT SAMPLE

1. Name of Venue _____
   Address   _____
   Contact person _____
2. Type of license _____
3. Type of Medicare certification, if any _____
4. Is copy of admission criteria attached? _____
5. Programs/Admissions. Are the following patients admitted?

	YES	NO
Stroke		
Ortho		
Head injury		
Pulmonary		
Cardiac rehabilitation		
Congestive heart failure		
Cancer		
Pain		
Spinal cord injury		
Substance abuse		
Psychiatric		

6. What are the venue's capabilities for performance of specific treatments and procedures?

PROCEDURES	LIMITATIONS/NOTES
Ventilators	
Oxygen	
Tracheotomy	
Swallow evaluation	
Suction	
Dialysis	
Cardiac monitoring	
Respiratory treatments	

Lab work	
X-ray	
Narcotics	
IV	
TPN	
Tube feeding	
Wound management	

7. What personnel is available?

PERSONNEL	LIMITATIONS/NOTES
ER physician	
Internist	
Surgeon	
Pathologist	
Physiatrist	
Obstetrician	
Radiologist	
Podiatry	
Anesthesiologist	
Other specialties	
Psychologist	
Social work	
Discharge planner	
PT	
OT	
Speech	
Recreational therapy	
Respiratory therapy	
Respiratory therapy 24 hours	
Registered nursing 24 hours	
On-site physician daily	
On-site physician 24 hours	
Orthotics/prosthetics	

8. Does the venue have specialized beds/units?

TYPE	YES/NO	NUMBER
ICU		
Rehab		
Pediatric		
Subacute care		
Isolation		
Telemetry		
Psychiatric		
Observation		
Other (please list)		

9. What is the average cost of care per day in this venue? Please detail any significant differences for varying diagnoses. How is this cost arrived at? Please explain.

_____

_____

10. Sense of quality (please describe). _____

_____

_____

11. Is there an internal outcome monitoring system or program evaluation program in place? What results are achieved?

_____

_____

_____

Tool #5 Cost of Care Identification

One of the most critical aspects of the situational audit is analyzing the cost of care. At a minimum, the average cost of care for each venue to be included in the continuum must be known. Ideally, cost of care for the primary diagnoses receiving treatment at each site should also be included in the analysis. Unbelievable as it seems to anyone outside the healthcare industry, most facilities are still unable to determine the exact cost of care either by venue or by diagnosis. There are a number of reasons for this, the simplest being that until recently there was no need for this information. Bills were sent out and they were paid. Moreover, organizations such as healthcare systems and hospitals file Medicare cost reports that require the costs from distinct units or venues to be aggregated together. For example, the cost of the emergency department is spread out over the various services of the hospital. Although the true cost of care of a patient who had a knee replacement should not include an allocation for the emergency room, it does under Medicare cost-accounting methodology. In most healthcare settings, it is next to impossible to obtain a true cost of care by sites of care without the allocation or addition of costs that are not directly related. Although cost of care is one of the most fundamental pieces of information to possess, it is often the most difficult to obtain.

Therefore, the best course of action for the case management design team is to enlist the assistance of the finance/reimbursement department of the healthcare provider to arrive at a cost calculation or approximation. If a sophisticated cost accounting system is in place, the job is done. Simply access the information by venue of care and by diagnosis. Select the top 30 diagnoses by two factors: length of stay and amount of Medicare uncompensated care as determined by the DRG analysis, which was the first step of the situational audit. The more likely scenario is that the design team working with the finance department will need to approximate the average cost of care by venue and by diagnosis.

The worksheet in Box 4–7 provides a useful methodology in determining that cost of care. The sample provided displays the cost of care for average patients in a rehabilitation unit as well as for three primary diagnoses treated within that venue: stroke, hip replacement, and head injury. The methodology starts with the assumption that each venue has fixed costs and variable costs. Fixed costs are those items that remain generally constant regardless of the type of patient treatment. Fixed costs in the sample provided include administrative overhead, laundry, and dietary. Variable costs must be calculated in connection with clinical input from each venue and from a review of patient bills. In the rehabilitation unit depicted in the sample worksheet, variable costs include nursing hours, therapy delivery,

BOX 4-7

SAMPLE COST ANALYSIS BY VENUE
(Rehabilitation Unit)

Mix of Cases

BUDGET FACTORS	STROKE	HIP REPLACE	HEAD INJURY	AVERAGE OF ALL CASES
Number of cases	24	16	17	174
Average collected revenue per case	$17,310	$12,500	$37,125	$19,840
# of patient days—ALOS	21	17	35	21
Resources				
Daily nursing hours	6	4	9	6.75
Costs	$192	$128	$288	$216
Daily therapy hours	4	3	6	4.25
Costs	$168	$126	$252	$179
Total supplies, lab, x-ray, pharmacy, misc.	$3,100	$2,250	$9,110	$4,300
Total resource costs	$10,660	$6,568	$28,010	$12,595
Fixed costs allocated by patient days including:				
General and administrative	$162	$162	$162	$162
Laundry	$9	$9	$9	$9
Dietary	$14	$14	$14	$14
Total daily fixed costs	$185	$185	$185	$185
Total fixed costs	$3,885	$3,145	$6,475	$3,885
Total costs	$14,545	$9,713	$34,485	$16,480
Average daily cost	$692	$571	$985	$785
Profit/loss per patient	$2,765	$2,787	$2,640	$3,355

laboratory, x-ray, and pharmaceuticals. (Physician care, while certainly a variable cost, was not calculated in this model.) These costs were arrived at by reviewing patient charts and bills as well as working with clinical staff to determine number of nursing hours per average patient and by the three identified diagnoses.

The next recommended step in the cost analysis is to determine what it presently costs an organization to treat its

patients across a continuum. Again, start with the same 30 selected diagnoses and chart out the cost of care in each venue utilized. Box 4–8 is a worksheet that delineates the cost of care for
the average stroke patient who has required several venues of
care within an integrated continuum. Again, this information
was obtained by first determining the cost of care in each venue,
and secondly, by reviewing a representative sampling of all
stroke patient files to determine their average lengths of stay at
the various venues used.

Several striking conclusions must be drawn about the organization represented in the sample. First, the organization fa-
vors utilization of inpatient rehabilitation for its stroke patients
and also encompasses significant home healthcare in its discharge planning. At this point, subacute care and CORF services
do not seem to be available to the organization's stroke patients.
The cost of inpatient acute care and rehabilitation will be a key
factor to the case management design team in determining if
venues of care, those not presently available, should be considered as necessary components of the continuum. Moreover, this
type of cost analysis allows the case management design team
to understand present patterns of venue utilization to assess
whether cost savings could be achieved through a different combination of venues or by altering the length of patient stay at

---

BOX 4 – 8

**AVERAGE STROKE PATIENT IN A MULTIPLE VENUE OF CARE
MODEL (Sample Based on Historical Utilization)**

	AVERAGE COST OF CARE	ALOS	TOTAL COST BY VENUE
Acute	$845/day	7 days	$ 5,915
Rehabilitation	$692/day	21 days	$14,532
Subacute	$421/day	0 days	$ 0
CORF	$750/day	0 days	$ 0
Home health	$389/day	30 days	$11,670

Total cost of care $32,117

the varying sites. In sum, it is critical that the design team accumulate all available information on cost of care by venues of care. Along with quality and outcome achieved by venue of care, cost will be one of the determinant factors in patient placement and situs of care delivery.

Tool #6 Medicare Reimbursement by Specialized Venue of Care

As long as Medicare and other forms of noncapitated coverage remain significant payment sources, cost of care is not the only financial factor to be considered. Available reimbursement must also be carefully assessed. This is particularly true for any organization serving a substantial number of patients covered under the Medicare system. Medicare reimbursement is and is likely to remain a morass of complicated and contradictory schemes of provider reimbursement. Depending on the venue of care, the provider will receive differing reimbursement for the same service to the same patient. Differing providers offering precisely the same service may receive vastly different amounts of reimbursement. At different times, some providers have incentives to utilize one unit over another for patients who will need costly care. For instance, most new skilled units are cost-based reimbursed; units that have operated for more than 3 years are not. Some hospitals receive TEFRA incentive payments because their cost of care is less than the ceiling of reimbursement.

In order to understand fully the financial incentives an institution has regarding Medicare, it is suggested that the design team collect selected data on Medicare reimbursement by venue of care. Again, working with a financial and/or reimbursement representative of the provider organization, the case management team can fairly easily extrapolate the necessary facts. The worksheet in Box 4–9 provides an outline of the primary Medicare-recognized venues of care for which specialized reimbursement may be available.

AN ANALYSIS OF THE SITUATIONAL AUDIT

The first step of the situational audit was data collection. The second step is analysis. Situational analysis for case management

BOX 4-9

MEDICARE REIMBURSEMENT BY SPECIALIZED VENUES OF CARE

PPS EXEMPT				
	TEFRA CAP PER DISCHARGE	**Incentive Payment**		
		YES	**NO**	**AMOUNT**
Rehabilitation hospital				
Rehabilitation unit				
Psychiatric unit				
Long-term care hospital				
Children's hospital				
Cancer hospital				

SKILLED		
	YES	**NO**
Cost-based unit or facility		
Hospital-based routine limit (amount)	$	
Freestanding routine limit (amount)	$	

OTHER SPECIALIZED FORMS OF MEDICARE REIMBURSEMENT	**TYPE OF REIMBURSEMENT**
CORF	
Ambulatory surgery	
Partial day hospitalization	
Hospice	
Home health	

involves examination of the data of a complex healthcare system into its component parts and their relations. It allows for individual scrutiny of the various elements that make up a healthcare system in order that the whole can be improved through the implementation of case management. Its forms of analysis are both statistical and grammatical. Ideally, the case management design team will collect the necessary information and review it for trends, variances, and issues related to the major themes of case management. These may include:

- overutilization or inappropriate utilization
- lack of discharge options for patients
- patterns of uncompensated care
- increased capabilities of non–hospital-based venues exceeding expectations
- unexpected or not clearly understood Medicare reimbursement issues related to patient placement
- emergence of issues not being well met by critical paths
- other areas where the intervention of case management may improve healthcare quality, long term wellness, and reduce cost of service delivery

The case management design team should prepare a written report with its findings and recommendations. In general, the report must answer the two questions posed initially: Which patients should be followed and what venues are preferred discharge options? Of course, the audit report may also include additional information that will be helpful in the later design phases of the system. A brief sample of key findings and their implications for case management appear in Box 4–10, and several hypothetical recommendations for a hospital-based system are given in Box 4–11. Once the design team has completed its initial report, the sponsoring organization should, working in concert with the design team, determine what are the articulated goals of the system of case management that is under development.

GOALS OF THE SYSTEM OF CENTRALIZED CASE MANAGEMENT

Following the situational audit, the senior management of the organization sponsoring the case management system must articulate the intended goals of the system. Of course, the nature of the sponsoring organization will largely influence the function of case management. If the model is to function in a primarily capitated network, alternative venue placement as well as decreased resource utilization will be chief objectives. If the case management system is being operated by a managed care organization, preadmission authorization, primary care gate-

BOX 4 – 10

EXCERPTED KEY FINDINGS OF SITUATIONAL AUDIT FOR CASE MANAGEMENT A Sample

FINDING			IMPLICATION FOR CASE MANAGEMENT SYSTEM
The following 15 DRGs result in the most uncompensated care:			These are likely diagnoses to be included in the group of patients to be followed for case management. It is believed that the intervention of case management may reduce revenue loss and improve patient outcome.
DRG	**DEFINITION**	**TOTAL LOSS**	
148	Major sm and lg bowel procedures w/cc	$400,000	
403	Lymphoma and non-acute leukemia w/cc	$150,000	
483	Tracheostomy for face, mouth, neck	$175,000	
14	Specific cerebrovascular disorders except transient ischemic attacks	$150,000	
79	Respiratory infection and inflammation, age over 17 w/cc	$120,000	
88	Chronic obstructive pulmonary disease	$75,000	
475	Respiratory system diagnosis w/ventilator support	$275,000	

	FINDING		IMPLICATION FOR CASE MANAGEMENT SYSTEM
DRG	**DEFINITION**	**TOTAL LOSS**	
107	Coronary bypass w/o cardiac cath	$180,000	
110	Major cardiovascular procedures w/cc	$350,000	
124	Circulatory disorders except acute myocardial infarction w/cardiac cath and complex diagnosis	$275,000	
127	Heart failure and shock	$200,000	
121	Circulatory disorders w/acute myocardial infaction and cardiovascular complication	$100,000	
1	Crainiotomy age over 17 except for trauma	$125,000	
191	Pancreas, liver, and shunt procedures w/cc	$200,000	
413	Other mycloprobifration disorders or poorly differentiated neoplasms w/cc	$250,000	

Cardiac diagnoses are the most costly. The payor group is 60% non-Medicare (mostly capitated) and 40% Medicare.

Again, these are diagnoses that should be considered for inclusion by case management. Moreover, case management will need to design follow-up and wellness service interventions such as weight checks, blood pressure, primary care visits, smoking cessation classes, followup, etc.

FINDING	IMPLICATION FOR CASE MANAGEMENT SYSTEM
The intensive care unit provides the most expensive care, yet the long-term care hospital provides in many cases equally intensive care at less cost. The long-term care hospital's TEFRA cap is $48,000.	The long-term care hospital should be a preferred discharge option. This is especially true for Medicare patients.
Nursing homes and home health venues of care are referring significant numbers of patients with urinary tract infections for E.R. trips and hospital admissions.	Case management should consider utilizing geriatric nurse practitioners in the nursing home setting to reduce these admissions.
Orthopedic care maps are not functioning as well as intended as ALOS still greatly exceeds the goal.	Case Management system must identify appropriate discharge options for these patients including a Medical Day Hospital, when available.
The network owns several nursing homes, which it has a strong interest in utilizing for acute discharge options.	Case management must access the capabilities of these venues and determine when these options are appropriate for discharge.
The network does not have a CORF or other outpatient setting offering comprehensive services to patients requiring rehab or other restoration of function.	An affiliation with such a venue should be expanded or, alternatively, such a venue may need to be developed.
The hospital based skilled units routine costs are exceeding the available Medicare reimbursement.	Seek to treat less intensive patients in this venue and utilize the other venues within the continuum.
Cardiologists and internists are responsible for the largest number of hospital admissions and also, as a group, utilize nonhospital venues the least.	The design team must determine the souce of these practice patterns and seek to put together a plan of action addressing the identified issues.

BOX 4-11

SAMPLE RECOMMENDATIONS

1. Implement a system of case management that is acute care-based but follows patients regardless of payor source within all continuum components, including:

   - Ambulatory surgery
   - Primary care physician office/clinics
   - Skilled care
   - Home health
   - Rehabilitation
   - Long-term care hospital
   - Outpatient rehabilitation
   - Medical day hospital

2. Initiate the case management system within 4 months to follow any patient with one of the diagnoses listed below:

88	COPD
475	Respiratory system disorder
483	Tracheotomy
14-16	Cerebrovascular disorders (TIA/strokes)
148	Major small and large bowel procedures
107–110	Coronary bypass and major cardiac procedures
121	Circulatory disorders with myocardial infarction and cardiac complications

3. Establish a system that has three high-risk areas of diagnoses to follow:

   - Respiratory
   - Cardiac
   - Neurologic

4. Seek to include additional diagnoses within each area as the case management systems begin to have an established track record.

5. Incorporate ongoing followup (up to 18 months) of intervention for any patient to be included in system.

6. The up to 18 months of case management intervention should include specific postacute strategies to reduce the need for ongoing healthcare services. These strategies should be developed as per the general needs of patients in the identified three areas of respiratory, cardiac, and neurologic focus.

7. Identify and/or alternatively develop a medical day hospital and long-term care hospital for inclusion into the continuum.

8. Continue to assist home health providers and skilled nursing programs in understanding how to meet the complex needs of patients in the three identified diagnosis areas.

keeping, and controlled utilization may be identifiable goals. With today's variety of ownership, organizational, and operational structures, it is critical that goal development for the system of case management is consistent with its sponsoring organization. Well-defined goals will ensure project direction and measurable goals will enable the impact of case management to be validated.

Close examination of the organizational policies guiding case management development, related administrative mandates, and professional standards promulgated by both case management organizations and managed care organizations* can set the context for the goals of the case management system.

The following potential goals of a centralized case management program have been arranged by primary functional category. Clearly, not all goals are appropriate for all organizations. The key is to set realistic goals that can be achieved yet challenge the system to perform to its fullest extent. It is the goals of the system that dictate the design of the program. For instance, if episodic intervention is desired, there will be no need to include postdischarge followup in the system. Selected goals can include:

---

*For example, the standards drafted by the National Committee for Quality Assurance (NCQA), NCQA Standards for Accreditation of Managed Care Organizations, are an important resource tool to understand the objectives of quality managed care organizations. A review of these standards will be instrumental in setting goals of case management that reflect consistency of philosophy and purpose with managed care.

Patient Advocacy and Care Delivery

- To ensure the coordination and integration of services to achieve treatment continuity for a specific spell of illness or disease.
- To monitor and ensure the quality of service delivery.
- To serve as a patient advocate to ensure that healthcare needs are identified and fulfilled.

Reimbursement and Financial

- To engage in cost and resource management through ensuring efficient utilization of all healthcare resources.
- To promote use of the most cost-effective and outcome-oriented venues of care.

Community and Social Integration

- To offer social support to people with identified needs because of their health who may be isolated or stigmatized.
- To provide intervention to patients to execute the tasks of daily living.

Wellness and Prevention

- To maintain ongoing communication with patients following a spell of illness or with patients suffering a chronic disease or disorder for purposes of monitoring health status and behavior.
- To encourage health risk modification behavior of patients in preidentified high-risk categories.

This list certainly does not exhaust the possibilities of goals, given the uniqueness and diversity of case management services. Yet the variety of potential goals reflects the inherent challenge in designing a workable program within clearly defined parameters. Program goals can and often do conflict in practice. The objectives of the program reflect the differing parties served by the system of case management—the sponsoring organization, the patient, the community, and the payor. The resulting goal mix may naturally create a dilemma: How can the system effectively serve patients with numerous and complex needs while simultaneously trying to reduce utilization and costs? The key to reconciling these issues is threefold. First, the various interests represented by the program should offer input into the selection of goals. Second, the sponsoring organization must commit to clearly prioritizing the goals of case management. And, finally, there must be latitude within the system design to address specific clashes of goals as reflected in a patient's particular situation. The methodology by which goals are implemented will depend on the individual tactics of the system design, as will be discussed later in this chapter.

ORGANIZATIONAL STRUCTURING AND LINES OF AUTHORITY

As a centralized system, case management must be organized to respond across several management and accountability levels. A well-functioning system will not long maintain itself through serendipity. Ideally, case management, when sponsored by a larger organization such as a hospital or health network, should be a recognizable division or organizational department. Not to organize case management within the context of a cohesive unit undermines its potential. For instance, when a case manager reports to a specific venue, he or she is unable to represent equally well the interest of all venues within the continuum. Moreover, consistency of philosophy, goals, and outcomes is requisite to any well-functioning system. A unit method of structuring is essential to accomplish these aims. When case management is the sole or primary function of the host organization, the structure should more closely resemble an entrepreneurial entity. Since organizational structuring is more complex in situations where the host is engaged in a variety of other activities, this section discusses a recommended course of action for these scenarios.

Today, organizations use a variety of structures for their case management services. Departments of utilization review, nursing, and social work are often charged with the task of case management under their existing departmental auspices. In all likelihood, this structure may not foster delivery of the most productive service. First and foremost, as these departments are typically organized along professional training and licensure, there is little room for a transdisciplinary approach to case management. To believe that case management must be practiced by a single discipline, any discipline, is anachronistic and sorely underestimates the complex and varied issues facing present-day case managers.

Second, healthcare organizations with preexisting departments that fulfill case management functions rarely vary the reporting and accountability structures of the case managers. For instance, a utilization review department of a hospital will often report to the vice president of nursing. This same reporting structure can include staff inpatient nurses, home health nurses, utilization review nurses, and others. The issues and decisions that must be made by case management are often at odds with other departments within a hospital. For example, nursing supervisors will naturally seek to ensure sufficient nursing hours and staff for their floors whereas case managers will be directed to move patients off of acute floors as soon as medically appropriate. A confrontation over resource utilization and need will undoubtedly emerge and the vice president of nursing may be brought in to settle the dispute. This situation is untenable.

In most institutions, case management still has no clearly defined champion. In order to realize the hard objectives of case management, the system of case management must be structured under a line of authority that is not subject to the conflicting priorities of the same organization. This is not to say that all conflict must be eradicated, but that surely most of it can be avoided by not resorting to historical discipline-based lines of reporting. Indeed the concept of a defined champion for case management is instrumental to the establishment of an effective program. Whether it is a vice president of HMO operations, the chief financial officer of the hospital or the medical director of a PPO, some individual with a position of real institutional power and autonomy must ultimately be the advocate and defender of system of case management and its employees. Horror stories abound about the lack of organization-wide support for case management. It is common to hear narratives such as a case manager losing her job because she sent the mother of a prominent physician to a subacute care rehabilitation program at a local nursing home instead of keeping her in the hospital for the same service. If an organization is truly dedicated to a centralized program of case management, it must provide

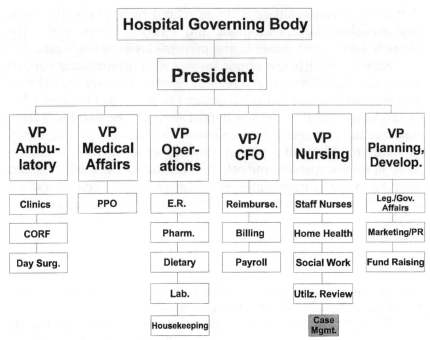

FIGURE 4–3. Historical Organization of Hospital-Based Case Management

the requisite administrative autonomy and authority to its leadership. Figures 4–3, 4–4, and 4–5 illustrate the traditional method of organization as well as two recommended options for a hospital network.

In both of the alternative organizational charts depicted, case management is relocated to a position of priority. In the first scenario, case management is put under its own vice president. Given the ultimate importance to a hospital of an effective program of case management, this can be a particularly prudent course of action. This course of action ensures that there is organizational support for the objectives of case management and sends a clear message to this effect. In the second alternative, case management is moved to a reporting line where internal conflicts are less likely yet where significant authority remains, as the vice president of operations becomes the champion of the system. It is also interesting to note the dotted line of authority for case management with the CFO. This is particularly useful because many

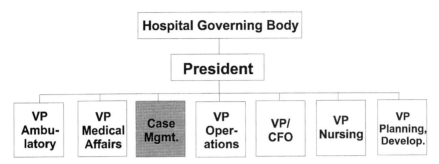

FIGURE 4–4. Alternative #1 Recommended Organizational Structure for Hospital System of Case Management

of the functions of centralized case management bear direct relevance to the financial performance of the organization. Naturally, a number of structuring possibilities exist depending on the particular characteristics and desires of an individual organization. Regardless of the exact methodology employed, it is critical that staff case managers have the ability and means to perform their jobs despite the controversial issues that may ensue.

In order to ensure that staff is vested with the ability to achieve the stated goals of the case management system, clearly defined areas of responsibility and reporting must be determined for all staff. At this stage in the system design, it has been recommended that a case management program be spearheaded by leadership with systemwide authority in the sponsoring organization. In a network or healthcare system, case management could be under the ambit of a single hospital only if appropriate safeguards to protect the interests of the whole system are put into place. Notwithstanding these caveats, the organizational success of the program will depend on granting the case manager in the field a significant amount of authority and autonomy to do the job. This can best be accomplished through drafting an outline of the job and listing the primary duties and responsibilities of the position. A sample job description appears in Box 4–12 to provide guidance in this process. Five additional job descriptions, including several with criteria-based performance appraisals, have been included in Appendix 1 for review and reference.

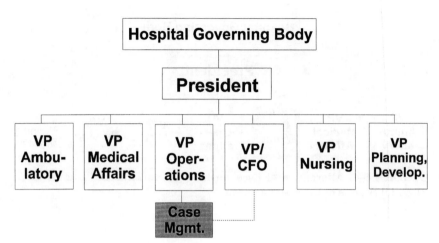

FIGURE 4–5. Alternative #2 Recommended Organizational Structure for Hospital System of Case Management

SERVICE DELIVERY DESIGN

The phase of service delivery design is initiated as soon as: (1) the patients to be included in the system have been identified, (2) the venues of care that will constitute the continuum have become known, and (3) the goals of the system have been determined and prioritized. The system must be designed to provide specific interventions for the patients who have been determined to be in the greatest need of case management or have high risk conditions that could be improved through such contact. Whereas centralized case management addresses the needs of these patients across a continuum, interventional activity must occur at the various venues of care included in the continuum. These interventions must be designed specifically to fulfill the stated goals of the sponsoring organization. The service delivery design phase serves to outline the case management process itself. Please see Figure 4–6.

A number of issues and procedures must be determined in concert with the development of the outline of the process. These include:

Initiation and Termination of Service

- When will case management intervention begin?
- When should case management intervention be terminated?

BOX 4-12

SAMPLE JOB DESCRIPTION

Provider-Based Case Manager [For Multiple Venue/Full Care Health System]

I. Description of Position—The case manager coordinates, negotiates, processes, and manages the care of an identified set of patients to facilitate achievement of quality and cost-effective patient outcomes. The case manager works with patients who are already admitted to the health system and patients who are being considered for admission to the health system. Work is conducted collaboratively with interdisciplinary staff internal and external to the organization.

II. Organizational Relationship—This position reports directly to the case manager supervisor, but works closely with the other case managers to assure cohesiveness of communication. The Case Manager Supervisor reports directly to the vice president of system operations.

III. Qualification

A. R.N., L.P.N., or other individual with sufficient medical background and at least two years of work experience in the field of health service.

B. Knowledgeable and articulate about the venues of care of the full healthcare continuum including applicable regulation and financing issues.

C. Familiar with various reimbursement mechanisms, insurance carriers, and third-party payors.

D. Strong sense of presence with excellent verbal and written skills.

E. Self-motivating and able to conduct various projects.

F. Strong preference for certification in care management.

IV. Duties and Responsibilities of Position

A. Review system admissions to determine which patients are likely candidates for services based on preexisting guidelines for case management.

B. Develop working relationship with social workers and discharge planners who are associated with hospitals and other venues outside the health system in order to assess which patients are likely candidates for services offered by the health system.

C. Conduct personal visits to physicians to ensure open line of communication with primary referral sources.

D. Interview and review medical charts of patients to be followed for case management.

E. Assess the patients to identify needs, issues, financial factors, available reimbursement, care goals, and discharge and continuing care options.

F. Ensure that patient care plans are being followed and the appropriate services are administered at the appropriate times.

G. Establish discharge planning consistent with the overall outcomes/goals according to the specific clinical setting for each venue included within the system.

H. Develop working relationship with insurance carriers and other third-party payors in order to assist the system with insurance verification and reimbursement issues as required and obtain any necessary precertification for care within the continuum or for community care.

I. Actively participate in discharge planning process of patients from time of admission into any program or service offered by the system.

J. Ensure that any clinical paths adopted by the system are being fully and appropriately utilized. Determine patterns and trends regarding variances in clinical pathways and reports to director of case management for study and reconciliation.

K. Remain current as to reimbursement and other trends in capitation, Medicare, and Medicaid.

L. Maintain professional competence through participation in appropriate professional societies and groups.

- Should initiation and termination be the same for all patients followed?

Tactics

- Which specific tactics of case management will be required to fulfill the goals of the system?

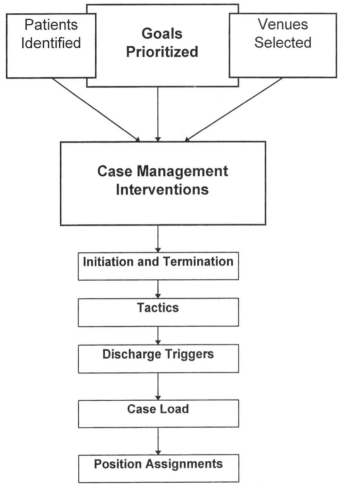

FIGURE 4–6. Designing the Service Delivery Component

- How will these tactics be arranged into a smooth and orderly process of case management?
- Will the tactics vary by venue of care as well as diagnosis?

Discharge Triggers

- What role do discharge triggers play vis-à-vis patient outcomes?
- How do case managers use discharge triggers to assist with venue utilization and placement?

The design phase provides the standards organization an opportunity to develop consistent procedures, processes, standards, and protocols for case management. Such an approach allows for a coherent and cohesive program of case management that will enable the greatest benefit to be realized from its establishment.

INITIATION AND TERMINATION OF SERVICE

The design team must initially address and review the timing of case management interventions. Oftentimes, issues related to timing will depend on who is the sponsoring organization, what is the payor source for the individuals covered by the system, and what is the budget likely to be for case management? If a healthcare network or managed care organization is the host entity, case management will likely begin when the client has a condition that requires more than routine outpatient medical service. If the goals of case management are to reduce the overall cost of care delivered to enrollees and to reduce enrollee's dependency on the medical system, case management should be initiated as soon as it appears an individual's health status could benefit from such activity. Conversely, unless a service provider is fully capitated, usually there is little financial incentive to begin case management until the patient has had an inpatient stay. For service providers who have some capitation, the best strategy to employ may be to provide early case management services only to patients whose care is covered under capitated arrangements. Therefore, capitated patients would be a subset of the already identified group of patients to be followed.

Again, questions about the termination of case management service will depend on the overall objectives of the sponsoring organization. It would be very rare, however, to see intervention limited to a single venue of care with no followup. This is true regardless of the patient's payor source. Although followup for capitated patients is essential to control costs and improve overall wellness, it is less financially justifiable for patients with other payor sources. Most healthcare organizations, managed care or service-based, are today mandated by a variety of accreditation standards (NCQA, CARF, JCAHO) to conduct ongoing followup of patients after they have received care. Therefore, even if a goal of the system is not to improve overall health status, followup becomes a recommended strategy. Followup would occur at that point in time when active intervention is no longer necessary. Examples of followup include a six-month postdischarge status phone call; mailed notices for annual diagnostics such as Pap smears and blood pressure screening; exercise classes conducted through the facilitation of case management; and other related activities occurring after a significant contact with a health service provider has taken place.

INTERVENTIONS

Case management is a powerful approach to managing the care of patients, including those with complex conditions, over the care continuum. It is the interventions of the individual case manager that largely determine the success of the system. Although the case manager executes the intervention, the range of possible interventions is usually preselected by the design team. Each intervention must respond to one of the overall objectives of the system. Figure 4–7 outlines this connection.

Which interventions need to be performed by case managers will depend on resource allocation and the particular functions of other departments within the institution. If clearly articulated goals have been outlined for the case management program, the necessary interventions are naturally derivative. If patients from a number of venues will be followed by case management, interventions will most likely occur at each venue.

At this point, the focus of the design team should be directed at the establishment of flow charts detailing the combination and course of such interventions. Given that a set of diagnoses have already been preselected as appropriate for case management services, a diagnostic orientation may be most useful in establishment of the flow charts. If case management is following 15 diagnoses that generally fall into three broad categories, (e.g. cardiac, respiratory, neurological), three flow sheets should be developed. The flow sheet identifies the intervention, the venue, and the timing. It serves as a general road map for case managers to guide their activities, but allows for sufficient

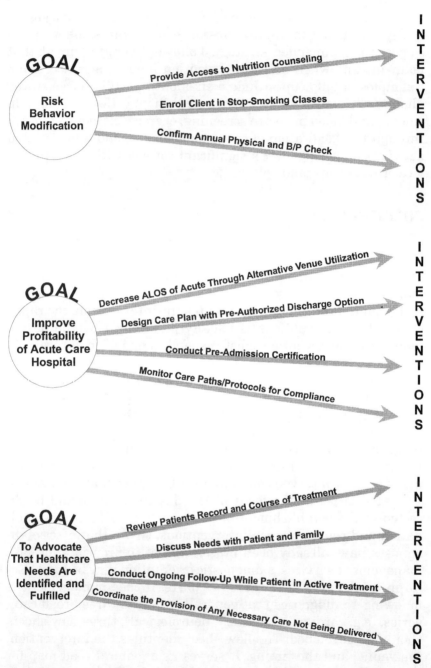

FIGURE 4–7. Identifying the Nexus Between Goals and Case Management
Interventions

customization and deviation given a set of particular facts and circumstances. It is certainly possible to perform case management without the benefit of a flow sheet. However, in a large and centralized system, it becomes an important tool in promoting consistency of approach and outcome. It is case management's equivalent of a care map. A sample flow sheet may look something like Box 4–13 if being used by a service-based provider such as a hospital.

FUNCTIONAL OUTCOMES PER VENUE

The flow sheet of interventions should naturally correspond to the likely or expected outcomes to be achieved in each venue of care. In this context, outcomes are the end result of care. What specific functional problem has been reduced or eliminated? What has been achieved? In order for the case manager to implement the right intervention at the right time, a functional outcome per venue of care should be developed for each diagnostic group to be followed. Such a tool answers a number of questions faced by the case manager. First, it profiles what the likely functional deficits are for a specific diagnosis. This assists case managers who may be unfamiliar with the appropriate intervention for a particular diagnosis. The detailing of the typical functional deficits is similar to a problem checklist so that the case manager can ensure that he or she has identified those areas needing the intervention of case management.

Moreover, the functional venues of care, stated on a venue-specific level, and by diagnosis, are the expected functional outcome goals of the patient. Attainment of these goals indicates that discharge to another venue is warranted. This approach also establishes the parameters of the level of care in each venue. For instance, in the case of a stroke patient, a functional outcome goal at the CORF may be to ambulate independently with adaptive aids. Clearly, this goal could also be achieved in the comprehensive inpatient unit (CIR) or in the subacute rehabilitation program. However, given the cost efficiencies of a CORF, primarily because it is an outpatient program of comprehensive rehabilitation care, it is the strongly preferred venue for particular aspects of care of the stroke

B O X 4 – 13

SAMPLE FLOW SHEET

ACTIVITY	TIMING	VENUE
I.D. patient for case management	Upon Admission	E.R./acute
Review medical record	Day 1–2	Acute
Project discharge date	Day 1–2	Acute
Interview patient/family	Day 2–3	Acute
Determine post-acute care plan with team approval (M.D., patient, etc.)	Day 3	Acute
Obtain precertification for postacute care	Day 3	Acute
Facilitate transfer to subacute/CIR	Day 5	Acute
Review/set outcome goals and care plan	Day 5	Subacute
Review goal process/status	Day 7	Subacute
Arrange for admission/CIR including precertification	Day 12	Subacute
Establish condition qualifies for admission under regulations	Day 12	Subacute
Facilitate transfer	Day 16	Subacute
Review goal/care plan	Day 17	CIR
Arrange primary care consult	Day 19	CIR
Establish ADL equipment needs for home and orient family to status	Day 21	CIR
Review status and project discharge date and identify postdischarge needs	Day 24	CIR

Task	Day	Location
Set up predischarge evaluation by CORF	Day 30	CIR
Facilitate discharge home and confirm CORF appointment	Day 33	CIR
Review goals/care plan	Day 35	CORF
Conference with primary care physician	Day 39	Clinic
Review attainment of goals and project discharge date	Day 60	CORF
Arrange for additional diagnostics	Day 65	Outpatient Center/CORF
Status call and followup survey	Postadmission 6 months	Home
Health risk modification check	Postadmission 1 year	Primary care physician

patient. Adherence to a functional outcome by venue of care approach simplifies the entire care process for the case manager. It enables the case manager to make discharge and placement decisions based primarily on the outcome that should be achieved. Although many factors (regulatory, financial, clinical, and individual venue capabilities) determine which venue can and should achieve what outcomes, at the individual case manager level the focus is only patient outcome. Additionally, consistent reference to functional outcomes by venue of care eliminates some of the problems associated with subjective decision making. Patients are assured consistency of treatment and understand that venue placement relates first and foremost to goal attainment rather than to financial or other factors. Figures 4–8, 4–9, and 4–10 are samples of functional outcomes by venue of care that illustrate these principles.

SYSTEM EVALUATION AND ACCOUNTABILITY

Case management is the means for a healthcare provider to combine optimal resource management with quality care delivery. Juxtaposition of these two objectives, cost and quality, forces a critical evaluation of which case management strategies promote the best outcomes. Each system of case management must include a means for accountability and evaluation. Such a mechanism should be built into the overall system design and should answer the questions:

1. How is the program working?
2. Are the articulated goals of the system being met?

System evaluation and accountability is the barometer of actual effectiveness and efficiency of resources expanded. In other words, is case management worthwhile? Is the program achieving the success expected from those who support and encourage its utilization? When an organization implements a case management program, such an evaluation plan must be developed to measure the program's benefits so that the organization can assess whether its investment in the program is worthwhile. The process begins with the construction of a conceptual model and reference to the previously identified programs goals to give focus and structure to the evaluation plan or design.

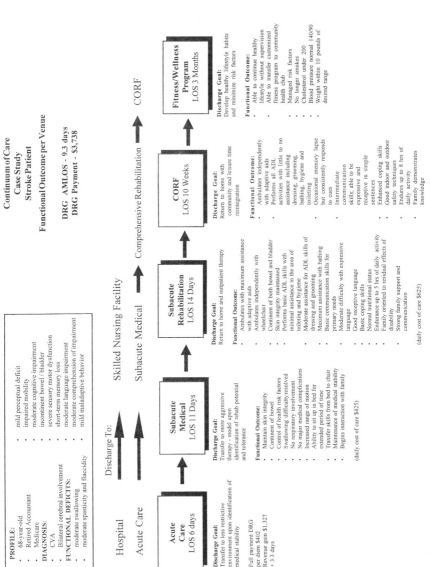

PROFILE:
- 68-year-old
- Retired Accountant
- Medicare

DIAGNOSIS:
- CVA
- Bilateral cerebral involvement

FUNCTIONAL DEFICITS:
- moderate swallowing
- moderate spasticity and flaccidity
- mild perceptual deficit
- impaired mobility
- moderate cognitive impairment
- incontinent bowel / bladder
- severe sensory motor dysfunction
- short-term memory loss
- moderate language impairment
- moderate comprehension of impairment
- mild maladaptive behavior

Continuum of Care
Case Study
Stroke Patient

Functional Outcome per Venue

DRG AMLOS - 9.3 days
DRG Payment - $3,738

Discharge To: Skilled Nursing Facility

Hospital

Acute Care   Subacute Medical   Comprehensive Rehabilitation   CORF

Acute Care
LOS 6 days

Discharge Goal:
Transfer to less restrictive environment upon identification of medical stability

Full payment DRG
per diem $402
Revenue gain $1,327
+ 3.3 days

Subacute Medical
LOS 11 Days

Discharge Goal:
Transfer to more aggressive therapy - model upon identification of rehab potential and tolerance

Functional Outcome:
- Maintain skin integrity
- Continent of bowel
- Control of health risk factors
- Swallowing difficulty resolved
- No respiratory involvement
- No major medical complications
- Increased range of motion
- Ability to sit in bed for extended period of time
- Transfer skills from bed to chair
- Maintenance of medical stability
- Begins interaction with family

(daily cost of care $425)

Subacute Rehabilitation
LOS 14 Days

Discharge Goal:
Return to home and outpatient therapy

Functional Outcome:
- Ambulates with maximum assistance with adaptive aids
- Ambulates independently with wheelchair
- Continent of both bowel and bladder
- Skin integrity maintained
- Performs basic ADL skills with minimal assistance in the area of toileting and hygiene
- Moderate assistance for ADL skills of dressing and grooming
- Maximum assistance with bathing
- Basic communication skills for primary needs
- Moderate difficulty with expressive language
- Good receptive language
- Basic coping skills
- Normal nutritional status
- Endurance up to 5 hrs of daily activity
- Family oriented to residual effects of disability
- Strong family support and communication

(daily cost of care $625)

CORF
LOS 10 Weeks

Discharge Goal:
Return to home with community and leisure time reintegration

Functional Outcome:
- Ambulates independently with adaptive aids
- Performs all ADL activities with little to no assistance including dressing, grooming, bathing, hygiene and toileting
- Occasional memory lapse but consistently responds to cues
- Intermediate communication skills; able to be expressive and receptive in simple sentences
- Enhanced coping skills
- Good indoor and outdoor safety techniques
- Endures up to 8 hrs of daily activity
- Family demonstrates knowledge

Fitness/Wellness Program
LOS 3 Months

Discharge Goal:
Develop healthy lifestyle habits and minimize risk factors

Functional Outcome:
- Able to continue healthy lifestyle without supervision
- Able to transfer customized fitness program to community health club
- Managed risk factors
- No longer smokes
- Cholesterol under 200
- Blood pressure normal 140/90
- Weight within 10 pounds of desired range

FIGURE 4-8. Continuum of care case study, stroke patient. Functional outcome per venue, DRG AMLOS—9.3 days, DRG Payment—$3,738.

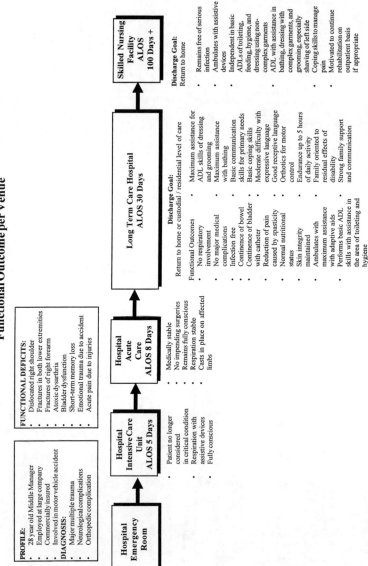

Continuum of Care
Case Study
Major Multiple Trauma Patient
Functional Outcome per Venue

PROFILE:
· 28 year old Middle Manager
· Employed at large company
· Commercially insured
· Involved in motor vehicle accident

DIAGNOSIS:
· Major multiple trauma
· Neurological complications
· Orthopedic complication

FUNCTIONAL DEFICITS:
· Dislocated right shoulder
· Fractures in both lower extremities
· Fractures of right forearm
· Ataxic dysarthria
· Bladder dysfunction
· Short-term memory loss
· Emotional trauma due to accident
· Acute pain due to injuries

Hospital Emergency Room

Hospital Intensive Care Unit
ALOS 5 Days

· Patient no longer considered in critical condition
· Respiration with assistive devices
· Fully conscious

Hospital Acute Care
ALOS 8 Days

· Medically stable
· No impending surgeries
· Remains fully conscious
· Respiration stable
· Casts in place on affected limbs

Long Term Care Hospital
ALOS 30 Days

Discharge Goal:
Return to home or custodial / residential level of care

Functional Outcomes
· No respiratory involvement
· No major medical complications
· Infection free
· Continence of bowel
· Continence of bladder with catheter
· Reduction of pain caused by spasticity
· Normal nutritional status
· Skin integrity maintained
· Ambulates with maximum assistance with adaptive aids
· Performs basic ADL skills with assistance in the area of toileting and hygiene

· Maximum assistance for ADL skills of dressing and grooming
· Maximum assistance with bathing
· Basic communication skills for primary needs
· Basic coping skills
· Moderate difficulty with expressive language
· Good receptive language
· Orthotics for motor control
· Endurance up to 5 hours of daily activity
· Family oriented to residual effects of disability
· Strong family support and communication

Skilled Nursing Facility
ALOS 100 Days +

Discharge Goal:
Return to home

· Remains free of serious infection
· Ambulates with assistive devices
· Independent in basic ADLs of toileting, feeding, hygiene, and dressing using non-complex garments
· ADL with assistance in bathing, dressing with complex garments, and grooming, especially shaving of left side
· Coping skills to manage pain
· Motivated to continue rehabilitation on outpatient basis if appropriate

FIGURE 4–9. Continuum of care case study. Major multiple trauma patient. Functional outcome per venue.

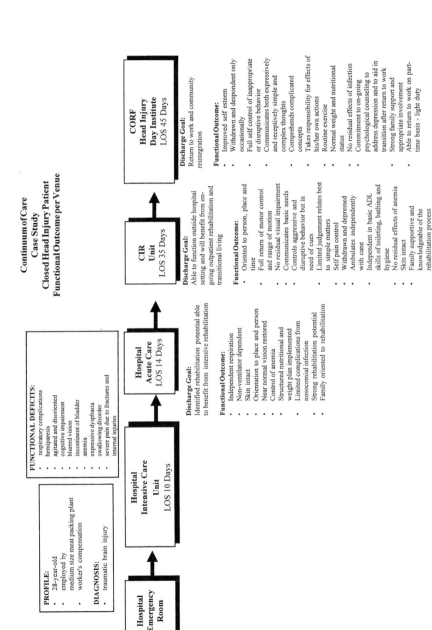

Continuum of Care
Case Study
Closed Head Injury Patient
Functional Outcome per Venue

PROFILE:
- 28-year-old
- employed by
- medium size meat packing plant
- worker's compensation

DIAGNOSIS:
- traumatic brain injury

FUNCTIONAL DEFICITS:
- respiratory complications
- hemiparesis
- agitated and disoriented
- cognitive impairment
- blurred vision
- incontinent of bladder
- anemia
- expressive dysphasia
- swallowing disorder
- severe pain due to fractures and internal injuries

Hospital Emergency Room

Hospital Intensive Care Unit
LOS 10 Days

Hospital Acute Care
LOS 14 Days

Discharge Goal:
Identified rehabilitation potential able to benefit from intensive rehabilitation

Functional Outcome:
- Independent respiration
- Non-ventilator dependent
- Skin intact
- Orientation to place and person
- Near normal vision restored
- Control of anemia
- Structured nutritional and weight plan implemented
- Limited complications from nosocomial infection
- Strong rehabilitation potential
- Family oriented to rehabilitation

CIR Unit
LOS 35 Days

Discharge Goal:
Able to function outside hospital setting and will benefit from on-going outpatient rehabilitation and transitional living

Functional Outcome:
- Oriented to person, place and time
- Full return of motor control and range of motion
- No residual visual impairment
- Communicates basic needs
- Controls aggressive and disruptive behavior but in need of cues
- Limited judgement relates best to simple matters
- Self pain control
- Withdrawn and depressed
- Ambulates independently with cane
- Independent in basic ADL skills of toileting, bathing and hygiene
- No residual effects of anemia
- Skin intact
- Family supportive and knowledgeable of the rehabilitation process

CORF Head Injury Day Institute
LOS 45 Days

Discharge Goal:
Return to work and community reintegration

Functional Outcome:
- Improved self esteem
- Withdrawn and despondent only occasionally
- Full self control of inappropriate or disruptive behavior
- Communicates both expressively and receptively simple and complex thoughts
- Comprehends complicated concepts
- Takes responsibility for effects of his/her own actions
- Routine exercise
- Normal weight and nutritional status
- No residual effects of infection
- Commitment to on-going psychological counseling to address depression and to aid in transition after return to work
- Strong family support and appropriate involvement
- Able to return to work on part-time basis - light duty

FIGURE 4–10. Continuum of care case study. Closed head injury patient. Functional outcome per venue.

No matter what design is chosen, the program evaluation tool must: (1) operationalize the program's objectives; (2) select measurement tools to collect data; and, (3) use the collected data to assess achievement of program objectives and make changes in the program as warranted.

When evaluating the effectiveness and efficiency of a centralized system of case management, outcomes can be characterized as financial, clinical, or related to satisfaction, and each outcome category is meaningful both by itself and in concert with the other two. Decreased or controlled cost of care is the primary financial outcome. This can be measured by calculating total cost of care per DRG category followed by case management, and the frequency or duration of specifically defined resource indication can provide additional information to what contributes to the total cost per case. As with any research, it is essential to the future acceptance of the program that the measurement tools have evidence of reliability and validity. Clinical outcomes that can be measured include mortality, length of stay, complications such as wound infection or atelectasis, and readmission. These clinical outcomes are both meaningful and measurable but are only useful for evaluating the efficacy of short-term, episode-based case management intervention. Long-term issues of patient functionality or quality of life are not addressed through episodic clinical goals alone. Measures of functional capacity would be useful to link healthcare delivery with ongoing health status. However, independent service providers have little incentive to measure anything but outcome relative to service provided. Healthcare providers who are components of an integrated delivery system, conversely, will want to encourage greater reliance on functional capacity and other global measures of health. Such an approach should be incorporated within the evaluation and accountability design of the case management system. Linking resources used with the health outcomes achieved throughout the continuum of care is the fundamental accomplishment of any case management's system of accountability.

Satisfaction outcomes can be measured by patient satisfaction surveys developed by the case management organization. Satisfaction can also be expressed through consistency of plan enrollment. Specific responses about how patients and their families perceived care provided by a model of case management may be useful information, but may not be true expressions of the state of satisfaction. The program evaluation design form in Box 4–14 should provide useful guidance to the team seeking to establish a means of case management accountability.

The culmination of data collection and outcome measurement is analysis. Program evaluation is designed to make analysis of the case management program as objective as possible. The measures and tools used should be chosen to maximize the likelihood that objective decisions and analysis can be made. Such analysis should be conducted on a quarterly basis and should provide recommendations based on both qualitative and quantitative data generated by implementation of the program evaluation design. In this way, a comprehensive assessment of the outcomes of case management can be obtained objectively. Accountability at the delivery level entails answerability only for clinical outcomes. Accountability at the level of case management incorporates responsibility for both short-term and long-term financial, clinical, and patient satisfaction goals. Accountability assesses whether the authority necessary to act or intervene has been acquired. In fact, accountability is only expected of those in their highest phase of professional growth and role development. Accountability begins with knowledge and skill, adds responsibilities, and ends with authority. To hold case management accountable is to acknowledge that it has matured sufficiently as a system to be challenged.

Case management is a valuable resource within a healthcare organization. Accordingly, it must be developed, planned, and nurtured in a strategic way. This requires careful selection of the design team and ongoing support and development of the individuals who assume the case manager leadership. This chapter has provided the healthcare manager with a detailed description of the design process and its pitfalls; numerous worksheets and forms have been included for reference and to serve as future guidelines in the development process. The result of such a design process is a customized and centralized system of case management. An effective system is produced only through a sufficient investment of time and resources in careful development.

BOX 4-14

PROGRAM EVALUATION DESIGN FOR CASE MANAGEMENT

REL WT	OBJECTIVE	MEASURE	EXPECTANCIES		
			Min	Goal	Opt
25%	Appropriate and effective utilization of multiple venues of care	% of patients referred through the case management system, to the appropriate venue of care, based on preestablished functional outcome expectations by diagnostic categorization; as determined by utilization review	75%	85%	90%
20%	Minimize recidivism to acute hospitalization	% of patients readmitted to an acute care hospital venue for the same medical condition within a period of 12 months	25%	20%	15%
15%	Minimize overall cost of patient care	% of patients whose stay in an acute hospital bed does not exceed length of stay targets by diagnoses utilizing PPS as the benchmark, thereby reducing DRG revenue loss	75%	85%	90%
15%	Minimize health risks among patients within designated disease management categories	% of patients reporting reduced health risks related to individual disease or condition	50%	60%	70%

10%	Maximize postmedical intervention contact with patients in order to preempt medical crisis through ongoing monitoring and education	% of patients who have missed no more than three follow-up contacts during a 12 month period	70%	75%	80%
10%	Maximize retention of functional capacity	% of patients, within control group, who report no loss of functional gains	65%	70%	75%
5%	Support community outreach to minimize patient isolation because of chronic disease or other health factors	Achieve targeted attendance of program enrollees at monthly community outreach meetings	85%	90%	95%

Health risks = e.g., weight, blood pressure, cholesteral level, smoking

Follow-up contacts = primary care physician office visits and/or nurse practitioner, follow-up telephonic visits

Functional capacity = physician and cognitive functioning

MIN = minimum, OPT = optimum

5

Case Management as an Information System

Case management has gained stature within the healthcare system because it is one of the few areas where both financial and clinical information overlap. The case manager's job is to see that the patients stay well and at the same time that care is delivered in a cost-effective manner. As a result of sitting in the financial/clinical crosshairs, there is a significant informational and organizational burden placed on the case manager. Success on the job is tied to the ability to access and organize the information needed to stay current regarding quality cost-effective medical care. In addition, the case manager must be able to manage and schedule patients navigating through today's complex and often disjointed healthcare system. Historically, case management systems have emphasized decreasing inpatient costs and controlling resource utilization, which was largely sufficient in the early phases of managed care contracting. With the growing assumption of greater financial risk and ultimate responsibility for the health status of a defined population, sophisticated information management tools become necessary.

The advent of case management in healthcare has occurred in parallel with another revolutionary change in the world at large: computers and information technology. It is through this second revolution, electronic information management, that case management can truly blossom to its full potential. With the right tools, an individual can now access, as needed, specific information related to an individual patient, a population, a disease, a treatment methodology, or essentially any other piece of relevant information that can be represented in a computerized flow chart.

This revolution in information handling has allowed medicine to move from an institutional or hospital-based view to a patient-based view of the services it provides. As a result, information generated from many sources, such as hospitals, doctor's offices, dental clinics, fitness clubs, senior centers, and home health agencies, must now be brought together to be used to care for the patient. The case manager can act as the agent for this process, computers can be the tools to facilitate the task. An analogy from the building trades is particularly illustrative. It is possible to build great edifices with brute strength and massive numbers of people; witness the pyramids of ancient Egypt built over a period of years by multitudes with manual tools and labor. In contrast however, a modern skyscraper can be constructed in the middle of a bustling center of commerce with modern tools in a period of months. More can be accomplished more efficiently by fewer people using modern tools.

Specifically, information tools allow the case manager to take pieces of information and organize them to yield useful knowledge. For example, individual facts related to the care of a patient can be coalesced to create a clear picture of the patient's present and projected health. The information tool helps to organize and categorize pieces of data into a useful clinical view, such as a diagnostic problem list, medications, appointments, living arrangements, social and vocational supports, and current functional condition.

Although it is possible to replicate the same clinical view using pen and paper, a properly designed computer system allows easier conversion of data into knowledge. In comparison with a manual system, an electronic information management tool can transform case management data into actionable knowledge more cheaply, accurately, and with more speed than any other available means. Many of the tasks involved in the care of managed patients are repetitive between patients.

Computers are uniquely capable of efficiently organizing and implementing repetitive tasks.

Within the continuum of care the following informational needs are apparent: (1) There is a need to combine both clinical and fiscal information to present a clear view of the quality of and resources expended for patient care; and (2) it is imperative to track patients and resources among organizations. An individual with a stroke is treated in the emergency room, the acute hospital, the rehab hospital or the subacute facility, by home health, and as an outpatient. This course of care occurs over a three- to six-month period. In a typical health system in the 1990s, most of the information related to the care of this patient would be unavailable for further use once a patient has been discharged from a particular venue. Accordingly, much of the available outcomes data is never used because it is too hard to retrieve from the many organizations involved in care. As a result, it is currently very difficult to comprehensively track patients through a continuum of care. The endpoint is duplication of care, perhaps a barium swallow or MRI is repeated because a previous test result is unavailable. Resources are overutilized by the healthcare system and optimal clinical care may not be delivered. From a systems perspective, feedback is lost. One of the elementary attributes of a well-designed system in engineering is one in which the actual output is measured and compared with the desired output. The system is then changed to try to get the real output to match the desired output. The results of the system interaction are fed back before new inputs start into the system. In this way, over time the system is optimized to achieve the desired output. The same process is happening in healthcare. Case managers and information tools define feedback within the healthcare system today. Experience in treating groups of patients leads to better and more efficient care. For example, it used to be standard practice that after a heart attack, six weeks of bed rest was mandatory. Over time, by evaluating outcomes and trying new strategies, it has become clear that immobility itself can cause problems and that early mobilization within a few days, depending on the severity of the heart attack, can optimize patient outcome. In addition, the healthcare system is no longer paying for unnecessary days spent in the hospital.

What specifically can an information system do for the case manager to orchestrate feedback and optimal care? It can facilitate communication, strategic analysis, education, and most importantly, work flow:

Communication: Computers allow a new type of communication called electronic mail or *E-mail*. It is different from the postal system because of its speed, which is nearly instantaneous. Unlike a telephone or face-to-face meeting, two communicators do not have to be in the same place to interact. Furthermore, it can be a "one to many" communication avenue with the inclusion of several recipients in the address line. A message is not degraded in quality when it is forwarded, a digital copy is identical to the original. It is possible to add a reply to the document that has been sent. This functionality keeps people on track by allowing them to have access to the issue at hand in an immediate fashion.

Strategic Analysis: By categorizing data in an organized fashion, computers allow a user to see information that would otherwise be unobtainable. Moreover, it is possible to access trend data by simply looking at a global view of a list of patient records that are recorded as part of routine workflow. The daily work flow is leveraged into being a strategic data input tool simply by computerizing it to capture the daily information necessary to manage the patients.

Education: The same computer that is used for day-to-day work activities can be used for education by accessing some of the vast resources available on the Internet. Box 5–1 provides addresses for web sites and further information via the Internet.

Work flow: For a case manager, work flow is the area in which the computer will have its most profound effect. The scheduling of meetings and tasks, maintaining and prioritizing to do lists, accessing and organizing phone contacts, and storing summary information on various venues of care in the referral network are some of the ways in which an electronic information system can improve work flow. In addition, a properly designed system should house all relevant clinical, financial, and functional information related to the patients being managed.

BOX 5-1

CASE MANAGEMENT SITES ON THE INTERNET

HealthCase, Inc.
Comprehensive client and/or server medical case management software
http://www.healthcase.com/

BJB Geriatric (Elder Care) Services
Elderly case management
http://pages.prodigy.com/bjbservices/geriserv.html

Pacific. Pacific Case Management, Inc.
Specializing in medical case management of workers' compensation and health insurance
http://www.pcmgmt.com/

Florida Health Consultants
Geriatric case management services
http://www.flahealth.com/

Ridgemoor Case Management Services, Inc.
A group of registered nurse/rehabilitation case managers who specialize in catastrophic medical and rehabilitation case management
http://www.alliance.net/rcms/—size 8K—24 Sep 96

APLA HIV-LA: Case Management
HIV case management
http://www.apla.org/apla/hivla/casemgmt.html

CASE MANAGEMENT AIDS
Maricopa managed care systems in Arizona
http://aztec.asu.edu/cirs/service/CASE_MANAGEMENT_AIDS.html

CASE MANAGEMENT DEVELOPMENTALLY DISABLED
http://aztec.asu.edu/cirs/service/CASE_MANAGEMENT_DEVELOPMENTALLY_DISABLED.html

NO/AIDS - HIV Case Management
NO/AIDS works to ensure that support systems for people affected by AIDS are always available
http://www.bigeasy.com/noaids/caseman.html

The ARC Connection—Case Management Services
The ARC—Case Management is a collection of coordinating,

brokering, advocacy, assessment, and administrative activities for children http://204.253.122.7/thearc/ARCICM.HTM
Case Management http://www.quikpage.com/C/casmgmt2/
Case Management of New Jersey MEDICAL MANAGEMENT http://www.quikpage.com/C/casemgmt/
The Center for Case Management, Inc. Founded in 1986, The Center for Case Management health care consulting firm http://www.cfcm.com/
HOMI. Assurance Case Management Systems http://www.homi.com/casemgmt.html
CorVel Corporation—Advocacy Medical Case Management http://www.worldsys.com/corvel/net/about/advocacy/
Wildwood Case Management Medicaid Case Management Services assists individuals with developmental disabilities http://www.wildwood.edu/casemgmt/
Case Management for Persons with Traumatic Brain Injury Objective: Assure timely and appropriate access to rehabilitation services http://140.254.20.2/ovchome/proj3-1/
MIDS, Inc. Case Management http://www.midsinc.com/web/prod-info/
Intensive Case Management http://www.multnomah.lib.or.us/div/corcas.html
Case Management Support services to help frail seniors live at home as independently as possible http://pen.ci.santa-monica.ca.us/pen/community-center/seniors/directory/sr2.html
IMS Software http://www.work-web.com/ims/
First Integrated Health Prospective Case Management Solutions for MCOs http://www.fih.com/fihhmo3.htm

Prodigy's Elder Lovin' Care http://www.mindspring.com/ ~ eldrcare/prodigy.htm
VNSNY Elder Care Home page http://ourworld.compuserve.com/homepages/VNSNY_Elder_ Care/
Austin Elder Care Austin Elder Care, Austin, TX http://www.gen.com/margie/
Elder Web http://www.ice.net/ ~ kstevens/elderweb.htm

In addition to the benefits of the computer as a management tool, software system vendors are enhancing and expanding their products to support real-time, concurrent approaches to case management that are provider-based and incorporate both clinical, financial, and situs of care considerations. A significant change is occurring to support decision making at the point of service rather than only at an organizational level, to manage care from a distance. A well-designed system should identify and assist in the daily management and treatment of potentially high cost, resource-intensive cases. When evaluating the software packages that are emerging in the market, the provider should consider a number of critical issues:

- To what extent does the organization sponsoring the system of case management have utilization review and case management integrated with claims, enrollment, and provider services?
- Does the organization, particularly if it is a service provider, want the option to integrate its own care guidelines and protocols into the case management program and be able to arrange or amend any predetermined rules for patient treatment and placement?
- How much customization of the system's rules will be desired, particularly as to referral, venue utilization, and preauthorization?

- What reports are available from the system and how quickly can they be obtained?
- To what extent does the organization need to have in-depth drill-down and focus on specific venues of care?

It must be determined which software system or other management tool meets an organization's needs. This can best be accomplished through an informational management planning process. The process should be undertaken to identify and prioritize requirements based on business goals and objectives; risk requirements; medical management needs; internal and external data needs; sophistication of market, including payor mix considerations; and other organizational parameters. Box 5–2 provides a checklist to use when evaluating a case management information system:

B O X   5 – 2

CHECKLIST OF INFORMATION SYSTEM FUNCTIONALITY FOR CASE MANAGEMENT

	YES	NO
Single master patient index		
Single data entry used many times		
Minimal typing for standard and repetitive data functions		
Voice, pen, or pointing device input		
Graphical user interface (Microsoft Windows type)		
Clinical and financial data integration		
Case mix		
Census		
Insurance verification		
Admission, discharge, and transfer summary information		

	YES	NO
Track healthcare resources used by the patient		
Number of hospital days		
Number and type of institutional stays		
Number of clinician visits by clinician type		
Amount and type of durable medical equipment used		
Cost of medications		
Track clinical and social aspects of patients		
Diagnostic problem list		
Medication list		
Allergies		
Appointments		
Living arrangements		
Social and vocational supports		
Current functional condition		
Scheduling		
Patient		
Disease-specific clinical pathways		
Ongoing appointments		
Preventive interventions (mammograms, prostate exam, etc.)		
Case manager		
Client load		
Personal schedule		
Electronic communication (E-mail)		
Case management resource manager		
Phone list		
Task list		
Contact list of resources in the local region		
Capabilities		

	YES	NO
Quality		
Personnel		
Computer program specific		
Open database (communicates with other computer programs easily)		
Ad hoc reporting (does not require programming to evaluate information contained in the database)		
Client server (works on a small personal computer, can communicate throughout an organization)		
Audit trail (can review who did what when in relation to a patient)		
Confidentiality ensured		
Encrypted data files when transferring information on a network		
Easily controlled user access		

Healthcare has changed to demand both strong clinical and fiscally responsible care. Case managers have emerged to occupy one of the leadership domains in managing this health delivery revolution. Information systems have matured at the same time as healthcare has been evolving; they now allow functional group work flow interaction, accessible to a nontechnical person. The combination of electronic information management and case management allow cohesive and rational delivery of clinical care. The growing complexity of healthcare information needs is driving the development of more sophisticated case management systems in order to provide appropriate care. It is care that can be evaluated for clinical and financial effect, and thus evolve into the optimal healthcare delivery system.

6

CHAPTER

The Professional
Case Manager

Case managers today come from many different groups, with diverse educational backgrounds and professional experiences. Many case managers began their careers as nurses or social workers. It is common for professionals such as vocational counselors, rehabilitation therapists, insurance specialists, and paralegals to reorient their careers to case management. The increase in case managers is further evidenced by the growing membership of the Case Management Society of America (CMSA), the largest organization of case managers in the country. In 1995, the CMSA grew from 3,500 to 5,000 members. In 1996, the CMSA merged with the Individual Case Management Association (ICMA) creating a total membership in excess of 7,500 case managers. The Center for Healthcare Information maintains a database listing of approximately 9,300 case managers. In 1995, there were approximately 15,000 certified case managers and 40,000 case managers who were not certified in the United States.

What is the explanation for this rapid increase in the creation of case manager positions? The explanation is twofold involving the wider variety of resources that have been incorporated into the continuum of care as well as the growing need to utilize those resources in the most cost-effective manner for all the parties involved. The case manager has become an important player in this new era of healthcare reform, guiding patients through the maze of providers and services.

THE ROLE OF THE CASE MANAGER

Indeed, the role of the case manager is to assess, facilitate, plan, evaluate, and coordinate healthcare delivery and services on behalf of the patient. CMSA defines the role of the case manager as follows:

> The case manager should facilitate communication and coordination between all members of the healthcare team involving the patient and family in the decision-making process in order to minimize fragmentation of the healthcare delivery system. The case manager educates the patient and all members of the healthcare delivery team about case management, community resources, insurance benefits, cost factors and issues in all related topics so that informed decisions may be made. The case manager is the link between the individual, the providers, the payer and the community. The case manager should encourage appropriate use of medical facilities and services, improve quality of care and maintain cost effectiveness on a case-by-case basis. The case manager is an advocate for the patient as well as the payer to facilitate a win-win situation for the patient, the healthcare team and the payer.[1]

The case manager functions as a link in the chain of services to be provided in the variety of venue options. The specific role of the case manager varies depending on his or her employer, but overall, the position demands that the case manager identify the physical and psychosocial needs of the patient and determine what services and venues would be appropriate for the patient's care. First, the case manager must identify which patients most require case management services. For each patient, the case manager must then develop care goals guiding the patient through the system. This guidance may include consulting clinical pathways, care plans, and standards of care, and acting as the patient's advocate to utilize resources in the most cost-effective manner. Throughout this process, the case manager must strive to maintain continuity of care and quality of care for the benefit of both the patient and the family.

The case manager walks a fine line serving the needs of both the payor or provider and the patient. Financial concerns must be balanced with the delivery of quality healthcare. The payor or provider is best served when the case manager uses resources in a way that optimizes cost effectiveness. These cost savings are realized when the case manager is able to move the patient appropriately along the continuum of care. The dual tasks of reducing acute inpatient lengths of stay when 24-hour acute care delivery is no longer necessary and directing the patient to more appropriate venues of care is the daily focus of the case manager.

In the last five years, there has been an explosion in the number of venues and care options available, including sub-acute care facilities, long-term care hospitals, medical day hospitals, comprehensive outpatient rehabilitation facilities, skilled nursing facilities, rehabilitation hospitals, ambulatory surgery facilities, home health services, and alternative medical clinics. In order to distinguish among venue options, the case manager must become an expert in the intended distinctions among each care delivery venue and pose the hard questions about the capabilities and outcome expectations of these many providers. In order to effectuate a continuum of care, the individual case manager must be thoroughly knowledgeable on all aspects of the continuum, comprehending the differences in venues relative to admission requirements, reimbursement structure, purpose of venue, and intended length of stay.

The case manager serves the patient by exploring the treatment alternatives and coordinating the variety of care delivery services. It is the case manager's responsibility to communicate with the patient and his family to ensure that they have the opportunity to make informed decisions regarding the patient's treatment. The case manager must also monitor and reevaluate the patient's condition to ensure that optimum care is being provided and that the patient is satisfied with the care received. The case manager must establish a system to track the patient's progress throughout the system, communicating with physicians and other healthcare providers as to the patient's needs.

SKILLS OF THE CASE MANAGER

The case manager must acquire specialized skills in order to maintain this delicate balance between payor/provider and patient. Most importantly, the case manager must be able to communicate effectively with the patient and his or her family, the healthcare providers, and the payor. It is essential that the case manager be able to educate the patient by explaining which resources are being utilized and why. At the same time, the case manager is responsible for communicating to the insurance company or managed care organization why he or she believes a certain venue or provider to be most appropriate and how this choice will achieve cost savings.

Clearly, this is not a simple task. Most importantly, case managers must ensure that their clinical knowledge remains current so that they can properly meet the patient's needs and be able to justify their choices to the payor. This can be achieved through the many continuing education courses and seminars that are widely available and via the ever-increasing number of case management publications. The case manager must be able to critically analyze the available options based on his or her clinical knowledge as well as familiarity with reimbursement structure. The case manager is a professional facilitator who has a strong commitment to ensuring quality care in a cost-effective manner. In order to do this, the case manager must be a visionary, able to see the overall picture of the patient's care delivery while focusing on maneuvering the patient through the healthcare system.

Given the complexity of navigating the healthcare system, the minimum level of education for a case manager position should be a bachelor's degree. Ideally, case managers would have master's level training, but this type of curriculum is not widely available. The case manager must acquire a vast body of knowledge, which should include:

- A general understanding of the healthcare industry
- Knowledge of the functional uses and admission criteria/ discharge triggers of the various available venues of care
- Regulatory requirements pertaining to the individual care delivery vehicles

- Reimbursement information relative to specific venues and payors
- Understanding of resources available within the continuum of care
- Knowledge of specific requirements of various payors.

STANDARDS OF PRACTICE

The Case Management Society of America has published Standards of Practice that encompass both Standards of Care and Standards of Performance. The Standards of Care include criteria for the following: assessment/case identification and selection, problem identification, planning, monitoring, evaluating, and outcomes. These standards delineate the process by which the case manager evaluates the patient's status, identifies opportunities for intervention, implements a case management plan, monitors care delivery, evaluates the patient's progress, and reports outcomes.

The Standards of Performance serve the purpose of measuring how the case manager fulfills his or her responsibilities in the following areas: quality of care, education/certification, collaboration, legal, ethical, advocacy, resource utilization, and research. These standards of performance measure whether the case manager is achieving positive outcomes, maintaining continuing education, communicating with all parties, acting in accordance with laws and regulations, resolving ethical issues appropriately, assisting the patient and family in their needs, utilizing appropriate venues and providers, and utilizing clinical data.[1]

It is important that the CMSA has created these Standards of Practice in that they provide for self-regulated professionalism in the industry. As noted, the discipline of case management is based on the sometimes conflicting goals of the payor or provider and the patient. For this reason, the standards are helpful in defining the case manager's role and priorities that can assist in resolving the inherent conflicts of the profession. Additionally, practitioners do not necessarily have common professional and educational experiences. Therefore, it is important that they have common standards to guide them through the process of case management. Finally, adherence to standards may provide protection for both case managers and consumers in an era where litigation is commonplace.

Aetna Health Plans and the Individual Case Management Society of America have also collaborated to create a set of guidelines for case managers.[2] According to Margaret St. Coeur, an author of the Aetna/ICMA Case Management Guidelines, these guidelines will "help define how case management differs from other medical management approaches, promote consistency within the practice, serve as a teaching tool, and help focus on outcomes."[3] The guidelines focus on the patient as the central aspect of the case management process although they recognize the need to satisfy payors and providers. The guidelines describe the process of case management including the steps of patient assessment, planning, implementation, evaluation, and documentation. Both generic guidelines and disease-specific guidelines are outlined. As with the CMSA Standards of Practice, the Aetna/ICMA Case Management Guidelines are important in defining the role of a case manager and bringing commonality to a profession with much variability.

CERTIFICATION

As the profession of case management has emerged, so has the certification of the case management professional. The trend towards certification in core areas of case management is vital in that case management is practiced by individuals with different disciplinary backgrounds in diverse practice settings. Certification serves to verify that a case manager possesses a certain level of work experience, education, and practical skills. Several types of certification exist corresponding with different practice areas such as rehabilitation counseling (CRC), disability management (CDMS), or general case management (CMC). Other credentials exist such as Care Manager, Certified and Continuity of Care Certification, Advanced (A-CCC).

Certified Rehabilitation Counselor

The oldest case management credential is the Certified Rehabilitation Counselor, or CRC, which has existed since 1973. This certification ensures that rehabilitation counseling is recognized as a distinct practice area within the rehabilitation field with counseling at its core. The Commission on Rehabilitation Counselor Certification administers the program, which began as a result of a desire on the parts of the American Rehabilitation Counseling Association (ARCA) and the National Rehabilitation Counseling Association (NRCA) to establish professional standards for practitioners within the field. The Commission defines rehabilitation counseling as "a systematic process which assists persons with physical, mental, developmental, cognitive, and emotional disabilities to achieve their personal, career, and independent living goals in the most integrated setting possible through the application of the counseling process."[4] The techniques used may include: assessment and appraisal; diagnosis and treatment planning; career counseling; individual or group counseling; case management, referral, or service coordination; program evaluation; intervention to remove environmental, employment, or attitudinal barriers; consultation services; and job placement services.[4]

The certification can be achieved by satisfying certain educational and employment requirements and passing the certification exam. The education and work prerequisites are specifically delineated in the CRC Certification Guide, which may be obtained from the Commission. In general, one must have obtained a master's degree or be working toward one in a recognized field and have a certain level of experience in rehabilitation counseling. The certification is valid for a period of five years and recertification is generally based on proven continuing education.[5]

Certified Disability Management Specialist

This credential was originally designated Certified Insurance Rehabilitation Specialist when the program was designed in 1984. In April 1996, the name was changed to Certified Disability Management Specialist to reflect changes in the field of insurance rehabilitation. Disability management is defined by the Certification of Disability Management Specialists Commission as "the practice of providing preventative and remediative services to minimize the impact and cost of disability and to enhance productivity" with the goal of "promot[ing] the ill or injured individual's maximum recovery and function."[5]

As with other case management services, the specific steps of disability management may include: assessment; planning and coordination of services; communicating and collaborating with the client, the payor, and the healthcare providers; and evaluating outcomes. Such services are often state or federally mandated under laws governing worker's compensation, social security disability, and the like. Like the CRC credential, there are certain educational and employment requirements that one must satisfy as well as passing the exam. This certification is distinct in that the professional must be engaged in "providing direct services to individuals with disabilities receiving benefits from a disability compensation system."[5]

The certification exam is offered twice a year and covers the following areas: job placement and vocational assessment, case management and human disabilities, rehabilitation services and care, disability legislation, and forensic rehabilitation. The initial certification is good for five years with recertification based on reexamination or continuing education. The CDMS Certification Guide and Application may be obtained from the Certification of Disability Management Specialists Commission in Rolling Meadows, Illinois.[5]

Certified Case Manager

In 1991 the Individual Case Management Society sponsored a meeting to discuss the possibility of developing a certification program for case managers. The meeting was attended by 29 different organizations in the industry who decided to create the National Task Force on Case Management. The task force identified a case management philosophy, definitions, and existing standards of practice, and accepted a proposal from the Certification of Insurance Rehabilitation Specialists Commission (CIRSC) to develop the program along with the Foundation for Rehabilitation Certification, Education, and Research. Collaborating with case management specialists, these two organizations defined eligibility criteria and identified content areas for the certification exam.[6]

Developing a certification exam was and continues to be a challenge in that the specialty of case management includes practitioners from a variety of professions in many different practice settings. Given the transdisciplinary nature of case management, a nationwide study of case managers was conducted in order to identify their job roles and functions and their knowledge and competency. The results of this original research assisted in the creating of the content design for the original exam as well as identifying areas requiring further development for future exams.[6]

Further research is conducted by the Commission for Case Manager Certification on an ongoing basis in order to identify and refine the core body of knowledge that is common to all case management professionals. (See Box 6–1.) As industry practices evolve, so do the exam content and eligibility criteria. The Commission for Case Manager Certification became the credentialling body for the CCM program in 1995.[7]

BOX 6–1

ESSENTIAL ACTIVITIES OF CASE MANAGEMENT

All applicants must hold a professional license or certification that allows the holder to legally and independently practice WITHOUT THE SUPERVISION OF ANOTHER LICENSED PROFESSIONAL, AND TO PERFORM THE FOLLOWING SIX ESSENTIAL ACTIVITIES OF CASE MANAGEMENT:

1. ASSESSMENT

    Assessment is the process of collecting in-depth information about a person's situation and functioning to identify individual needs in order to develop a comprehensive case management plan that will address those needs. In addition to direct client contact, information should be gathered from other relevant sources (patient/client, professional caregivers, nonprofessional caregivers, employers, health records, education/military records, etc.).

2. PLANNING

    The process of determining specific objectives, goals, and actions designed to meet the client's needs as identified through the assessment process. The plan should be action oriented and time specific.

3. IMPLEMENTATION

The process of executing specific case management activities and/or interventions that will lead to accomplishing the goals set forth in the case management plan.

4. COORDINATION

The process of organizing, securing, integrating, and modifying the resources necessary to accomplish the goals set forth in the case management plan.

5. MONITORING

The ongoing process of gathering sufficient information from all relevant sources about the case management plan and its activities and/or services to enable the case manager to determine the plan's effectiveness.

6. EVALUATION

The process, repeated at appropriate intervals, of determining the case management plan's effectiveness in reaching desired outcomes and goals. This might lead to a modification or change in the case management plan in its entirety or in any of its component parts.

The Commission is an independent credentialling body with a mission to promote professional case management certification to advance the quality of case management services provided to individuals. The Commission is responsible for: (1) establishing the criteria for certification eligibility; (2) developing and maintaining the credentialling process; (3) developing and administering the certification examination; (4) encouraging accountability and consumer protection; and (5) supporting the certification process through public education and other means.[8]

The CCM credential is meant to be a supplement to a case manager's already existing professional identity in the health and human services arena. The first eligibility requirement mandates that the applicant be currently licensed or certified by a government or nongovernment agency. This license must enable the applicant to practice the following components of case management: assessment, planning, implementation, coordination, monitoring, and evaluation. Furthermore, the applicant must be legally able to practice these activities independently and without the supervision of another professional. This license or certification has to have been awarded as a result of the applicant passing an exam in his or her area of concentration, following a post-secondary program in this area.[9] Therefore, under these standards, to be eligible for certification, the case manager must already be actively involved in case management or be trained for such practice. This first eligibility request is actually a validation by CCMC of existing training and/or experience.

The second eligibility requirement mandates that the applicant have acceptable employment experience. The applicant must use the six components of case management in five core areas: coordination and service delivery, physical and psychological factors, benefit systems and cost benefit analysis, case management components, and community resources. These components must be applied across the continuum of care in multiple venues of care delivery and involve interaction with all of the relevant parties (healthcare providers, payors, clients and family, etc.). This employment experience must have been gained over 12 months of acceptable full-time employment or its equivalent as a supervisor of case managers who provide direct case management services; over 12 months of acceptable full-time employment or its equivalent under the supervision of a Certified Case Manager; or over 24 months of acceptable full-time employment or its equivalent.[9]

The Commission for Case Manager Certification requires that each application be accompanied by the applicant's official job description and employment verification, both of which must be signed by the applicant's manager, supervisor, or employer. The job description must clearly indicate that the applicant engages in the six essential activities of case management and that the applicant provides or supervises the provision of direct case management services at least fifty percent of the time. The job description must also evidence that the case management services being provided address the client's ongoing needs, not simply dealing with a single episode of care. As noted, these services must be provided across multiple venues of care delivery.[10]

According to the Commission for Case Manager Certification, as of November 1996, approximately 17,500 individuals have been credentialed as certified case managers and approximately 1,000 more were scheduled to take the exam in December 1996. The exam is administered twice per year, in June and December, and has an approximate 80 percent pass rate. The Commission believes that the passage rate is very high because of the screening process employed by the Eligibility Compliance Committee.

Initial certification is valid for five years. To maintain the certification, it must be renewed according to the Commission's certification renewal plan. The objectives of the plan are to: (1) obtain information on current trends; (2) acquire knowledge in specific content areas; (3) master new skills and techniques; (4) expand client management approaches; and (5) develop critical inquiry skills and achieve more balanced professional judgment. To renew the certification without re-examination, individuals are required to complete 80 hours of documented continuing education over the 5-year period. More specific information regarding certification renewal may be obtained from the Commission for Case Manager Certification.[9]

Continuity of Care Certification, Advanced (A-CCC)

The National Board for Certification in Continuity of Care (NBCCC), based in Hartford, Connecticut, sponsors a certification program for continuity of care professionals. The NBCCC has published the following definition of continuity of care:

> Continuity of care is a goal of health care achieved through an interdisciplinary process involving patients/clients, families, health care professionals and providers in the management of a coordinated plan of care. Based on changing needs and available resources, the processes optimize quality outcomes in continuity of care and in the health status of clients.
>
> The NBCCC recognizes that continuity of care includes many factors beyond those traditionally associated with discharge planning and case management, and that these important components of the total health and social support system are included in continuity of care.
>
> Professionals from many different disciplines within multiple systems are involved in continuity of care.[11]

To be eligible to take this exam, one must have obtained a bachelor's degree and have had 2 years of full-time employment experience (or 4,000 hours part-time experience) in continuity of care within the last 5 years. This credential is valid for a period of five years. Recertification may be obtained by reexamination and/or documented evidence of fifty hours of continuing education activity within the five-year period.[11]

The exam consists of 250 multiple-choice questions in the following categories: (1) continuity of care process; (2) healthcare delivery systems; (3) professional issues; (4) standards; (5) reimbursement, regulations, and legal issues; and (6) clinical issues.[11] The first category covers the steps of case management, including assessment, planning, implementation, evaluation, and documentation. The continuum of care is explored in the second category with questions on the various venue options. The professional issues section speaks to the role and skills of a continuity of care specialist. In the standards section, different guidelines, protocols, and standards of care are explored. In the final category, clinical issues are addressed. For further information regarding this certification, one may contact the NBCCC or the Professional Testing Corporation, New York, New York.

Care Manager, Certified (CMC)

This certification program is administered by the National Academy of Certified Care Managers, which is an independent nonprofit organization formed in 1994 by the Case Management Institute of Connecticut Community Care Inc. and the National Association of Professional Geriatric Care Managers. As with the certifications already discussed, this credential was developed in response to the evolution of care management as an area of expertise being practiced by a variety of professionals in several different practice settings. As the practice grows, standards, skills, and job roles and responsibilities must be defined.[12]

To be eligible to take the exam, the applicant must meet both educational and employment criteria in one of the three categories below:

1. Two years of supervised, full-time care management experience that includes interviewing, assessment, care planning, problem solving, and followup subsequent to obtaining a master's degree in a field related to care management such as social work, counseling, nursing, psychology, or gerontology.

2. Four years full-time direct experience with clients in fields such as social work, nursing, mental health, counseling, or care management, two years of which must be supervised care management experience, including activities listed in Category 1. This experience must be obtained subsequent to obtaining a BA/BS in a care management-related field.

3. Six years of full-time direct experience with clients in fields such as social work, nursing, mental health, counseling, or care management, two years of which must be supervised care management experience, including activities listed in Category 1. This experience must be subsequent to obtaining a high school diploma or a degree in a field unrelated to care management.[13]

The CMC exam was developed over an 18-month period by more than 500 care management professionals. It consists of 200 multiple-choice questions relating to six areas of care management practice[12]:

1. Assessment and identification of consumer strengths, needs, concerns, and preferences
2. Establishment of goals and plan of care
3. Coordination and linking of formal and informal services and resources
4. Managing and monitoring the ongoing provision of care
5. Understanding legal, professional, and ethical issues
6. Providing continuous quality evaluation

The initial certification is valid for a period of three years. In order to be re-certified, one must (1) provide care management services for a minimum of 1,500 hours during the 3-year period, (2) earn 15 hours per year of continuing education for a total of 45 hours over the 3-year period, and (3) document continuing education and/or academic credit hours.[13]

Holding a professional credential is important in the field of case management in that the field encompasses many different disciplines being practiced across a wide variety of settings. The particular certification is significant because it denotes for the employer or the consumer the specific area in which the case manager specializes. The case manager is able to represent himself or herself as having met the eligibility requirements and standards established by others in the field and as having certain skills or a specific knowledge base. This promotes accountability, giving the case manager more credibility in the profession. For these reasons, certification is favored by potential employers, healthcare providers, insurance companies, and managed care organizations. As case management becomes more commonplace, credentialing may become a requirement for reimbursement by third-party payors. Certification may also give case managers a competitive edge in the marketplace. While few employers actually require certification as a prerequisite to hiring a case manager, credentialed case managers are certainly preferred and many employers are encouraging their case managers to obtain certification.

WHO ARE CASE MANAGERS?

A wide variety of opinion exists in the case management industry and literature as to who makes the best case manager. Many groups claim that they are the only possible case managers, including nurses, social workers, discharge planners, and utilization reviewers. The main turf battle exists between nurses and social workers. Historically, acute care nurses have had a strong claim on case management, but as the healthcare system evolves and moves beyond the walls of the acute care hospital, social workers are being employed because of their familiarity with outside resources. In fact, each of these groups has strengths and weaknesses when it comes to the process of case management. The strength of acute care nurses in a hospital setting is their clinical knowledge. Although this is very beneficial in managing a patient through that setting, their area of expertise often does not extend to postacute venues or reimbursement issues. Allied health professionals may lack the medical expertise of nurses, but their strength lies in their ability to access resources and plan care so that the resources are utilized in an appropriate manner.[14]

No single group may claim a monopoly on the practice of case management because case management is a discipline unto itself. In a survey of 11,109 individuals applying for the CCM credential, 5,098 noted that their job title was "case manager" (Table 6–1).

Other job titles included registered nurse, rehabilitation counselor, administrator/manager, social worker, utilization reviewer, and discharge planner. The actual practice of case management requires individuals with skills from all of these professions. It should not be limited to simply a nursing approach or a social services approach because each patient has many and various needs. Please see Table 6–2 for a comparison of recognized case management credentials. Effective case management calls for a multidisciplinary approach employing skills and experience from each of these professions. The patient can be served best by a collaboration among professionals with each case manager acquiring broad-based skills and knowledge.

TABLE 6–1

Respondent Job Titles

Job Title	Frequency	Percent
Discharge planner	223	2.0
Case manager	5,098	45.9
Utilization reviewer	295	2.7
Bill auditor	21	0.2
Insurance benefits manager	99	0.9
Admissions liaison	117	1.1
Vocational evaluator	35	0.3
Social worker	369	3.3
Physical therapist	23	0.2
Occupational therapist	27	0.2
Medical doctor	12	0.1
Rehabilitation counselor	1,208	10.9
Work adjustment specialist	6	0.1
Administrator/manager	849	7.6
Registered nurse	2,202	19.8
Other	393	3.5
Missing	132	1.1
TOTAL	11,109	100.0

T A B L E 6-2

Comparing Case Management Credentials

Certification	Certifying Agency	Elegibility Requirements	Length of Certification	Primary Industry Indentification
CCM Certified case manager	Commission for Case Manager Certification Rolling Meadows, IL	▪ Professional license or certification that allows the individual to practice the components of case management. ▪ Acceptable employment experience practicing the six components of case management. ▪ Job description. ▪ Passing score on certification exam.	5 years	Independent firms, hospitals, commercial insurers, and managed care companies
A-CCC Continuity of care certification advanced	National Board for Certification in Continuity of Care Hartford, CT	▪ Bachelor's degree. ▪ Two years full-time employment in continuity of care. ▪ Passing score on certification exam.	5 years	Hospitals, managed care, and others
CMC Care manager certified	National Academy of Certified Care Managers Hollywood, FL	▪ Specific amount of care management experience paired with specific educational experience. ▪ Passing score on certification exam.	3 years	Geriatric care
CRC Certified Rehabilitation counseling	Commission of Rehabilitation Counselor Certification Rolling Meadows, IL	▪ Completed or in the process of completing master's program. ▪ Acceptable employment experience. ▪ Passing score on certification exam.	5 years	Rehabilitation
CDMS Certified disability management specialist	Certification of Disability Management Specialists Commission Rolling Meadows, IL	▪ Educational requirement such as Bachelor's, Master's or Doctorate degree in certain disciplines. ▪ Acceptable employment experience. ▪ Passing score on certification exam.	5 years	Disability programs

WORK SETTINGS

In the 1993 survey of applicants for the CCM credential, individuals were also asked to note their work setting.

Of the 11,109 respondents, 2640 or 23.8% of the individuals worked for an independent case management company (Table 6–3). The number has significantly declined since 1993 as case management has shifted from a vendor-supplied service to an internal department of a wide variety of organizations. Yet, this type of organization is seen by some as the ideal place to practice case management because it sometimes allows for more objectivity than in provider organizations and enables case managers to see the "big picture" of patient management. The second most common workplace in this survey was hospi-

TABLE 6–3

Respondent Work Settings

Work Setting	Frequency	Percent
State/federal agency	234	2.1
Rehabilitation facility program	835	7.5
Independent case management company	2,640	23.8
Independent rehabilitation/insurance affiliate	1,218	11.0
Workers' compensation insurer	674	6.1
Mental health center	26	0.2
Hospital	1,301	11.7
Health insurance company	888	8.0
Third-party administrator	156	1.4
Managed care company	701	6.3
Life/disability insurer	50	0.5
Liability insurer	40	0.4
Veterans' administration agency	12	0.1
Community residential program	23	0.2
HMO, PPO, EPO	455	4.1
Home care agency	695	6.3
Reinsurer	25	0.2
Other	1,099	9.9
Missing	36	0.3
TOTAL	11,109	100.00

tals, with 1,301 people or 11.7 percent of those surveyed noting this as their place of employment. Case management is also a growing trend in hospitals, with utilization review and discharge planning departments often being combined or phased into a case management department. Unfortunately, some hospitals are making the mistake of simply renaming these departments with a case management title and not actually changing the structure or function of the departments. Clearly, this will not benefit the hospital or the patient. Effective case management is not just synonymous with an existing hospital department. It demands its own organizational structure and focus. The third and fourth most frequent job settings were independent rehabilitation/insurance affiliates and insurance companies with 11 percent and 8 percent of those surveyed, respectively. These entities are increasingly interested in case management to improve cost savings as well as clinical outcomes. A recent survey by the Health Insurance Association of America found that insurance companies saved thirty dollars for every one dollar invested in case management programs.[15] Case managers are needed by many employers in a variety of settings including managed care organizations, home health agencies, and government agencies. The demand for case managers has increased significantly over the last decade and, given the changes taking place in the healthcare arena, this trend is likely to continue well into the years to come.

REFERENCES

1. Case Management Society of America. *Standards of practice for case management*. Little Rock, AR: CMSA, 1995.
2. St. Coeur M. *Case management practical guidelines*. St. Louis: Mosby, 1996.
3. St. Coeur M. Care management guidelines. *Case Review* 1:46, 1995.
4. Commission on Rehabilitation Counselor Certification. *CRC certification guide*. Rolling Meadows, IL: Commission on Rehabilitation Counselor Certification, 1996.
5. Certification of Disability Management Specialists Commission. *CDMS certification guide*. Rolling Meadows, IL: Certification of Disability Management Specialists Commission, 1996.

6. Foundation for Rehabilitation Certification, Education, and Research. *Validation of essential knowledge dimensions in case management.* Rolling Meadows, IL: Foundation for Rehabilitation Certification, Education, and Research, 1994.

7. Thorson RK. The credentials. *Case Review* 1:43, 1995.

8. CIRSC/Certified Case Manager. *CCM update.* Rolling Meadows, IL: CIRSC/Certified Case Manager, 1994.

9. Commission for Case Manager Certification. *CCM certification guide.* Rolling Meadows, IL: Commission for Case Manager Certification, 1996.

10. Holt E. Eligibility for the CCM exam: Job descriptions. *J Care Management* 2:77, 82, 1996.

11. National Board for Certification in Continuity of Care. *Continuity of care certification examination.* New York: Advanced Professional Testing Corp., 1995.

12. Whitman CM. Certifying long term care. *Case Review* 2:71–73, 1996.

13. National Academy of Certified Care Managers. *Handbook and application for candidates for certification examination.* Hollywood, FL: National Academy of Certified Care Managers, 1994.

14. Burgess C. Will the real case manager please stand up? *Case Review* 2:11–12, 1996.

15. Hurley ML. Case management—Communicating real savings. *Business and Health* 14:29–36, 1996.

7

CHAPTER

Conflict Resolution: Balancing Legal Duty, Cost, and Expectations in Healthcare Decision Making

Almost everyone is familiar with the old TV series "M*A*S*H," a television sitcom that humorously dealt with the activities of a field hospital during the Korean War. Several episodes highlighted the concept of triage. A medical personnel, usually a nurse, would survey those arriving at the hospital and would make swift decisions, based on available information, on how best to use limited resources, thereby directing patient treatment and prioritization. Patients were directed to receive immediate surgery or available surgery or to be treated by allied health personnel and later examined by a physician. It was a single-payor system in which the limitations were time, personnel, equipment, and technology. It was chaos as the triage nurse balanced information and resources. However, it was an efficient form of conflict resolution under the circumstances.

Today, efficient case management is concerned with the resolution of conflict in the delivery of healthcare. It involves the juxtaposition of limitations on areas of responsibilities, conflicts of interest among patient, provider, and payor, as well as legal barriers and limitation of resources that affect healthcare delivery. On this quagmire, the case manager must build an efficient delivery and decision-making process to develop an appropriate and effective medical care plan. As in most emerging trends, the law, as it exists and as it will evolve, will have a far-reaching impact on the development of case management.

The changes in the delivery of health services and treatment are exerting an enormous effect on decision making, that is and has been the basis of liability for medical malpractice. As the control of the delivery of services shifts from the physician to the system, so too does the liability.

Historically, the physician and the nurse, that is, licensed practitioners, were the only parties to deliver healthcare and be held responsible for its negligent delivery. A hospital, the primary venue of healthcare delivery outside of the physician's office, was originally viewed more as an innkeeper than a healthcare facility. It merely housed the equipment and beds, providing a centralized location for the physician to practice his or her profession. Generally speaking, in the world of medical malpractice, the hospital was not held liable for any negligent medical treatment received by a patient at its facility. The courts consistently held that hospitals were not licensed to practice medicine and therefore were not liable for medical malpractice. One may ask, did not the hospital provide the physical plant? Did not the hospital provide and employ the support staff? The answer is affirmative, of course, for these areas were under the control of the hospital, and if they were provided negligently, the hospital could face liability for the resulting injuries. Nevertheless, the question of the quality of care and the adequacy of treatment provided at the hospital were the responsibility of the physician. The physician admitted, provided treatment, and discharged the patient once treatment was concluded. The hospital merely provided the building. This era of holding only the physician and other licensed healthcare practitioners liable for the delivery of healthcare is long past. Liability has been extended to hospitals and other healthcare facilities, to insurance companies and other third-party payors who have denied or limited coverage for treatment, and, of late, to those entities arranging for the provision of healthcare services.

This chapter will highlight the conflicts faced by case managers in the performance of their duties. It will identify the theories of liability that may be used to hold the case manager's organization liable for the decisions made vis-à-vis the design and implementation of a medical care plan. Finally, it will provide guidance on how to minimize the risks associated with the activities of case management. Specific case studies will be used as examples of the liability problems faced.

CASE MANAGEMENT DILEMMA

The case manager can be employed by a provider, an HMO, an insurance company, or even by the employer of the beneficiaries of the health plan. One definition of case management provides a clue to the case manager's dilemma.

> Case management is a process of coordinating an individual client's health services to achieve optimal, quality care delivered in a cost effective manner. The case manager establishes a provider network, recommends treatment plans that assure quality and efficacy while controlling costs, monitors outcomes, and maintains a strong communication link among all parties. The case manager can play a pivotal role in the provider/patient/employer relationship.[1]

Analysis of the definition provides the framework for discussion of the inherent conflicts.

case management
is a process of coordinating an individual client's health services to achieve optimal, quality care delivery in a cost-effective manner.

This statement highlights two conflicts for the case manager: (1) the employment conflict and (2) the treatment conflict.

EMPLOYMENT CONFLICT

The case manager refers to the patient as a client. Webster defines a client as one who is under the protection of another;

a person who engages the professional advice or services of another, or a person served by or using the services of a social agency. Each one of these relationships implies a consensual relationship usually based on contract between the parties. However, the patient does not have a direct contractual relationship with the case manager, who is usually employed by a third party, such as an HMO or the patient's employer. The case manager's employer is usually a cost-conscious organization. The paycheck and the performance evaluation (and thus employment career) of the case manager is in the hands of an organization whose mission, at least in part, is to limit the use of healthcare while still providing an acceptable level of care.

The case manager is torn between two often conflicting criteria. What is in the best interest of the patient? What is in the best interest of the case manager's employer? Managed care programs, by nature, have third parties participating in decisions traditionally made by physician and patient. Pressure is placed on physicians by financially rewarding them for prescribing treatments, referrals, and tests that ultimately reduce costs for the plan provider. There may be disincentives if they are not. Many a physician and health care group have found themselves de-selected by the HMO if they do not live up to the expectations of the control group in reducing costs and the utilization level of healthcare. If physicians, who may not be directly employed by the HMO, feel this pressure, what resistance can the case manager, who is a direct employee, provide?

Many times the case manager directs the treatment plan without direct contact with the client. The case manager works with the treating physician or allied health personnel, approving or rejecting treatment options that affect the patient. When there is interaction between the patient and the case manager, there is most likely no disclosure of any possible conflicting loyalties caused by the employment situation. Patients many times are not allowed access to case managers or may not even know they exist. Even if patients had this knowledge and access, there is not a mechanism in place to evaluate objectively the case manager. It may be only after something goes wrong and 20-20 hindsight is applied that the patient will focus on the performance of the case manager. If the performance complies with the criteria of care established for the conduct of a case manager in designing and implementing a medical care plan, the risks of liability for the case manager's organization will be substantially minimized.

THE TREATMENT CONFLICT

Optimal quality care delivered in a cost-effective manner—the HMO and the insurance industry believe that the important words in this phrase are *cost effective.* The emphasis on cost-effective care delivery as opposed to optimal care delivery is a national problem with few ready answers. In 1995, the Robert Wood Johnson Foundation[2] funded a study of five central issues in this area:

1. How incentives for physicians to provide fewer medical services may affect the quality of patient care, as well as patient-doctor relationships
2. The legal implications of limiting procedures and treatments for patients
3. Assessing quality of care in managed care organizations and developing just and ethical standards for quality
4. The role of technology management
5. The relationship between plan administrators and physicians

The five areas of the study frame the conflict between cost of treatment and quality of treatment. Just as physicians in managed care plans, through financial incentives, face a conflict between containing costs and producing a sufficient level of care to appropriately treat the patient, the case manager faces a conflict between providing the best medical care plan to ensure the health of the patient and the limitations placed upon the case manager by his or her organization to be cost conscious. A further conflict may arise between the treating physician's recommendations, which may have a self-interest component, and the case manager's desire to place the patient in the most cost-effective venue of care.

In a time of transition, abuses are abundant because there is no way to differentiate quality of care in a meaningful way.

Thus, at the early stages of managed care, everyone was being told that the highest quality of care was being delivered without reference to a standardized measuring stick. The discussion often centered on price alone. The patient had a difficult time discerning the differences in quality, especially when the physician and the hospital may have been the same even though the payment process for healthcare delivery was completely different (capitation versus fee-for-service).

There was also an information conflict component. It took time to ferret out the fact that many managed care contracts contained restrictions on the physician concerning the amount of information on available treatment that could be shared with the patient. These gag rules were resisted by physicians, but were often imposed as the result of the differing bargaining positions of the physician versus the managed care organization. For example, the physician may have been forbidden to advise the patient that certain referrals were restricted to a limited preferred provider list constructed by the managed care organization.

The manner in which the patient's care is directed may be affected by many parties, including the treating physician, the hospital, the insurer, and the managed care organization, based on many conflicting goals. The case manager has the responsibility to overcome these conflicting perspectives and do what is best for the patient within the confines of the resources available and the reimbursement methodology used for payment of the care.

FIDUCIARY RELATIONSHIP

As part of the physician/patient relationship, the former owes a fiduciary obligation to the latter. A fiduciary is one who is bound, in equity and good conscience, to act in good faith and with due regard for the interests of another with whom he or she has a special relationship. The fiduciary is to act according to the highest standards, with discretion, sound judgment, and in the other person's best interest. Can a physician who has a financial incentive not to provide services act as fiduciary for a patient in the matters of health treatment? The answer is yes, but a great deal of discipline is required.

The case manager, on the other hand, does not share this fiduciary responsibility to the patient. Rather, as an agent for the employer, such as the managed care organization or the health plan sponsor, the case manager owes a fiduciary obligation to the employer who is the principal. This is based on the well-established law of agency. The duty owed by the agent to the principal is one of obedience, care, and loyalty. The agent is required to obey the principal and carry out all tasks directed by the principal. When conflicts arise between the employer's interests and the patient's interest, the case manager must follow the instructions of the employer or principal. In this situation, the case manager's role as patient advocate may quickly become adversarial in nature. The case manager will still owe a common-law duty of care to the patient and the case manager's employer will expect that the case manager will take no action that will adversely affect the health of the patient. Depending on the professional certification or licensure of the case manager, there may be industry or professional ethical guidelines for such conflict situations. Otherwise, the ultimate legal duty is owed to the principal, the case manager's employer.

It has been said that the system of managed care has often hindered the fiduciary relationship between physician and patient, particularly when it came to advising the patient of all the pertinent treatment options available. The managed care industry has, at times, inserted a gag clause in the contract with the physician, limiting the information available to patients to those treatments and providers available under the health plan rather than treatments and providers available generally. Secondly, the contract with the physician often contained financial incentives that were intended and did influence the physician to direct care in a calculated manner. The physician was turned into a classic gatekeeper directing and restricting the type of care and specialty of provider made available to the patient. Because of the negative publicity resulting from the existence of gag rules (which the industry claims did not exist in the first place), many states have regulated them out of existence and some managed care organizations are now removing the semblance of any gag rule language from their contracts.

Although the case manager will generally not face these types of conflicts, he or she will face conflicts in constructing the medical care plan to fit the parameters of the health plan or insurance covering the patient. To an extent, a case manager's duties involve rationing care based on what is contractually available to the patient. It has been argued that the case manager is thus required to provide information not only on the medical care plan possible under whatever plan or insurance program the patient has, but on treatments not covered in case the patient chooses to voluntarily pay for the uncovered care. In practice, this rarely occurs. For conflict resolution purposes, however, it may be advisable for the case manager to inform the patient, directly or indirectly, of all options available to deflect any criticism that the patient was misinformed of treatment options.

This raises the issue of applicability of the doctrine of informed consent to the case manager's duties. Informed consent is a doctrine based on the patient's right to be informed about the material risks of the proposed treatment, the benefits from the treatment, and the consequences of refusing treatment. The doctrine is said to serve six salutary functions:

1. Protection of individual autonomy
2. Protection of patient status as a human being
3. Avoidance of fraud or duress
4. Encouragement for doctors to consider carefully their treatment decisions
5. Fostering rational decision making by patient
6. Involvement of the public generally in medicine

The courts in the United States have been almost uniform in their decisions that informed consent requires not only an understanding of the procedure or treatment to be initiated and the effects of refusal of treatment, but that alternative treatments must be discussed and presented so that consent is based on enough information and detail as to be truly informed. Over time, the courts have identified six essential elements to be disclosed under the doctrine of informed consent:

1. Diagnosis
2. Nature and purpose of proposed treatment
3. Risks of proposed treatment
4. Probability of success

5. Treatment alternatives

6. Risks of foregoing treatment

The duty to properly inform the patient, however, was originally designed for and remains primarily with the treating physician and has not been expanded to encompass case managers. Case managers do not treat patients although they may dictate the plan of treatment. It arguably will remain the responsibility of the treating physician to inform and obtain the consent of the patient for treatment received.

THE PATIENT AS KNOWLEDGEABLE CONSUMER

Another conflict that has arisen that may affect the case manager is the conflict between what a patient knows and what a patient can understand. Information regarding treatments and drugs used to flow almost exclusively downstream from the physician to the patient. In this information age, the patient is much more likely to be cognizant of the most recent technologies and advances in care and treatment, and demand the same regardless of their applicability. The information on available treatments is on-line and is being accessed. The implications for increased requests for specific treatments because of the expansion of the patient knowledge base are becoming increasingly obvious.

In fact, the public is being targeted directly by pharmaceutical companies bypassing the initial involvement of physicians completely. Recent magazine publications have contained ads for a brand-name, rapidly acting insulin.* The ad invites consumers to ask their healthcare professional about this particular brand of insulin. This may encourage patients to request perhaps more expensive and possibly unnecessary treatments, denial of which will cause great consternation among patients who have now been "educated" as to the benefits of such treatment. This direct marketing of information has brought a warning from the physician community that is upset with the bypassing of the physician in this data dissemination.

---

*One should also keep in mind that the federal government does regulate the information that must be provided in pharmaceutical advertisements.

The message (the ad) was delivered without ever once mentioning the word "physician" or even the less prestigious "doctor" as if by some magical process, obtaining reliable advice and then getting the insulin are all part of one seamless process. It is a masterful manipulation. Not surprisingly, the profit margin on (this drug) is higher than on ordinary insulin. This should provide extra incentive to get the message out.

If this is tomorrow's medicine, then I must agree with Milton Friedman's prescription. Let's get rid of medical licensure and let everyone do his or her thing. Caveat Emptor. And in the resulting free-for-all, drug companies will share more of the blame for mishaps. HMOs are discovering that patients are treating them as if they themselves are providers of care— the penalty for the success they have had in pre-empting physicians. So it ought to be if the "ethical drug industry" (doesn't the very phrase sound outdated?) positions itself as being closer to patients and more trustworthy than their own physicians.[3]

With knowledge comes power and the case manager should be prepared to deal with a more powerful patient in the future. This is particularly true in the case of experimental or investigative treatment to be discussed later in this chapter.

CASE MANAGEMENT LIABILITY

The year 1965 was a watershed year for the delivery of healthcare services in the United States. The introduction of Medicare shifted the resources of the federal government behind the growth of hospitals. Whereas before medicine was delivered in the physician's office or the patient's home, these delivery sites gave way to the mandate of Medicare (and later Medicaid) that stressed providing covered services within the confines of a hospital. This shift in emphasis to hospital-based healthcare delivery and control did not go unnoticed by the courts and has a historical impact on the evolution of case management liability.

Darling v. Charleston Community Memorial Hospital

Darling v. Charleston Community Memorial Hospital[4] changed the way courts looked at hospitals and their liability in the delivery of healthcare services. It was the first breach in the strong demarcation line separating the hospital, as merely adminis-trators and providers of brick and mortar, from the medical staff as the actual providers of healthcare services. The court es-tablished a duty on the part of the hospital that was inde-pendent and separate from the duty owed by the treating physician. This was a duty of care based on public reliance. The duty of care was breached by:

1. Failure to have the patient examined by a qualified member of the medical staff
2. Failure to review the treatment received by the patient
3. Failure to call for a consult to insure proper treatment

Hospitals now had a duty to properly monitor and super-vise the delivery of healthcare within the hospital. *Darling* was the first case to take seriously the entire body of hospital law as it related to licensing, accreditation, medical staff investiga-tions, and credentialing, and incorporate it into a new theory of hospital liability. The court determined that if these responsibil-ities were to be meaningful, then the hospital must follow its precepts and be responsible, overseeing any care provided to en-sure compliance with the standards adopted for the delivery of care within its own facility. The language used in the *Darling* case was prescient because it seems to address the concerns of the present environment as much as the changing environment of 1965:

> The conception that the hospital does not undertake to treat the patient, does not undertake to act through its doctors and nurses, but undertakes instead simply to procure them to act upon their own responsibility, no longer reflects the fact. Present-day hospitals, as their manner of operation plainly demonstrates, do far more than furnish facilities for treatment. They regularly employ on a salary basis a large staff of physi-cians, nurses, and interns, as well as administrative and manual workers, and they charge patients for medical care and treat-ment, collecting for such services, if necessary, by legal action. Certainly, the person who avails himself of "hospital facilities" expects that the hospital will attempt to cure him, not that its nurses or other employees will act on their own responsibility.[4]

If we substitute the words *health system* for *hospital*, does not the rationale seem the same? If we substitute *HMO* or *case management system* for *hospital,* does not the rationale for liability hold just as true? The courts after the *Darling* decision have continued to expand the obligations and resulting liabilities for hospitals, including the duty to properly select and retain medical staff. This is relevant to the imposition of liability on the case management system. In the 1990s the trend has been to move healthcare from a hospital-based environment to a managed care environment, rearranging the way healthcare is delivered. Just as moving the focus from physician's office to the hospital resulted in increased liability for the hospital, the focus on healthcare delivery arranged by a third party has created liability exposure for those third parties, including case management organizations.

Part of the change in healthcare delivery can be attributed to payment methodology and the increased use of expensive technologies in medical treatment. Third-party payors, because of increased costs, began searching for ways to better control these costs and have become increasingly reliant on case management and utilization review as methods of determining the availability and appropriateness of treatment as a covered benefit under the respective health plan. Provider organizations as well adapted their techniques as a means of controlling their own internal costs. These parties would examine the type, extent, manner, and duration of the treatment sought in order to determine whether the treatment was justified and would be covered under and paid by the patient's benefit package. If the third-party payor, for example, found that the treatment sought was unnecessary or otherwise lacking, it would restrict or even deny coverage for the treatment. Such restriction or denial of coverage for the treatment sought may result in potential liability exposure to the party making such a decision.

Although insurance companies have always faced liability for breach of contract and bad faith claims in the context of coverage denial, the three cases about to be discussed were arguably the start of expanding liability to those third parties who more directly affected the provision of healthcare by denying payment for care sought or by determining what care was appropriate. The focus of these and similar cases is on third-party payors, but the rationale is just as applicable for organizations providing case management services that also restrict or deny treatment. The three cases most regularly cited in the area of utilization review and thus by extension case management are *Wickline v. State of California,*[5] *Wilson v. Blue Cross of So. California,*[6] and *Corcoran v. United Healthcare, Inc.*[7] The primary issue involved in these cases was whether the utilization review provider should be liable for its decision that resulted in the discontinuation or limitation of the medical treatment sought by the patient.

In *Wickline,* the California Court of Appeals held that where the third-party payor did not override the medical judgment of the treating physician, it could not be held liable for harm suffered by the patient deprived of medical care. Subsequently, in *Wilson,* the California Court of Appeals reversed the lower court's grant of summary judgment for the defendants stating that there were triable issues of fact regarding whether the denial of healthcare benefits played a substantial factor in the decedent's demise. In *Corcoran,* the Fifth Circuit stated that, under an ERISA* plan, even if the third-party payor made the medical decision resulting in harm to the plaintiff, all state law claims were preempted, thus depriving plaintiff of any remedy for the injuries resulting from the deprivation of medical care. The lesson to be learned by case managers from these cases is how to develop prophylactic measures to protect against the type of allegations attempting to find those parties liable who are effectively making medical care decisions for a patient, particularly if one substitutes *case management* for *utilization review.***

Wickline v. State of California

Wickline can be examined in terms of the ramifications of utilization review and the effect on the medical care provided. This case, at least factually, would appear to support the proposition that the final decision maker regarding necessity and

---

*Employment Retirement Income and Security Act of 1974, 29 U.S.C. sec. 1001 *et seq.;* see, especially, 29 U.S.C. at sec. 1144(a) which provides that "Except as provided in subsection (b) of this section, the provisions of this subchapter and subchapter III of this chapter shall supersede any and all State laws insofar as they may now or hereafter relate to any employee benefit plan . . . ."

**Cases to date have generally focused upon utilization review services, but there is a strong argument that under similar factual scenarios, case management organizations would be even more at risk for liability.

appropriateness of medical care and treatment is the treating physician because the physician is in the best position to determine the medical necessity of treatment. However, it does illustrate the proposition that if a case manager dictates a care plan contrary to that recommended by the treating physician, any negative outcome may result in a claim of negligence against the case manager. The injured patient will allege that the necessary and appropriate medical treatment was not provided as a result of the case manager's negligent formulation and implementation of the care plan.

In *Wickline* the utilization reviewer was found not to be liable for the adverse outcome because the treating physicians were responsible for the apparently premature discharge from the hospital and the utilization reviewer did not participate in that decision. Although the utilization reviewer denied additional hospitalization based on the information that was currently available, the court determined that, because a mechanism existed to appeal that decision of denial of an additional stay, and the parties did not avail themselves of that mechanism, the utilization reviewer had no liability for the adverse outcome. The saving grace for the utilization reviewer in this case was that, despite its apparent erroneous decision in denying an additional hospital stay, it made available a mechanism for the physician or patient to contest the denial.

This case highlights an important question for the case manager to ask. Does your organization have available a formal appeal process for a patient to contest the medical care plan developed and executed by the case manager? If not, and the outcome is adverse, the patient may have a claim that he or she was denied adequate care because of his or her inability to contest the case manager's initial care plan determination. An important component of any case management system should be a formalized appeal process.

Wilson v. Blue Cross of So. California

Although the utilization reviewer escaped liability in the *Wickline* case, the case of *Wilson v. Blue Cross of So. California* represented an important progression in the potential liability a third-party payor (and, by analogy, case manager) may have in terms of its role in determining the medical care a patient receives. In this case, the same court that decided *Wickline* determined that a third-party payor may have liability for its role in the medical treatment provided to a patient. As in *Wickline,* the claim against the third-party payor centered around denial of coverage for the medical treatment recommended by the treating physician. The decision resulted in discontinuance of further medical care for the patient who then committed suicide (the patient had been receiving inpatient mental health services). The court concluded that the decision to deny coverage, thus ending treatment, may have been a substantial factor in causing the patient's suicide and thus required factual adjudication.

The court in *Wilson* focused on whether defendant Western Medical, the utilization review provider, had the actual authority to make the decision to deny coverage and thus treatment. This was particularly true because the language of the policy seemed to empower the patient's treating physician with the right to make the decision as to whether treatment was medically justified. If the physician made such a decision, then the patient/insured was entitled to the coverage afforded under the policy. Additionally, although the Court focused on whether the coverage denial may have been a substantial factor in the injury claimed, the key was whether the third-party payor and its surrogate followed the proper process in making that determination of coverage.

This decision provides important clues for the case manager. If the case management services are being provided as part of a health benefit plan, the case manager should be well-versed in the contractual provisions of the health plan and know the extent and limit of the type of case management services contracted for under the plan. If the case management services are being provided under the provider's own internal processes, the case manager should be well aware of the internal policies and procedures as to how the organization will execute its case management system. With this knowledge, the case manager will be better able to comply strictly with any contract requirements or internal policies and procedures, thus minimizing claims alleging contract breach or other similar claims.

What is of additional interest in *Wilson* and relevant to the case manager is the court's backtracking on its opinion in

Wickline. Whereas most commentators thought *Wickline* determined that the third-party payor had no liability if the physician makes the decision to discharge the plaintiff and the payor plays no actual role in the medical decision-making process vis-à-vis that discharge, the court now stated that the third-party payor was not liable because it met "the usual standards of medical practice in the community"[5] in performing the utilization review and made its decision in full compliance with the statutory requirements and in accordance with public policy.

The guidance this provides for case managers is to know and adhere to the standards applicable to their profession for the proper formulation and implementation of a medical care plan. If case managers adhere to accepted practice, they will minimize the inherent risks associated with their duties.

Corcoran v. United Healthcare

The *Corcoran* case explored another arena of conflict management for patients facing medical care denial through third-party involvement. In this instance, and of great importance to the outcome, was a health plan that involved ERISA, the uniform national standards for benefit plans offered by employers pursuant to federal law.[8] These benefits include healthcare plans that often replaced traditional health indemnity insurance obtained directly from the private insurance sector. ERISA contains an express preemption section which states that the provisions of the Act supersede any and all state laws as they relate to the employee benefit plan. The patient in *Corcoran* was seeking care and treatment under an ERISA plan. The lawsuit was brought to recover damages for the negligent conduct of the defendants and the defendants alleged that ERISA preempted any state law claims against them. The court conducted an exhaustive analysis of the intent of the preemption provision and the intent of Congress to preempt state law. It concluded that, since the actions of the defendant, United Healthcare, were in connection with its duties under the ERISA plan, any state tort action was preempted and the defendants were without liability. This is consistent with the position other courts had been taking in regard to ERISA preempting state law.

The facts in the case involved the plan provider who made a medical care decision regarding course of treatment (as opposed to merely determining a plan benefit). The tragic result was the death of Mrs. Corcoran's baby. Despite this, the court concluded no state law action, such as for negligent design of care plan or improper utilization review, could be brought against Blue Cross, the plan administrator who had contracted for the alleged negligent utilization review services. The irony of this case is that the plan description stipulated that if the participant complied with the Quality Care Program requirements of contacting the utilization review provider concerning the course of treatment, but did not obtain the precertification approval, and obtained treatment contrary to the provider's decision, the benefactor could still receive full coverage for the "unauthorized" treatment should an internal appeal show that the treatment chosen was appropriate. Because the plan's second opinion stated that the treatment chosen by Mrs. Corcoran's treating physician was appropriate, she should have had no problem in eventually receiving full coverage for the recommended treatment. Her child therefore may have survived and a tragedy averted. However, Mrs. Corcoran apparently failed to avail herself of this option and contest the initial decision that hospitalization (which was the care plan sought) was unwarranted.

A case manager may take initial comfort in the results of *Corcoran* in that case management provided pursuant to a qualified ERISA plan may avoid any possible state negligence liability. Be forewarned, however, that the tide has been turning and a string of recent court decisions have held, for example, that ERISA does not preempt state law for claims of vicarious liability for medical malpractice against HMOs. Total reliance on the state law preemption of ERISA for qualified plans will be misplaced. However, *Corcoran* is another illustration of how liability may be minimized for improper care treatment plans if a formal mechanism exists for patient appeal of initial decisions regarding the course of treatment devised by the case manager. Although not totally insulating the case manager and his or her organization from liability, adverse claims are less likely to occur if a patient has a right to contest and appeal the plan of care devised.

A common thread through these three cases is whether the patient has full and complete knowledge of the process that determined the availability of care as well as the process available to contest the initial determination. Armed with this knowledge, the patients may have chosen to continue with the treatment recommended by the treating physician while initiating the steps needed to contest the initial decision.

After the *Wickline* decision, several commentators reflected on the extent of liability that a third party may face in the role of determining the appropriateness of the medical care sought. They speculated that a trend may develop exposing third parties, such as case managers, to substantial liability for their role in making medical care determinations and examined various theories that could be used in these attempts. The commentators' examination included the legal liability involving utilization review and case management. Utilization review was defined in a generic sense as the "external evaluations that are based on established clinical criteria and are conducted by third-party payors, purchasers, or health care organizers to evaluate the appropriateness of an episode, or series of episodes, of medical care."[9] Case management was defined as an extension of utilization review involving "use of an external case manager who not only reviews a particular case but also drafts an alternative plan of patient care."[9]

It had been earlier believed that the thrust of *Wickline* was that a utilization reviewer could not be held liable for negligently discharging a patient, because that decision is a medical one and falls outside the purview of third-party utilization review. However, the subsequent *Wilson* decision indicated that the third-party payor was not liable because it met "the usual standards of medical practice in the community"[5] regarding utilization review and made its decision in full compliance with the statutory requirements and in accordance with public policy. The belief that utilization review, and, by extension, case management, does not involve medical decision making was proved wrong in *Corcoran*. The court, in that case, determined that the utilization review provider *did* make medical decisions as part of its utilization review (although this appears to be the only reported case where a court has made such an explicit finding).

Laying out and directing an alternative course of treatment, as a case manager does, comes even closer to medical decision making as opposed merely to determining the appropriateness of the care being received from a coverage or payment standpoint. By making a medical decision, one has to be prepared for any adverse consequences flowing from that decision. At the very least, the case manager faces liability exposure for any negligence in the process of reviewing and choosing the proper medical care plan, whether the process is called medical decision making or not. This includes relying upon incomplete or inaccurate information.

Other potential liabilities are faced by case managers. Because case management involves a program designed to coordinate a patient's health services, usually between the treating providers and the paying parties, the case manager is clearly not making determinations as to the extent of coverage or lack thereof, but is providing a service to manage the actual care of the patient within the confines of the coverage provided by the payor. Because of the type of services provided by a case manager, some commentators have taken the position that liability exposure for case management is essential to create incentives for third parties to use reasonable care in their process. Without such incentives, it is feared that case management will focus solely on cost containment to the detriment of the patient's health.

This potential trend of expanding liability for case management once again highlights the importance of case management organizations establishing and following a formal and standardized process when it comes to instituting and implementing medical care treatment programs. The potential exists for the case manager's organization to be held directly liable if the case management system is defectively designed or negligently performed. Case management is very outcome oriented, but if the outcome is negative from the patient's viewpoint, allegations will be made that the case manager was negligent in his or her duties of either following the organization's established processes, or in devising the plan implemented, or that the organization's policies and procedures themselves were somehow defective.

Another legal commentator has examined the legal liabilities of third parties such as case managers. Her article specifically addressed HMOs and their utilization review programs designed to determine the medical necessity for all but the most routine care.[10] She made a very interesting observation regarding the standard of care applicable to the utilization process. The standards referenced included:

1. Review decisions should be made by qualified medical professionals, and any denial decisions should be made only by licensed physicians.
2. Reviewers should consult with specialist physicians as appropriate.
3. Efforts should be made to obtain all necessary information, for example by reviewing the patient's charts and consulting with treating physicians as appropriate.
4. The reasons for decisions should be clearly documented.
5. There should be a well-publicized and readily available appeal mechanism.
6. Decisions and appeals should be made in a timely manner as required by the exigencies of the situation.[10]

It is hoped that the case manager's organization has adopted standards akin to these and follows them religiously.

EXPERIMENTAL VS. MEDICALLY NECESSARY CARE

Another concern relative to conflict resolution is the situation where treatment is sought based on technology that is arguably experimental. How is the case manager to react? Should the patient's interest in exploring all possible avenues of treatment be paramount? Should the concern of the case manager's employer of cost-containment be the overriding element? How should this conflict be resolved? When medical care decisions reach this stage, how is one to judge what is "experimental" versus "medically necessary"? Because healthcare plans typically exclude experimental care, the patient will normally be denied such treatment even if it is recommended by the attending physician. Several good case studies illustrate the issues raised by a third party's attempted determination of what is experimental versus medically necessary treatment. They exemplify the type of scrutiny that a case manager's determination that a course of care is experimental and should not be pursued may undergo.

Clark v. K-Mart

A court's conclusion as to who can make the medical care decisions is partially determined by whether the health plan language determines who has that right. An illustrative example is *Clark v. K-Mart Corp.*[11] The court, in this case, indicated that where a plan administrator is given discretion to make determinations as to who is eligible to receive benefits and what benefits are covered by the plan, the arbitrary and capricious standard applies. This means that, as long as the decision made by the plan administrator and the process used to arrive at that decision was done properly, the courts will not disturb that decision. The court found in this case that the plan included specific and express language allowing the plan administrator to interpret discretionary matters such as the definition of *experimental*.

This case involved an employer-sponsored plan administered by Blue Cross/Blue Shield. The treatment in question was high dose chemotherapy with autologous bone marrow transplant (HDC/ABMT) to be used for the patient's breast cancer. The patient's condition had deteriorated despite six months of chemotherapy postradical mastectomy. The new treatment prescribed by the patient's physician was determined by that physician to be effective for some forms of cancer and thus "no longer experimental and investigative." However, because the plan language allowed the plan administrator to make discretionary decisions as to what was or was not experimental treatment, the court deferred to the plan's determination. According to the findings of the court, substantial supporting evidence existed as to the experimental nature of the treatment.

This case provides another example of a method for the case manager to resolve the conflict between patient care and plan coverage. The case manager needs a well-written health plan contract that expressly provides for sufficient power and authority for the case manager to determine whether a particular technology can be considered experimental or not. For example, does the plan define "experimental" and "medically necessary"? Does the plan provide the necessary language granting the authority and discretion to the case manager to make such decisions? If the case manager is not working within the confines of a health plan, but rather for a provider organization, the case manager must still be familiar with the type of coverage afforded the patient and the provider organization's policies and procedures for executing case management services. If the provider organization does not have the appropriate policies and procedures, they should be drafted accordingly. Without these tools, the case manager needs to tread lightly.

Kekis v. Blue Cross & Blue Shield

Kekis v. Blue Cross & Blue Shield of Utica-Watertown, Inc.[12] was another case involving a third-party denial of coverage for HDC/ABMT. Like *Corcoran,* the health care plan was an ERISA plan. The third-party payor had denied coverage based on a plan exclusion for experimental/investigative services. The plan described such services as "any service or procedure we do not recognize as accepted medical practice as we determine has no proven medical value."[12] Because the plan administrator had reserved the right, as in *Clark,* to make discretionary decisions regarding plan benefits, the court used the arbitrary and capricious standard* to decide whether to defer to the third-party payor and its decision to deny treatment.

The court analyzed the methodology that the third-party payor used in making its decision. The analysis resulted in the conclusion that the payor used "an impermissible standard when it refused Ms. Kekis' request."[12] It seems that the payor's medical director, who made the actual decision regarding the nature of the treatment, failed to apply the policy's definition of experimental/investigative and, instead, substituted his own.

---

*The court thus examines the plan administrator's process of making the determination. If the plan administration did not have the right to make such a determination, then the court would then make the determination based upon what is called the *de nova* standard. Under this standard, the court examines the entire issue anew as opposed to the arbitrary and capricious standard wherein the court merely determines whether the plan administration had the right, under the plan, to make the decision and if the decision-making process was in accordance with the express process stated in the plan.

The court found that the only question the medical director needed to answer in determining coverage was whether the treatment had any proven medical value.

The court further determined that, even if the medical director had used this permissible standard to determine coverage, the decision still would have been arbitrary and capricious. The third-party payor would have had to prove that there was no medical value to HDC/AMBT. Because there was incontrovertible testimony that this treatment has at least some medical value, the third-party payor could not have met its own definition.

Clearly, this case is another instance wherein the process used to determine the appropriateness of the medical care was defective. Further, even if the process had not been defective, the court appears to be using an objective standard as to whether the treatment sought has any medical value, not merely the subjective opinion of the third-party payor regarding medical value to the patient. This once again points out the need for case managers to have available and to follow objectively the policies and procedures of their employer in making medical care plan decisions.

Heasley v. Belden & Blake Corp.

Courts have long recognized that making decisions regarding the appropriateness of third-party involvement in treatment and care decision planning are difficult. In *Heasley v. Belden & Blake Corp.,*[13] the court very perceptively stated:

> We recognize that any determination of whether a particular procedure is experimental will necessarily turn on the facts of the particular case. Nor are we unaware of the context in which these cases arise. The archetypal case presents a gravely ill patient requesting an injunction after being denied benefits. Faced with the exigencies of such a claim and a wealth of conflicting and complex expert testimony, the trial court has a daunting task.[13]

Despite this recognition, the court attempted to lay out in its opinion an excellent road map for how to approach a case involving requests for seemingly experimental treatment.

Heasley was another instance wherein an ERISA health insurance plan fiduciary, on the advice and direction of its utilization review provider, had denied coverage for treatment the plan considered to be experimental. The patient had been seeking a liver/pancreas transplant as treatment for pancreatic cancer. When denied coverage under the plan, the patient sought redress through the plan itself. However, the plan provided no provision to contest the coverage denial. The plaintiff quickly filed suit to obtain an order that the treatment sought was not experimental and that the transplant should be authorized under the plan. The trial court directed that the plan authorize and pay for the treatment sought. The third-party payor appealed the trial court ruling in order to determine who ultimately would be liable for payment of the treatment.

On appeal, the appellate court concurred with the trial court that the third-party payor had not, through a "clear and unequivocal" statement in the policy, reserved the right to make discretionary decisions regarding the benefits under the plan. The policy language was such that, at best, it was ambiguous as to whether the plan reserved the right to make such discretionary decisions. Thus the court agreed that the trial court was correct in applying the *de novo* standard of review as opposed to the arbitrary and capricious standard. The court then went on to examine whether the trial court properly applied the standard in arriving at its decision that the treatment sought was not experimental.

The court noted that experts on both sides agreed that the treatment was not experimental in every situation, but was dependent on the condition of the particular patient. The court went on to discuss how the term "experimental" had been defined in other cases. It noted that there have been attempts made to "cure the inherent ambiguity of the term 'experimental.' Some plans enumerate particular conditions for which a given procedure is experimental or simply write into the plan specific exclusions for these conditions without reference to their experimental nature . . . Other insurers and employers resolve the definitional problem by specifying who will decide the meaning of the term 'experimental.' "[13]

The court noted that in this case the policy in question had no language defining the term or listing types of procedures considered experimental. It also noted that the evidence presented at the trial court level was insufficient to determine whether or not the treatment was experimental under the particular conditions of this patient and remanded it back for further proceedings. However, the court went on to say that whether a treatment is experimental hinges on its safety and efficacy, but realized that this description also was a generalization not properly defining the term "experimental." The court believed that "a more systematic approach is warranted than simply applying a general definition."[13] It then identified a nonexclusive list of factors to consider in determining whether a procedure is experimental. The factors[13] were:

1. Whether the treatment was considered experimental in the judgment of other insurers and medical bodies
2. The amount of experience with the procedure
3. The demonstrated effectiveness of the treatment

The conclusion the court reached was that unless the language of the health plan specifically and expressly excludes coverage for a listed treatment (for example, this plan does not cover heart transplants), a determination by the third-party payor as to whether the treatment sought is experimental, medically unnecessary, or inappropriate will hinge on evidence presented indicating that, by objective standards, there is reason to believe that the treatment sought will be safe (no harm to the patient) and effective (will have some medical benefit).

Close scrutiny will continue to be directed at those cases in which a third party is involved in developing, monitoring, or in some other manner, participating in the physician-patient medical care plan. It is critical for the case manager to learn from previous situations in which such involvement was successfully challenged. Too often, those organizations most likely to employ case managers have been slow in developing appropriate methodologies to assess objectively the medical necessity of expensive treatments that are becoming more readily available and frequently requested by patients. An emphasis should be placed on the need to properly draft the health plan contracts or whatever vehicles are used for the provision of case management. In this way, an objective process can be instituted to follow in designing and implementing medical care plans.

Appropriate and effective policies and procedures also need
to be developed and put in place to ensure compliance with
this objective process. In addition, a formalized appeal process should be constructed that permits aggrieved patients a
realistic avenue to contest adverse medical care plan decisions.
If these recommendations are undertaken, the conflicts faced
on an almost daily basis by case managers are more likely to
be resolved.

FACTORS TO CONSIDER TO MINIMIZE THE LIABILITIES CASE MANAGEMENT ORGANIZATIONS FACE

To assist the leadership of the case management organization in
assessing the potential risks an organization faces in providing
case management services, the following points may be of particular interest.

- The case manager should be cognizant of the various
  parties involved, for example, who is the payor, who are
  the providers, what type of organization is providing the
  case management services. In this way, the case
  manager will become more aware of the particular
  concerns each party may have and the conflicts that
  may arise from such concerns and will be better
  positioned to resolve them.
- The case manager should be aware of and be familiar
  with any contractual documents dealing with the
  provision of the case management services. Knowing the
  limitations and restrictions on the available medical
  care and treatment will be helpful in devising the
  appropriate care plan.
- The case manager should know whether the
  organization has internal policies and procedures to
  follow in devising and implementing case management
  programs and be familiar with them. If such policies
  and procedures do not exist, the case manager can be
  proactive in helping develop them.
- The case manager should be cognizant of any industry
  or professional standards for the case management
  services.

Additionally, the following questions may be asked.

- Are decisions for the medical care plan adequately discussed with the treating physician and relayed to the patient?
- Are all medical care plan decisions objectively based?
- Does the case manager follow the same process for each medical care plan decision? Are there exceptions and can the case manager substantiate the rationale for any exceptions?
- Does the case manager have sufficient clinical knowledge and background to make medical care plan decisions? What certifications, education, or licensure does the case manager have?
- Are all decisions and plans properly documented?
- Are all terms properly defined, such as "experimental" and "medically necessary"?
- Does the case manager possess the necessary patient medical information to make the medical care plan decision?
- Is there a formal appeal process permitting a patient to object and contest the medical care plan decision and receive a timely decision? Who hears and decides the appeal? Is it a disinterested party?
- Are there state laws regulating the services provided by the case management organization?

SUMMARY

A number of theories of liability exist related to the design and implementation of medical care plans by case managers. Direct liability may result from the negligent selection or retention of malpracticing physicians. Vicarious liability may arise from the negligent supervision/control of the medical care plan arranged for patients and carried out by the service providers. Liability may be the result of defects in the design of the cost-control system or of negligent implementation of the cost-control mechanisms. Claims may be brought regarding breach of contract issues. Alternatively, claims may be minimized through express contract provisions, such as a provision stipulating that the service is purely advisory in nature and that the decision to implement a particular case management plan rests with the health plan sponsor or treating physician. The intent is to contractually limit the liability between the case manager's organization and the party with whom it contracts. Additionally, a patient's consent may be obtained for the plan thus minimizing any subsequent complaints that the patient sought differing care, but was denied. When the health plan involved is a qualified ERISA plan, that fact may be used as a defense in any state law claims. However, if case management is part of the services provided by the ERISA plan, and if the case manager fails to provide the services the plan purports to deliver, or does so improperly, a contract enforcement action may arise between the relevant parties.

Potential liability also exists if the nature and type of medical information used by the case manager to formulate the medical care plan is somehow inadequate. The care plan should be based on data that a competent professional in a case manager's role would deem sufficient for clinical decision-making purposes. The information processed to arrive at the medical care plan should be both accurate and adequately protected against disclosure to unauthorized personnel. The case manager has an additional duty to protect the confidentiality of the patient and medical-provider information with the specific requirements often dependent upon federal and state law.

Another area of concern for the case manager is when the medical information review process uncovers incompetent or negligent practice on behalf of the service providers, be they staff or independent contractors. Does the case manager have a duty to report such conduct to any state regulators, to the patient, to the organization employing the case manager? Ideally, the case manager's organization has in place a methodology to report and review possible incompetent or negligent care on the part of the service providers, regardless of whether the providers are staff or independently contracted.

It is important that case managers and their employers be aware of any specific state requirements regarding the standards necessary for the use of case managers, including the need for any professional licensure of the case managers themselves.

This is especially true where case management involves the formulation of a treatment plan requiring a sufficient level of clinical background to be able to evaluate patients with complex medical problems and recommend appropriate medical venues based not simply on cost, but on the level of medical care to be provided.

This chapter has identified the types of liabilities that a case manager may face and has described steps to minimize those liabilities as the result of directing the medical care plan of the ill patient. The case manager plays an important role in acting as an advocate for healthier patients while devising a more cost-effective delivery of healthcare. If done properly, this can be accomplished with minimal liability risk to the case manager's organization.

REFERENCES

1. American Association of Occupational Health Nurses, Position Statement.
2. Grant awarded to the Hastings Center in Briarcliff, NY, by the Robert Wood Johnson Foundation press release, April 13, 1995.
3. Alper PR. The Wall Street Journal, Dec. 4, 1996, p. A16.
4. 33 Ill.2d 326, 211 N.E.2d 253, certiorari denied 383 U.S. 946, 86 S. Ct. 1204, 16 L.Ed.2d 209 (1966).
5. *Wickline v State of California,* 192 Cal.App.3d 1630; 239 Cal.Rptr. 810 (1986).
6. *Wilson v Blue Cross of So. California,* 222 Cal.App.3d 660; 271 Cal.Rptr. 876 (1990).
7. *Corcoran v United Healthcare, Inc.,* 965 F.2d 1321 (5th Cir. 1992).
8. §212.1 Three-day prior hospitalization, skilled nursing facility manual (HCFA Pub. 12).
9. Blum, J. An analysis of legal liability in health care utilization review and case management. 26 Houston > /R. 191, 192–93 (1989).
10. Tiano LV. The legal implications of HMO cost containment measures. 14 Seton Hall Legis. J. 79 (1990).
11. *Clark v K-Mart Corp.* 979 F.2d 965 (3rd Cir. 1991).
12. *Kekis v Blue Cross & Blue Shield of Utica-Watertown, Inc.* 815 F. Supp. 571 (N.D.N.Y. 1993).
13. *Heasley v Belden & Blake Corp.* 2 F.3d 1249 (3rd Cir. 1993).

CHAPTER

From the Field: A Discussion of the Pressing Issues Facing Case Managers

The success of case management and the resulting recognition of its value has been dependent on the contributions of a dedicated and visionary field of professionals. Those in the field shape and define the role of case management in the present healthcare system.

These individuals have collaborated to position case management as not only a significant tool of healthcare reform, but as a positive force in patient care delivery. Indeed, it is the field itself which is in the best position to spot trends and to discuss the pressing issues of tomorrow. To this end, the authors spoke with case managers across the nation and conducted a survey of more than 200 individuals working actively in the field. The responses were filled with enthusiasm, thoughtfulness, and urgency. Many identified challenges, conflicts, and possibilities of case management not only for today, but also for the twenty-first century.

T A B L E   8 – 1

Employment of Case Managers

Facility	Percentage
Acute Hospital or Specialty Hospital and/or Health System	58%
Nursing facility/Subacute Program	13%
Home Care or Other Health Facility	4%
Case Management Organization	4%
Self-Employed Case Manager	4%
Other	17%

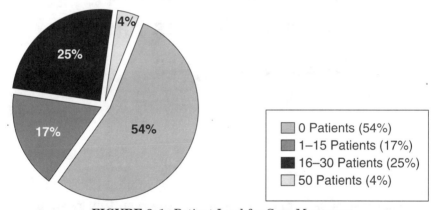

FIGURE 8–1. Patient Load for Case Managers

Survey respondents and interviewees are involved with case management in a variety of practice settings. A majority of the respondents interviewed work in an acute or specialty hospital or health system as depicted in Table 8–1. Figure 8–1 depicts the number of patients the individual case manager follows. When the respondents were asked whether or not their facility used a centralized case management system, the responses were as shown in Figure 8–2.

Table 8–2 summarizes responses to the question of how long the case management system had been in operation.

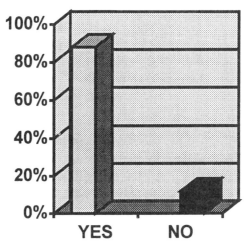

FIGURE 8–2. Utilization of Case Management System

TABLE 8 – 2

Case Managers' Tenure in Position

< 1 Year	4%
1 - 2 Years	33%
2 - 4 Years	21%
4 + Years	29%
"No System"	13%

The field of case management reflects the diversity and complexity of human service and healthcare delivery. The individuals who are the hands-on practitioners of case management are the fiduciaries of the system and the bellwethers of the future. Cognizant of their contribution to the development of centralized systems of case management, the authors queried leading case managers about a variety of issues facing the field today. The following represents a cross section of some of the most considered and thought-provoking opinion.

What is your definition of case management?

To help individuals at a crisis time in their lives, when they are asked to do difficult things after an accident or operation, to find the most resources available to them, and to help them get back to their normal lives. Case management should be structured to:

1. Help a patient assess his/her needs;
2. Help the patient prioritize his/her needs;
3. Find resources to help the patient; and,
4. Help the patient to utilize those resources in the most beneficial way.

During this process, there should be an ongoing educational component, not only for the patient, but also the family, to ensure that the patient gets the most help necessary to return him/her to the community.

Marlys Severson
SCM Associates
President, Case Management Society of America
Cypress, California

Case management is truly multidimensional and interdisciplinary. It involves the delivery of the highest quality of services to the patient and family within cost effective parameters. Case management is the key to the whole process, and should address the question of what works in the best interest of the patient and family.

Laura Deming, RN, MS, CS, CCM
President, Deming Neo/Pedi Consulting
Houston, Texas

I would define case management as a shared experience between the provider of care and a facilitator. The two need to be brought together as a source of information relative to patient education.

I prefer a model in which case managers can move throughout the continuum. They need to be involved prior to the admission of the patient and continue their involvement well after the patient is discharged.

Diane B. Williams, RN, MSHA
Editor in Chief
Nursing Case Management Magazine
Portland, Oregon

Case management is a transdisciplinary multipractice setting industry. Case management is a coordination role, it's not a hands-on role. The emergence and real explosion of case management has been in the last ten to fifteen years. Because case management is transdisciplinary, we have discipline issues related to the body of knowledge in each specific discipline. There is a body of knowledge specific to the broad field of case management which is irrespective of practice setting or discipline.

The process of case management, as defined by the Commission for Case Manager Certification, consists of six essential activities including: assessment, planning, implementation, coordination, monitoring, and evaluation. These six activities are applied through the following core components of case managing which encompass:

- coordination and service delivery;
- physical and psychological factors;
- benefit systems and cost benefit analysis;
- case management concepts; and
- community resources.

Carrie Ann Engen, RN, BSN, CCM
Director, Case Management Operations
Advocare, Inc.
Past Chairperson, Commission for
Case Manager Certification, 1995–1996
Past President, Case Management
Society of America, 1993–1994

I really think case management is multidisciplinary. In social work, case managers work with a totally different type of case, but manage care with the core components of coordination and service delivery, physical and psychological factors, benefit systems and cost benefit analysis, case management concepts, and community resources as identified by the Commission for Case Manager Certification. Case managers do this. They assess, they implement, they monitor, and they do it with a different population.

Rehabilitation counselors can also be case managers, but they do it a little differently than a nurse would do it. Case management is multidisciplinary, and includes many, many professions in this big globe. You make a big circle and call it illness, and wellness encompasses all of this. There will be all different types of case managers in that circle.

Eda Holt
Chief Executive Officer
Commission for Case Manager Certification

What is the goal of case management?

The primary goal of case management is to be cost efficient, provide quality care, and to utilize the appropriate healthcare resources available.

Jacqueline J. Birmingham, RN, MS, A-CCC, CHE
Director, Continuity of Care and Special Programs
Chartwell Home Therapies
New Haven, Connecticut

Maximizing the coordination of patient care services between family, patient, referral agency, third-party payor and hospital. This responsibility includes facilitating an effective utilization review program, which monitors the appropriate allocation of hospital resources for patients, and provides quarterly discharge planning.

Kathleen Bremer, RN, BS, CCM
Director, Case Management
New England Rehabilitation Hospital of Portland
Portland, Maine

The goal of case management is to assist the patient in receiving the right level of care in the most appropriate venue of care at the right cost. Appropriate care is synonymous with continuous quality improvement. Also, case managers must collaboratively manage the patient's care within the patient's benefit limits, and assist and act as a resource to primary medical physicians and nurses in advance practice.

Ann M. Long, RN, MSM, CAN, A-CCC, CCM
Director, Division of Continuum of Care Management
Saint Francis Hospital and Medical Center
Hartford, Connecticut

How would you structure an effective system of case management?

Case managers need to work in conjunction with administration and social work to assure that the patient has all resources available to him/her, so that the case manager can effectively move the patient through the continuum.

Dual case management would definitely be effective if the system was appropriately established. A social work case manager and a nurse case manager could be very effective in many situations. Most patient's medical problems cannot be resolved until some social aspects of the patient's life are corrected. There needs to be someone available to the patient *after* discharge.

In a rehabilitation setting, physical therapists or occupational therapists would be effective case managers because they have hands-on experience with patients and know what will be needed during the patient's stay and after the patient returns to the community.

The effectiveness of case managers depends on the case management system and the population being served. Different populations need different types of assistance, and it is the case manager's role and responsibility to know what those needs are. If the case manager is focused and knows their function in the system, the outcome will not only be beneficial to the patient, but also to the facility.

Marlys Severson
SCM Associates
President, Case Management Society of America
Cypress, California

Do you find a difference between the way hospitals and physicians structure their case management programs?

There is very little difference. Of course, hospitals have a broader base with a variety of patients and payor sources. I find that the physicians have a smaller group to deal with. However, I do not find either group more difficult to deal with one way or another. Each wants the cost savings advantage, but neither wants to deal with the other "stuff." I see typical passive aggressive behavior. Case managers having trouble communicating with the physicians and neither wanting the other person involved.

It may not be necessary for hospitals to seek additional personnel to operate their case management system. Many times a case manager can operate the system in conjunction with other personnel already in place. Case managers don't need to do it all. They should share the responsibility with others, including the social services departments. Do it hand in hand. Incorporate the two, while letting social services continue to operate the planning, financial and social end of it.

Diane B. Williams, RN, MSHA
Editor in Chief
Nursing Case Management Magazine
Portland, Oregon

Define the difference between case management and managed care.

There is very little difference. Managed Care is just one step of a case management system. Be it case management or managed care, the basic objective is to move the patient throughout the continuum and be accountable to the system. Nearly all facilities believe they are using some type of case management system and all of them like the way it sounds. However, many may not understand the true process of case management.

Many hospitals are changing the name of their discharge planning department to case management department. One hospital changed its department name to *care* management rather than *case* management because the physicians tend to feel more comfortable with the management of *care* rather than the management of their patient *cases*.

Jacqueline J. Birmingham, RN, MS, A-CCC, CHE
Director, Continuity of Care and Special Programs
Chartwell Home Therapies
New Haven, Connecticut

Do you think managed care is the driving force for case management?

Just the opposite. Managed care supported the expansion of the concept, especially with its development of the DRG system, which resulted in a decreased length of stay for the patient. Aetna, who initially started this concept with the Medicare patient, said if the Medicare patient could leave the hospital earlier then why couldn't those younger and healthier patients do the same. Those involved in the outset looked at what worked and what did not in a good case management system, and thus managed care came as a result of this case management.

Managed Care is the mushroom cloud of case management, not the other way around.

Jacqueline J. Birmingham, RN, MS, A-CCC, CHE
Director, Continuity of Care and Special Programs
Chartwell Home Therapies
New Haven, Connecticut

Define the difference between a discharge planner and a case manager.

I see case management embracing the other. It really depends on how utilization review is dealt with and what is done with the data collected. Utilization review tends to look at outcome data. Case management encompasses this, and so much more, including lengths of stay and cost data. There needs to be a balance between all of these. I believe discharge planning and utilization review are components of the case management process.

Diane B. Williams, RN, MSHA
Editor in Chief
Nursing Case Management Magazine
Portland, Oregon

How knowledgeable is the discharge planner? Do these individuals really know all the options?

For the most part they may know the next step or second level for the patient after acute care, namely home care or subacute/SNF care. Recently, while speaking at a conference, I asked participants what was the next step after acute care. I received over twenty-three different responses including everything from sending the patient to the physician's office or to the morgue.

The needs of the discharge planner are changing. As healthcare increasingly moves toward the managed care environment, discharge planners are ill prepared. Although many know the resources that are covered in their particular circumstances, many are not aware of those services that may not be covered. Specifically those patients requiring social services or those requiring the services from volunteer groups in their community. This will especially hold true when many patients from the Medicare and/or Medicaid population enter into the managed care playing field. Many of these patients have different physical, as well as, mental needs which must be met.

Today's case manager must know the needs of a mother with three young children at home, who has no one to care for them during her illness or injury. Case management will be treating a different type of patient with many different types of need. Those case managers who are not in tune with these types of issues may have trouble meeting the demands of this patient population. The future case manager needs to have some type of public health experience.

Managed care could be compared to the changes made by the U.S. Government in the 70s when it began to deinstitutionalize patients. I believe the homeless problem in America today began when the government started the deinstitutionalization program. As many as 50% of the homeless have some type of mental illness diagnosis.

By the government stepping in and mandating some type of Medicaid HMO, for which the private sector is responsible, it could result in the same problems that are attributable to the changes made in the 70s. With the government's "tough love" approach to today's welfare system, we could have the same disastrous effects, by jumping in bounds rather than small increments. These programs need to be dissolved in small steps with the comfort of some type of safety net. Otherwise, the street will become a haven for those with infectious diseases and crime will run rampant.

Jacqueline J. Birmingham, RN, MS, A-CCC, CHE
Director, Continuity of Care and Special Programs
Chartwell Home Therapies
New Haven, Connecticut

From which perspective do you feel case management should be looked at?

It is mostly looked at from the patient perspective, but it should also be looked at from a global perspective. Case managers are supposed to have an objective view of a patient's situation. However, it is also the case manager's responsibility to keep in mind other issues such as resource allocation, community resources, and other issues that may affect a patient's situation.

All goals should be equally addressed with the patient, so that the patient is aware of the process he/she will be going through, what aspects of the process will be the most difficult, and any other issues. It is the case manager's duty to assist the patient in working through the decision process. Ultimately, the decision is in the hands of the patient as to what he/she will be going through throughout their stay.

Marlys Severson
SCM Associates
President, Case Management Society of America
Cypress, California

In healthcare, we have gone from a straight fee for service environment, which is at one end of the spectrum, to moving toward a capitated environment. Capitation looks at outcomes, gives the risk to the providers of care, more than to the payors of care. As we move in that direction, other things are taking place, like utilization issues. And what I think will happen in the next few years, is a move back to the middle. I think we will need to come back to the middle because the public is going to demand it.

In the past, we have traditionally done case management in one way, and our clients, patients and competitors have been separate entities. The environment is confusing because today one organization could be a competitor and tomorrow that same organization could be a client. Those of us who have been in healthcare for a long time are not always ready for those kind of changes, and change is hard. As providers and physicians take on more of the financial risk for the outcome of their patients, you will see a burgeoning of case management to help them manage that risk. As our consumers get better educated, you will see much more case management happening, and referrals happening on the consumer level as opposed to what you have seen in the past. As managed care changes, more real case management will happen in the managed care industry. Today, with heavily managed care entities like HMOs, you don't always see much actual case management taking place. What you see is utilization management.

I have an approach to case management that is very different. I see case management as being an entity that could actually be a very important player in the healthcare delivery system. Possibly, even the driver of the healthcare delivery system. As you look at access, you look at utilization. Appropriate care is cost effective and that is the number one priority. We have created a system that is totally complex, totally fragmented, with a very high level of technology. It is very difficult to maneuver through the system, even if you are a healthcare professional. And it is going to be absolutely essential to have somebody guide the lay people.

If case managers can recognize that their marketplace is changing and be flexible and change with it, then they will survive. There are people who just aren't going to change, and for them the future is bleak.

Carrie Ann Engen, RN, BSN, CCM
Director, Case Management Operations
Advocare, Inc.
Past Chairperson, Commission for
Case Manager Certification, 1995–1996
Past President, Case Management
Society of America, 1993–1994

How important is an educational background for the case manager?

With the clinical element being such an important part of case management, I think a nursing background is extremely important especially in a hospital or subacute setting. It's difficult enough for a nurse to get a physician to speak to him or her let alone someone without this experience.

For the most part they should have at a minimum an RN. Anyone with less may not have the appropriate skills for the position. However, many times a nurse practitioner is appropriate and I know of a respiratory therapist who is a very good case manager.

Diane B. Williams, RN, MSHA
Editor in Chief
Nursing Case Management Magazine
Portland, Oregon

I just spoke to social workers yesterday about this issue. A social worker stood up to make a comment, and said, "years ago when discharge planning started in the hospital, the social workers thought it was beneath them and then the nurses decided they would do it. They did a very good job of it and now the social workers said 'Hey wait a minute, we want to do it.'" Now these two groups are struggling with these turf issues again. I think partly this is some of the cause for the panic in case management. Discharge planning departments are being renamed and the hospitals are restructuring their case management models. I think that we are seeing some of this influence and this may be one of the reasons we see so many social workers in case management roles. Not every social worker is a case manager, just like not every nurse is a case manager.

Having chaired the Commission for Case Manager Certification's Eligibility Commission, I have seen the spectrum of the jobs and the categories that we continue to have some difficulty defining. For instance, one such difficult category is the hospital based nurses, who are allocated to the Utilization Review Department. Case management is becoming a vogue term and hospitals are trying to do more with less. Hospitals are renaming departments from Utilization Review to Case Management, which may or may not truly change the role of the employee to a case manager. The employee may still be doing Utilization Review but they are just relabeling it and calling it case management. This is why the Commission for Case Manager Certification goes back to the core elements in the job description when reviewing applications for eligibility for certification.

Linda Chalmers, RN, CRRN, CIRS, CCM, WCLA
Managed Care Specialist
Zurich-American Insurance Group
Chairperson, Commission for Case Manager Certification

Nurses and social workers both act in the capacity of case managers. In acute care settings with high acuity levels, R.N.s are the preferred case managers. Social workers or R.N.s function effectively as case managers in many other settings. In managed care settings, however, I have mainly encountered R.N.s.

Certification is valuable since case management is relatively new, and certification serves to validate the scope of knowledge and expertise level of the practitioner as judged by national standards. I think it is preferable if a case manager candidate has either a CCM or A-CCC credential. The Case Management Society of America Statement regarding ethical case management practice (1996) provides guidance to the individual case manager in the development and maintenance of an environment in which case management practice is conducted ethically. This issue of the ethics will continue to be of great concern to all.

A case manager should also have the interpersonal skills to effectively communicate with patients, families, physicians, and all others involved in delivery systems to focus on goal directed activities.

Ann M. Long, RN, MSM, CAN, A-CCC, CCM
Director, Division of Continuum of Care Management
Saint Francis Hospital and Medical Center
Hartford, Connecticut

There are many, many turf battles out there and they are heating up. With the advent of managed care, and hospitals down-sizing and controlling their costs, we have, nurses, social workers, whoever, doing the work of more than one person. What's happening is that we are having these turf issues which are escalating.

There is a pervasive feeling in the nursing field that nurses make the best case managers. There are several reasons for that thinking. One of the key reasons is our level of technology. We have a very high level of technology for which medical expertise is absolutely necessary. But if you look at what is being served to the consumer and which entities are being served with case management, then you can identify who the appropriate professional in the field is to best serve the needs of the consumer. If it is a population of catastrophically medically ill and injured patients, then maybe the best person who can manage those cases is a nurse. Case management in a hospital is really team nursing with a few twists to it and a few more added responsibilities.

Substance abuse and return to work issues involve entirely different disciplines. With the level of technology and the present complexity of healthcare delivery systems, case management must be in some cases a multi-disciplinary approach. Sometimes, more than one case management professional is involved. Case management is predicated on the fact that as a case manager you already have an established professional identity. Case management is not a profession in itself at this point in time. Therefore, people in the field of case management who have already established professional identities, are contributing to case management. We have a terrific crisis right now with those discipline identity issues. This is a huge controversy in the field of case management today.

Carrie Ann Engen, RN, BSN, CCM
Director, Case Management Operations
Advocare, Inc.
Past Chairperson, Commission for
Case Manager Certification, 1995–1996
Past President, Case Management
Society of America, 1993–1994

R.N.s or social workers are preferred as case managers. R.N.s have a global knowledge base and interdisciplinary team practice experience over the continuum from wellness to illness and back to wellness. However, R.N.s can be pigeonholed.

I have found an LPN in the field who is a wonderful case manager. An essential qualification of a case manager is the ability to not think inside of a box. A case manager should be innovative, and a good problem solver and communicator, qualities which might not necessarily coexist with any particular educational background.

Laura Deming, MS, RN, CS, CCM
President, Deming Neo/Pedi Consulting
Houston, Texas

Is there a need for some type of formal training or education?

Although education is important, there is a need for the case manager to go through a structured certification process. I would like to see all case managers with some type of professional capacity. The risk is very great to the case manager and many of today's case managers are most likely under-qualified. I would like to see individuals in this position with a minimum of a Bachelor's Degree and those in a managerial position with their Master's.

The area of case management is new and changing and all case managers should be required to seek certification by an appropriate body conducting some type of certification. Additionally, case managers should attend inservices to keep them abreast of any changes to this area. In a structured certification environment, case managers would be required to have sufficient time in the field, as well as have completed a comprehensive examination.

Jacqueline J. Birmingham, RN, MS, A-CCC, CHE
Director, Continuity of Care and Special Programs
Chartwell Home Therapies
New Haven, Connecticut

I see case management being taught through a body of knowledge at the Master's level within the next five years, which will change the whole face of the certification process for case management.

Eda Holt
Chief Executive Officer
Commission for Case Manager Certification

Is there a need for a degree in case management?

Yes, I believe there is a real need for this. Case management as a profession is struggling for an identity. The more we do at the educational level, the better. Credentialling case managers will give credibility to the profession.

Presently, the only one I see with momentum is the CCM (Certified Case Manager) which is sponsored by one of the case management societies.

Society needs to stop looking at healthcare with tunnel vision. Its an evolving area.

Diane B. Williams, RN, MSHA
Editor in Chief
Nursing Case Management Magazine
Portland, Oregon

What are other challenges which tomorrow's case managers will face?

The elimination of adequate training facilities for tomorrow's case managers. With the number of acute beds continually decreasing, where are we going to send our nursing students for their training? Many of these students are stuck going to nursing homes for this type of education. However, the question now becomes whether this type of facility can prepare them to deal with the patients in an acute setting?

Nursing education is to blame. They have been extremely hesitant when it comes to the administrative side of nursing. These nurses must be made aware of the regulatory and financial implications associated with the decisions they are making in a patient's case management.

Many of these case managers are making medical decisions without ever seeing the patient. The managers must be aware of the disease process. Many times, these case managers are dealing with some pretty sophisticated stuff. The grand problem keeps coming back to education.

More case managers are needed at the provider level where the risk is greater. The future will dictate the need for providers to be closer to their patients, thus benefiting the patient.

Jacqueline J. Birmingham, RN, MS, A-CCC, CHE
Director, Continuity of Care and Special Programs
Chartwell Home Therapies
New Haven, Connecticut

Ethical concerns about being "forced" to discharge patients back into a community where there are limited resources available to patients or families because of limits on their outpatient benefits or lack of insurance at all.

Kathleen Bremer, RN, BS, CCM
Director, Case Management
New England Rehabilitation Hospital of Portland
Portland, Maine

What are the most pressing issues in the field of case management today?

Community support for outpatient services.

Edna Lee Kucera, RN, MS
Director, Medical Care
University Hospital
Stony Brook, New York

Managing the preadmission phase to better intervene with high risk patients and plan for home care or rehabilitation needs.

Mary L. Dunphy
Manager, Case Management
Beth Israel Deaconess Medical Center
Boston, Massachusetts

The obstacles case managers face include: confusion as to the true definition of a case manager, lack of consensus with case managers, lack of communication and cohesiveness between facility based, payor based, and postdischarge based case managers, lack of case management expertise in specialty areas such as pediatrics, confusion between the role of case manager and discharge planner, inability to be effective, and confusion with management.

Laura Deming, MS, RN, CS, CCM
President, Deming Neo/Pedi Consulting
Houston, Texas

Providing quality care to patients and families who are being admitted to our hospital sicker than ever before. Also, third-party payors are pushing patients out of the hospital faster than ever before.

Kathleen Bremer, RN, BS, CCM
Director, Case Management
New England Rehabilitation Hospital of Portland
Portland, Maine

Discharging elderly patients to their homes who have no family support, and arranging for home IV and ATBs for Medicare patients. Helping physicians to understand home care and what services and care can actually be provided in the home versus the hospital continues to be a challenge for case managers.

Teresa A. Hennick, RN, CCM
Director, Case Management
Park Medical Center
Columbus, Ohio

I believe that the most pressing issue in the field of case management is the identification of high-risk patients and having physicians understand the role of case management.

Susan J. Aldape
U.M. Nurse
Mercy Ventures, MSO
Westminster, Maryland

The dilemma case managers face is how to balance the HMO payment with the length of stay based on critical pathways. There is more work, less staff, yet patients are more acutely ill.

Jeanette Ekberg, MSN
Clinical Nurse Specialist
Methodist Hospital
Omaha, Nebraska

Declining lengths of stay and working within "HMO" products that have "no cognitive rehab benefits" for TBI patients.

Christine Hamele
Director, Managed Care and Marketing
Meadowbrook Rehabilitation
Gardner, Kansas

High tech needs, especially newborn/pediatric care on the home care front is a significant issue for case management.

Marilyn L. Abbott, RN, CCM
Intake Specialist
Olsten Kimberly Quality Care
Winter Springs, Florida

Cost quality outcomes, patient satisfaction, patient education, early intervention, prevention, and wellness are all case management issues today.

Janet K. Hunter
Director of Patient Care Services
DeKalb Memorial Hospital
Auburn, Indiana

Competencies in the field and communication with other case managers consistently challenge case managers.

Janie Hill
Case Manager
Children's Hospital
Birmingham, Alabama

Pressures from managed care to discharge patients while physicians and team members feel that the patient truly requires more time hospitalized. This is a constant ethical dilemma for case managers.

Alison Blum, RN
Director of Case Management
Transitional Hospital Corporation
Arlington, Texas

Getting nursing to buy into clinical efficiency and management and getting all departments to be pro-active!

Marianne V. Bailey, RN, ONC
Case Manager
Washington Regional Medical Center
Springdale, Arizona

Daily changes, mergers, and changing players constantly affect case management.

Chris Bartel, RN, CCM
Regional Director, Managed Care
GranCare
Novato, California

The change in the "mindset" of many health care providers regarding how and where patients may receive quality care is a key concern of case managers. Also, an information system infrastructure that promotes immediate access to pertinent data which ties quality, cost/financial, and patient satisfaction outcomes together, and also supports collaborative management of client needs by licensed professionals is essential to an effective case management system.

Ann M. Long, RN, MSM, A-CCC, CCM
Director, Division of Continuum of Care Management
Saint Francis Hospital and Medical Center
Hartford, Connecticut

Pressure to find resources quickly, limited benefit dollars, and managed care requirements.

Steve Jennings
Director, Case Management
Fairfax Hospital
Kirkland, Washington

Our position is viewed as that of an adversary by the injured worker's attorney, thus making case management even more challenging.

Barbara J. Armstrong, RN, BSN, MS, CCM, CLNC
Stage II Medical Reviewer
Omaha, Nebraska

Quality of care and cost effectiveness are pressing case management issues. The client needs and deserves good care, but it must be provided cost effectively.

Julia Gray Keeler, RN, CRRN, CCM
Medical Case Manager
Genex
Tyler, Texas

Outcome management, quality patient care, follow-up issues, and providing services for uninsured patients or patients within insurance limits, continue to be issues that case managers must address.

Sandra Cannon
Case Manager
Floyd Medical Center
Cedar Bluff, Alabama

Difficulty qualifying for CAM Certification.

Evelyn Brillon
Director, Utilization Case Management
Bronx Lebanon Hospital Center
Bronx, New York

Ethics, balancing care with reimbursement, and liability issues.

Eileen Bartlett
Director, Programs
HealthSouth Rehab Hospital
Concord, New Hampshire

How important is case management to the future of healthcare?

Pivotal.

Ann M. Long, RN, MSN, A-CCC, CCM
Director, Division of Continuum of Care Management
Saint Francis Hospital and Medical Center
Hartford, Connecticut

Case management is very prevalent in the future of managed care. It has become evident though, that case managers are getting too involved with superfluous issues.

Marlys Severson
SCM Associates
President, Case Management Society of America
Cypress, California

Vital, if we are going to make an impact on saving healthcare dollars for our children. If we do not get healthcare under control, we are not going to have a Medicare program in the future.

Laura Deming, MS, RN, CS, CCM
President, Deming Neo/Pedi Consulting
Houston, Texas

The Promise of Quality—Case Management's Continuing Agenda

Centralized case management is state of the art healthcare. It is the cornerstone of both managed care and an integrated or continuum approach to service delivery. Case management simultaneously addresses the three major issues confronting the American system of healthcare: cost, quality, and access. It is these issues that fuel the movement to reform the healthcare system. Despite the ultimate outcome of major policy reforms with respect to healthcare, it is marketplace dynamics that will continue to effect industry change. As costs are reined in, continuums of care are expanded through venue development, and the efficiencies of operations are realized, healthcare providers will boldly pursue the most appropriate forms of service delivery. What treatment and care is appropriate will be based on a balancing of often-conflicting priorities. It is within this context that the role and value of case management has a certain future.

Centralized case management is the perfect strategy for the new era of healthcare delivery. It is at once an exquisitely simple concept that has stood the test of time and a revolutionary process for change. It is indeed a recognized force in the redesign of the healthcare system of tomorrow. That system must be premised on competition between healthcare providers on the basis of price *and* quality. Much of the competition recently has evolved only on price. And although the incentives under the old system were for healthcare providers to do what many would describe as too much, the incentives today are often for providers to do too little. Definable and measurable quality has taken a secondary role to cost control. Critics of marketplace healthcare question whether quality can ever be equated with price when third parties are purchasing healthcare. In the recent past, questioners of managed healthcare have voiced their dissatisfaction with the system in the public forum. Patients routinely testify before Congress about care they see as life saving and the companies see as experimental. Newspapers are filled with reports of patients with rare conditions denied access to specialists. The healthcare system is being attacked by anecdote.

The fusillade is gaining in force and threatens to shake the very foundations of managed competition. In this new era of managed competition backlash, case management will define its own future role. Case management must remain the advocate of quality. Systems of case management will be challenged to measure quality so that choices can be made on the basis of what is best rather than on what will cost the least. Given that the industry is composed of numerous players motivated by many different kinds of ideological, political, and economic considerations, the task is a complex and yet unrealized objective. Cost control has been the mantra of the payor, quality has been the theme of the provider, and the government and public call for equal access. In the future, case management will be recognized as the best tool to both achieve and reconcile the often conflicting goals inherent in the system of healthcare.

G L O S S A R Y

Access   A patient's ability to obtain medical care. The ease of access is determined by such components as the availability of medical services and their acceptability to the patient, the location of healthcare facilities, transportation, hours of operation, and cost of care.

Adjusted average per capita cost (AAPCC)   HCFA's best estimate of the amount of money care costs for Medicare recipients under fee-for-service Medicare in a given area. The AAPCC is made up of 122 different rate cells; 120 of them are factored for age, sex, Medicaid eligibility, institutional status, and whether a person has both part A and part B of Medicare.

Ambulatory surgery centers   A distinct entity that: (1) operates exclusively for the purpose of providing surgical services to patients not requiring hospitalization, (2) has an agreement with HCFA under Medicare to participate as an ASC, and (3) meets the prescribed regulatory conditions for coverage.

Base year   For providers exempted from the prospective payment system, the base year (a full fiscal year) inpatient operating cost per discharge serves as the limit for future fiscal years, with minor yearly updates. It is generally the first or second full year of operations.

Capitation fee   A per-member, monthly payment to a provider that covers contracted services, and is paid in advance of the delivery of the service. In essence, a provider agrees to provide specified services to HMO members for this fixed, predetermined payment for a specified length of time (usually a year), regardless of the actual number or nature of services delivered.

Catastrophic care   A case or medical condition where total cost of treatment is expected to exceed an amount designated by the HMO contract with the medical group.

Certificate of need (CON)   Approval granted by the state to add new facilities, tertiary services, or to buy major equipment. Hospitals, nursing homes, ambulatory surgical centers, and home care agancies must comply with CON regulations.

Clinical pathway   A "map" of preferred treatment/intervention activities that outlines the types of information needed to make decisions, the timelines for applying that information, and what action needs to be taken and by whom. These pathways, which monitor care in "real time," are developed by clinicians for specific diseases or events. Proactive providers are working now to develop these pathways for the majority of their interventions and developing the software capacity to distribute and store this information.

Complementary medicine clinic A clinic generally part of a larger out-patient program offering diagnosis, treatment and therapy outside of conventional medicine. Under such a model, patients take primary responsibility for their own health and wellness. A multitude of resources, including physicians who are supportive of non-traditional medicine and healing, are readily available in the alternative health clinic. Common alternative therapies can include acupuncture, kinesiology, aromatherapy, biofeedback, diet and nutritional supplements, traditional Chinese medicine, herbal medicine, and osteopathy.

Comprehensive inpatient rehabilitation unit (CIRU) A Medicare recognized venue of care for rehabilitation which offers comprehensive therapy (PT, OT, speech, psychology, etc.) and medical care. By law, patients must be able to tolerate at least three hours of therapy daily and 75% of its patients must fall within 1 of 10 specific rehabilitation diagnoses. Reimbursement in comprehensive inpatient units are subject to a TEFRA cap as these units are exempted from the prospective payment system.

Comprehensive outpatient rehabilitation facility (CORF) An out-patient venue, specifically recognized by Medicare. CORFs are designed to provide a wide array of functional, therapeutic, and restorative care services to patients with diverse medical and rehabilitation needs. Product lines often included in a CORF are medical day hospital, neurological institute, industrial medicine clinic, bone and joint center, and pain management clinic. A CORF as recognized by 42 CFR § 485.50 is a non-residential public or private facility that: (1) is exclusively engaged in providing, under a physician's direction, diagnostic, therapeutic, and restorative services to outpatients for the rehabilitation of injured, disabled, or sick persons, at a single fixed location; (2) provides, at least, the following services: (a) physician's services (rendered by physicians who are available at the facility on a full-time or part-time basis), (b) physical therapy, and (c) social or psychological services; (3) maintains clinical records on all patients; (4) has policies established by a group of professional personnel (associated with the facility), including at least one physician to govern the services it furnishes, and provides for the carrying out of such policies by a physician; (5) has a requirement that every patient must be under the care of a physician; (6) meets all applicable state or local standards for licensing; (7) has in effect a utilization review plan in accordance with federal regulations; (8) has in effect an overall plan and budget in accordance with the requirements under the law; (9) meets any other conditions, as the secretary may find necessary, relating to the health and safety of individuals who are furnished services by the facility, including conditions concerning qualifications of personnel in these facilities.

Continuity of care A degree to which the care of the patient from the onset of the illness until its completion is continuous, that is, without interruption.

Continuum of care A range of medical and nursing treatments and social services in a variety of settings that provides services most appropriate to the level of care required.

Diagnosis related group (DRG) One of the 495 classifications of diagnoses in which patients demonstrate similar resource consumption and length of stay patterns. Medicare reimburses acute care hospitals by assigning specific payment to each DRG.

DRG payment system The DRG payment comprises two parts. One part is for labor and one part is a standard amount. The labor amount reflects the cost of employees needed to care for the patient and the standard amount includes the costs of supplies, drugs, and other expenses. These amounts differ for hospitals located in large urban, other urban, or rural areas and are updated annually on October 1. The DRG payments system is based on averages. That is, payment is determined by the resource needs of the average Medicare patient for a given set of diseases or disorders. These needs include the length of stay and the number and intensity of services provided. Therefore, the more efficiently a provider delivers care, the greater its operating margin will be.

Durable medical equipment Medical equipment that is owned or rented that can withstand repeated use; is primarily and customarily used to serve a medical purpose; generally, is not useful to a person in the absence of illness/injury and is appropriate for home use. This equipment is generally placed in the home of an insured to facilitate treatment and/or rehabilitation.

Enrollees A person eligible to receive benefits from an HMO or insurance policy. This includes those enrolled and their eligible dependents.

Exclusive provider organization (EPO) A form of managed care where enrollees are limited to using providers belonging to one group.

Fee-for-service A method of payment for healthcare whereby a fee is rendered for each service delivered. This traditional method contrasts with that used in the prepaid sector where services are covered by a fixed payment made in advance that is independent of the number of services rendered. Payment may be made by an insurance company, the patient, or a government program such as Medicare or Medicaid. Beneficiaries are free to use any legitimate provider they choose. Providers are paid based on the specific services furnished to beneficiaries. Payments may be based on billed charges, discounted charges, negotiated rate schedule, or the usual or customary charges in that community.

Fixed cost Costs that do not change with fluctuations in census or in utilization of services.

Gatekeeping A primary care physician who must authorize, oversee, and coordinate all aspects of a patient's medical care. In order for a patient to receive a specialty care referral or hospital admission, the gatekeeper must preauthorize the visit, unless there is an emergency.

Health and Human Services Department (HHS)   The U.S. Department of Health and Human Services, which is responsible for health-related programs and issues.

Health Care Financing Administration (HCFA)   The agency within the Department of Health and Human Services that administers federal health financing and related regulatory programs, principally the Medicare, Medicaid, and Peer Review Organization.

Health maintenance organizations (HMO)   A legal corporation that offers health insurance and medical care. HMOs are organized delivery systems that provide or arrange for comprehensive care. HMOs typically offer a range of healthcare services at a fixed price (see capitation). Enrollees typically have low out-of-pocket expenses in comparison to traditional fee-for-service insurance plans, however, enrollee's choice of providers is strictly limited to the HMO's network of physicians, hospitals, and ancillary providers. HMO patients are typically assigned a primary care physician to coordinate and authorize specialty care. HMO physicians often have strong financial incentives to carefully manage utilization, particularly use of hospital and specialty services. Over the past decade, a wide range of organizational models and characteristics have evolved with distinctions among different types of plans becoming blurred as hybrids (like point of service plans) are established. HMOs offer prepaid, comprehensive health coverage for both hospital and physician services. An HMO contracts with healthcare providers (physicians, hospitals, and other health professionals), and members are required to use participating providers for all health services. Members are enrolled for a specified period of time. Model types include staff, group practice, network, and IPA.

> **Staff model**   HMO owns its clinics, employs its salaried physicians and other health professional who provide care solely for members of one HMO.
>
> **Group model**   In a group model HMO, the HMO contracts with a medical group and/or a group of physicians, which is paid a set amount per patient to provide a specified range of services. The group of physicians determines the compensation of each individual physician, often sharing profits. The practice may be located in a hospital or clinic setting and generally all services except hospital care are provided under one roof. Both group and staff models are known collectively as prepared group practice plans.
>
> **IPA model**   Contract with an IPA that in turn contracts with individual physicians.
>
> > ■ **Independent Physician Association**   Contacts with individual physicians who see HMO members, as well as their own patients, in their own private offices. It is the ability of IPA physicians to see both IPA and private patients in their own offices that principally differentiates an IPA from a group or staff HMO. Physicians in an IPA are paid either on a capitation or a modified fee-for-service basis.
> >
> > ■ **Individual Practice Association**   An HMO model in which the HMO contracts with a physician organization that in turn contracts with individual physicians. The IPA physicians provide care to HMO members from their private offices and continue to see their fee-for-service patients.

- **Independent Practice Associates** Contract with groups of independent physicians who work their own offices. These independent practitioners receive a per-member payment or capitation from the HMO to provide a full range of health services for HMO members. These providers often care for members of many HMOs.

Direct contract model Contracts directly with individual physicians.

Mixed model Members get options ranging from staff to IPA models.

Health Maintenance Organization Act of 1973 The HMO Act of 1973 focuses on prepaid medical practices and freed up federal funds to be used for the study and development of individual HMOs. The Act also instilled the dual choice provision obligating employers with more than 25 workers to offer their employees the opportunity to enroll in a federally qualified HMO if one was available in their region.

Homebound Individuals are considered homebound if they have a condition, due to an illness or injury, that restricts their ability to leave their home, except with the assistance of another person or the aid of a supportive device (such as crutches, a cane, a wheelchair, or a walker), or if they have a condition such that leaving the home is medically contraindicated. While individuals do not have to be bedridden to be considered homebound, their condition should be such that there exists a normal inability to leave home, that leaving home requires a considerable and taxing effort, and that absences from the home are infrequent or of relatively short duration, or are attributed to the need to receive medical treatment [Soc. Sec. Act ¶1814(a).]

Home health agencies A public agency or private organization, or a subdivision of such an agency or organization, that [Soc.Sec. Act ¶ 1861 (o)]: (1) is primarily engaged in providing skilled nursing services and other therapeutic services; (2) has polices established by a professional group associated with the agency or organization (including at least one physician and at least one registered professional nurse) to govern the services, and provides for supervision of such services by a physician or a registered professional nurse.

Hospice A public agency, private organization, or a subdivision of either, that is primarily engaged in providing care to the terminally ill (individuals with a life expectancy of six months or less), has a valid provider agreement, and meets the conditions of participation specified in the law and in the regulations. [Soc. Sec Act ¶ 1861 (dd); Reg. ¶418.50 et seq.] A hospice may be dually certified as a hospice and as a hospital, skilled nursing facility, home health agency, or intermediate care facility. However, it must have separate provider agreements, must file separate cost reports, and must independently meet the hospice conditions. [Soc. Sec. Act ¶1861 (dd) (4).]

Integrated delivery systems (IDSs) This continuum of healthcare services is linked through information systems and a series of contractural or financially integrated organizations. Moreover, IDSs have several performance imperatives: improve health status, integrate delivery, demonstrate value, improve efficiency of care delivery and prevention, and meet patient and community needs.

Joint Commission on Accreditation of Healthcare Organizations (JCAHO)   A private not-for-profit organization whose purpose is to establish standards for the operation of health facilities and services, conduct surveys, and award accreditation for those that meet the standards.

Long term care hospital   A long term care hospital recognized under 42 CFR § 412.23 (e) must have a provider agreement under part 489 to participate as a hospital under the Medicare System. Long term care hospitals generally provide diagnostic and medical treatment or rehabilitation to patients with chronic disease or complex medical conditions. Medicare reimbursement is cost-based per a TEFRA limit established by each individual provider. Long term care hospitals can be physically located within existing acute care hospitals. Patients in aggregate must have an average length of inpatient stay greater than 25 days.

Managed care   A general term for organizing doctors, hospitals, and other providers into groups in order to enhance the quality and cost-effectiveness of healthcare. A relatively new term coined originally to refer to the prepaid healthcare sector (e.g., HMOs) where care is provided under a fixed budget and costs are therein capable of being "managed." Increasingly, the term is being used by many analysts to include PPOs and even forms of indemnity insurance coverage that incorporate preadmission certification and other utilization controls.

Medicaid   A federal program, run and partially funded by individual states, to provide medical benefits to certain low income people. The state, under broad federal guidelines, determines what benefits are covered, who is eligible and how much providers will be paid. Medicaid also is responsible for nursing home care for the indigent elderly.

Medical day hospital   Medical day hospitals provide a structured and specialized comprehensive rehabilitation and/or medical program for individuals with acute and chronic disorders, including post-surgical, respiratory, neurological, pain, and oncological conditions. Services will be provided, including assessment, diagnostic evaluation, treatment, and management and monitoring of patients. Structured in day-long programs, these entities can substitute and/or shorten inpatient admissions. Medical day programs are often certified as a CORF (comprehensive outpatient rehabilitation facility) for Medicare patients.

Medicare   A nationwide, federal health insurance program for people age 65 and older. It also covers certain people under 65 who are disabled or have chronic kidney disease. Medicare Part A is the hospital insurance program; part B covers physicians' services and other services.

Medicare risk contracting   Medicare risk contracting, first authorized in 1982, gives Medicare beneficiaries the option to enroll in HMOs, all of which offer Medicare-covered benefits and most of which offer coverage of cost sharing and supplemental services that replace Medigap policies.

National Committee for Quality Assurance (NCQA)   A nonprofit accrediting body for managed care companies created to improve patient quality and health plan performance in partnership with managed care plans, purchasers, consumers, and the public sector.

Outcome   The result of medical or surgical intervention or nonintervention. An outcome should be able to be measured as to its achievement or lack of attainment.

Partial day psychiatric program   A psychiatric hospital must be primarily engaged in providing, by or under the supervision of a psychiatrist, psychiatric services for the diagnosis and treatment of mentally ill persons; and it must generally meet the conditions of participation for a Medicare certified hospital and special conditions of participation for psychiatric hospitals.

Peer review organization (PRO)   An organization that reviews the appropriateness and quality of care delivered to Medicare patients. The PRO has the ability to deny approval for care and deny payment for care delivered.

Per diem cost   The cost of care per day in a hospital or other institution providing care.

Physician hospital organization (PHO)   An organization owned jointly by a hospital and a physican group. The PHO, in turn, contracts with the hospital and physicians for delivery of services to payors enrolled under the PHO contract.

Preferred provider organization (PPO)   A select group of medical care providers who have agreed to furnish services for discounted rates. Patients who go to a preferred provider get a higher benefit. For example, beneficiaries who use the network may be responsible for only 10% of the charges versus a 25–30% copayment if care is received outside the network. In return, providers expect growth in their volume of services. Beneficiaries are not formally enrolled in PPOs; instead, the PPO network is made available to them by their insurance sponsor. PPO users may decide at any point to utilize network providers, or to obtain care from non-network providers at increased out-of-pocket cost. PPOs employ financial incentives to encourage use of network providers. PPOs do not utilize primary care gatekeepers, but typically employ careful utilization review techniques.

Primary care   Basic or general healthcare usually rendered by physicians who are predominantly primary care physicians, including general or family practitioners, internists, pediatricians, and OB/GYN physicians.

Prospective payment system (PPS)   Medicare payment mechanism for inpatient operating costs established by the Tax Equity and Fiscal responsibility Act of 1982 (TEFRA 82). Places limits on reimbursable total inpatient operating costs on a per-case basis, with yearly adjustments. Providers are paid a predetermined amount per discharge according to diagnostic groupings.

Rehabilitation agency   A rehabilitation agency (with respect to determining its qualifications as a provider of outpatient physical therapy and/or speech pathology services) provides an integrated multidisciplinary program designed to upgrade the physical function of handicapped disabled individuals by bringing together as a team specialized rehabilitation personnel. At a minimum, a rehabilitation agency must provide physical therapy or speech pathology services and a rehabilitation program that, in addition to physical therapy or speech pathology services, includes social or vocational adjustment services [Reg. CFR 405.1702 (i)].

Risk contracting   An arrangement through which a health provider agrees to provide a full range of medical services to a set population of patients for a pre-paid sum of money. The physician is responsible for managing the care of these patients, and risks losing money if total expenses exceed the predetermined amount of funds.

Risk pool   Risk limiting procedure in which costs for individual enrollees or providers over a specified time period are aggregated in some manner in order to offset cost overruns; this practice can help stabilize the large variability in costs inherent in smaller group sizes.

Skilled nursing unit (SNU)   This is defined in Sec. 1891(a)-(d) as an institution (or a distinct part of an institution) that has in effect a transfer agreement with one or more participating hospitals and that:

1. is primarily engaged in providing to residents (a) skilled nursing care and related services for patients who require medical or nursing care, or (b) rehabilitation services for the rehabilitation of injured, disabled, or sick persons; and
2. meet detailed requirements relating to services provided, residents' rights, professional standards, health and safety standards, and administration. Facilities that primarily treat mental illness are specifically excluded.

Subacute   A transitional level of care designed to offer a wide range of medical and rehabilitation services. Typically these venues are licensed as skilled nursing units. Subacute is not a Medicare-designated reimbursement category. Reimbursement rates vary widely depending on the program services and intensity.

Tax Equity and Fiscal Responsibility Act (TEFRA)   TEFRA, enacted by the federal government in 1982, is best known in the healthcare industry for its sections defining and delineating reimbursement to those facilities that are exempt from the Prospective Payment System (PPS). Under TEFRA, Congress mandated that a proposal for Medicare Prospective Payment System be submitted by December 31, 1982. At the same time TEFRA provided for a transitional period of paid incentives or penalties to hospitals if Medicare Costs were less than or in excess of a predetermined target rate per admission. TEFRA is applied only to providers who are excluded from PPS which includes rehabilitation hospitals, psychiatric hospitals, children's hospitals, and long term care hospitals. Originally it was expected that diagnosis related groupings (DRGs) would soon be developed for these excluded providers and they would then be included within the Prospective Payment System.

Tertiary care   A level of medical care furnished by highly specialized providers such as neurosurgeons, thoracic surgeons and intensive care units and available in large medical facilities. Tertiary care often requires highly sophisticated technology and methods of therapy and diagnosis which involves equipment and personnel that would not be available in smaller facilities as a result of economic and utilization factors.

Utilization review   Evaluation of the necessity, appropriateness, and efficiency of the use of medical services and facilities; helps ensure proper use of healthcare resources by providing for the regular review of such areas as admission of patients, lengths of stay, services performed, and referrals. And, the various methods used by health plans to measure the amount and appropriateness of health services used by its members. These checks can occur before, during, and after services have been sought and received from health professionals.

Worker's Compensation   A state-mandated program providing insurance coverage for work-related injuries and disabilities.

Acronyms and Abbreviations

AAPCC	Adjusted average per capita costs
ABCs	Alternative birthing centers
A-CCC	Advanced continuity of care certification
ADS	Alternative delivery systems
ALOS	Average length of stay
ARCA	American Rehabilitation Counseling Association
ASCs	Ambulatory surgical centers
CARF	Commission on Accreditation of Rehabilitation Facility
CCM	Certified case manager
CCMC	Commission for Case Manager Certification
CDMS	Certified disability management specialist
CFR	Code of federal regulations
CIRSC	Certification of Insurance Rehabilitation Specialists Commission
CIRU	Comprehensive inpatient rehabilitation unit
CMC	Case manager certified
CMSA	Case Management Society of America
CON	Certificate of Need
COPD	Chronic obstructive pulmonary disease
CORF	Comprehensive outpatient rehabilitation center
CRC	Certified rehabilitation counselor
DME	Durable medical equipment
DRG	Diagnosis related group
EPO	Exclusive provider organization
GDP	Gross domestic product
HCFA	Health Care Financing Administration
HHS	Department of Health and Human Services
HIAA	Health Insurance Association of America
HMOs	Health maintenance organizations
ICMA	Individual Case Management Association
ICU	Intensive care unit

IPA	Independent Physician Association
IPA	Individual Practice Association
JCAHO	Joint Commission on Accreditation of Healthcare Organizations
LDL	Low density lipoprotein
LOS	Length of stay
LTCH	Long term care hospital
NBCCC	National Board for Certification in Continuity of Care
NCQA	National Committee for Quality Assurance
NRCA	National Rehabilitation Counseling Association
OT	Occupational therapy
PPOs	Preferred provider organizations
PPS	Prospective payment system
PRO	Peer review organization
PT	Physical therapy
RN	Registered nurse
SNF	Skilled nursing facility
SNU	Skilled nursing unit
TEFRA	Tax Equity and Fiscal Responsibility Act
TPA	Third-party administrators
UR	Utilization review

Case Management Job Descriptions

The following are five case manager job descriptions which have been graciously supplied by providers from across the country. The providers include:

St. Francis Hospital and
Medical Center
The Rehabilitation Hospital
of Connecticut   Hartford, Connecticut

Dekalb Memorial Hospital   Auburn, Indiana

GranCare   Novato, California

The Medstat Group   Nashville, Tennessee

Children's Hospital   Birmingham, Alabama

1. Saint Francis   THE REHABILITATION HOSPITAL OF CONNECTICUT
Hospital and Medical Center
Hartford, CT

CRITERIA-BASED JOB DESCRIPTION AND PERFORMANCE APPRAISAL

Job Title: Case Manager

Position Classification: Code: 20036

Department: Case Management (6700)   Pay Grade:
                   Division of Continuum of Care Management

Reports to (position):   Manager, Case Management

Supervises (positions):

FLSA Status: Exempt   EEO Classification:

Approved by: _____   _____
                    Department Head/Date   Human Resources/Date

JOB SUMMARY

The Case Manager coordinates, negotiates, procures, and manages the care of complex patients to facilitate achievement of quality cost-effective patient outcomes. Works collaboratively with interdisciplinary staff internal and external to the organization. Participates in quality improvement and evaluation process related to the management of patient care. In most Clinical Program Lines, the activities are carried out with a particular focus on the adult and geriatric patient age group; the pediatric, adolescent, and young adult population represent the focus in the Women and Children's Clinical Program Line. These activities are carried out in varying models specific to the dynamic needs within the established Clinical Program Lines but always guided by the Philosophy and Vision Statement of Saint Francis Hospital and Medical Center and the Philosophy of the Division of the Continuum of Care Management. Position may require working at either campus. The Standards of Practice for Case Management (Case Management Society of America) and the Code of Ethics and Standards for Hospital Continuity of Care (American Association for Continuity of Care) are incorporated in all policies and activities.

JOB QUALIFICATIONS

Education: Bachelor of Science in Nursing Masters in Nursing.
Experience: Two to five years of diversified, progressive experience in acute
                    care and/or other settings within the continuum.
Licensure: Current Registered Nurse - State of Connecticut
Certification: Certification in Case Management (CCM)/Certification in Continuity
                    of Care - Advanced (A-CCC) preferred.
                    OR
Education: Masters in Social Work.
Experience: Two to five years of diversified, progressive experience in acute
                    care and/or other settings within the continuum.
Licensure:
Certification: Certification in Case Management (CCM)/Certification in Continuity
                    of Care - Advanced (A-CCC) preferred.

Skills:

This position requires a person with a positive attitude who is self directed, pleasant, cooperative, assertive yet compassionate displaying a professional demeanor with patients, families, physicians, and fellow employees. The position requires the knowledge of social work or nursing principles and practice and the ability to remain productive under stress; ability to adequately use or learn computer software and hardware applications. Basic knowledge of statistics, HCFA-OBRA regulations, ISDA criteria, JCAHO, levels of care in the continuum, and dynamics occurring in health care delivery systems a necessity. The ability to function in a fast-paced, integrated interdisciplinary model of Patient Focused Care to improve patient care and outcomes.

PHYSICAL AND MENTAL EFFORT

Much walking and stair-climbing involved throughout the day. Mental effort: Critical decision-making involving multiple variables which determine/influence quality and cost outcomes for the patient and System. Position requires ability to frequently push/pull/lift light objects less than 20 lbs., perform moderately difficult manipulative, arm-hand steadiness, and eye-hand coordination skills; walk and stand; see objects closely and hear normal sounds with some background noises. Position requires ability to concentrate on fine detail with constant interruption and attend to tasks or functions for 10-20 minutes at a time. Individual must be able to understand and relate to theories behind several related concepts and remember multiple tasks given over long periods of time and be able to communicate in written word using advanced written skills.

ENVIRONMENTAL AND WORKING CONDITIONS

Spends most of the day in patient areas specific to the continuum; starts and finishes in the Case Management Office (physically or via modem). A combination of direct contact with patients, families, other disciplines internal and external to the organization. High levels of telephone communication, computer use, and documentation requirements. Employee may frequently be exposed to blood; body tissues or fluids; hazardous waste materials; dust; and electrical hazards.

JOB DUTIES

The following description of job responsibilities and standards are intended to reflect the major responsibilities and duties of the job, but is not intended to describe minor duties or other responsibilities as may be assigned from time to time.

CRITERIA-BASED JOB DESCRIPTIONS AND PERFORMANCE APPRAISAL
Please place the appropriate rating 0-4 in each of the boxes below.

1.0 Supports the Saint Francis/Mount Sinai commitment to World Class Service by demonstrating a continuous commitment to deliver a level of service that exceeds all personal expectations. As a provider of "World Class Service", we must:

Weight 90 points

1.1 Continuously pursue excellence in meeting the needs and expectations of all customers (patients, families, guests, fellow employees, physicians, payors, and the communities we serve.) Must demonstrate a commitment to the highest standards of care, compassion, and service while maintaining a safe environment for all customers. Ensures that all care is delivered with the utmost respect and dignity.

1.2 Continuously earns the highest levels of confidence and respect of all customers we serve. Must communicate with all customers by listening and appropriately responding to their needs while demonstrating moral and ethical values consistent with the vision of Saint Francis Hospital and Medical Center and Mount Sinai Hospital.

1.3 Embrace change and continuously identify opportunities for improvement by demonstrating a commitment to creativity and innovation, learning from others and ourselves, and working together to make things simpler and better.

1.4 Efficiently and effectively use resources to ensure the financial viability and continued success of Saint Francis Hospital and Medical Center and Mount Sinai Hospital. In order to best serve our customers, we are committed to offering services of superior value by taking responsibility and ownership for hospital property and resources, embracing cost management practices, striving for accuracy, and reducing waste.

1.5 Recognize that people are the key to our success and the only way our shared goals can be achieved is through team effort. Each employee must respect and appreciate their fellow workers' talents, abilities, and cultural background to ensure that every individual is an integral part of the Saint Francis/Mount Sinai team.

1.6 Have achieved the goal(s) established during the last performance review relative to "World Class Service".

CRITERIA BASED JOB DESCRIPTION AND PERFORMANCE APPRAISAL

Please place the appropriate rating 0-4 in each of the boxes below.

2.0	Assesses patients and patient populations needs for Case Management services at multiple points within the health care continuum.	Weight 30 Points

2.1 Identifies appropriate patients/caseloads within designated specialty area requiring case management intervention via established high-risk screening criteria and individual professional decision-making.

2.2 Provides evaluation of patients identified through high-risk screening and referral according to established procedures using creativity and flexibility.

2.3 Introduces self to the patient/family, explains the Case Manager's role, and provides them with a business card.

2.4 Assesses the patients within the caseload to identify needs, issues, financial resources, and care goals; demonstrates comprehensive knowledge of reimbursement mechanisms and the ability to research same.

2.5 Assesses the multidimensional domains of
- physical functioning
- psychological functioning
- social supports
- financial resources

2.6 Demonstrates ability to proactively research patients' financial resources for meeting health care needs, i.e., health care insurance plans (indemnity and managed care), entitlement programs, and personal resources.

2.7 Collaborates with primary nurse and physician in identifying patients appropriate for Case Management intervention, i.e. selected Level II patients (those requiring home health care services) and all Level III patients (those requiring care in another health care facility) as defined in the nursing admission data base.

2.8 Evaluates and collaborates with all members of the health care team to document patient status and variances, working toward achievement of patient goals/optimum quality and cost outcomes utilizing specific tools where applicable, i.e., CareMaps TM, Cost-Benefit Analysis Reports, etc.

2.9 Assumes responsibility for ongoing assessment of patient case management needs through frequent patient rounds and communication with physicians and other appropriate members of the health care team.

2.10 Conducts admission and concurrent utilization activities according to established criteria and guidelines, i.e., CONNCUR, ISDA, etc.

CRITERIA BASED JOB DESCRIPTION AND PERFORMANCE APPRAISAL

Please place the appropriate rating 0-4 in each of the boxes below.

3.0	Plans for high quality, realistic, and cost-effective/resource driven continuum of care arrangements for identified patients consistent with JCAHO Accrediting Standards and the Philosophy and Mission of Saint Francis Hospital and Medical Center System.	Weight 30 Points

3.1 In conjunction with the patient, physician, family, and other members of the health care team, the payor and available resources, formulates a plan to address assessed needs in the most appropriate setting, thus achieving optimum quality and cost outcomes.

3.2 Identifies patient discharge needs, making appropriate referrals, and utilizing available community/regional resources.

3.3 Establishes optimum discharge planning goal that is consistent with the overall outcome/goal according to specific clinical setting, Interdisciplinary Patient Care Planning Rounds, CareMaps, etc.

3.4 Prioritizes case management activities in order of greatest patient and system need to achieve optimum quality and cost outcomes.

3.5 Is accountable for all activities specifically related to the Nursing Home Admission process.

3.6 Conducts all Nursing Home Pre-Admission Screening activities according to guidelines from the State of Connecticut, Department of Social Services, Alternative Care Unit, as evidenced by documentation and behaviors observed by Managers/Case Managers.

3.7 Collaborates with the Case Management Team, the extended clinical team, and with appropriate administrative personnel (Manager/Case management).

3.8 Develops a network of the usual services and disciplines required by the typical patient within the caseload.

3.9 Maintains a working knowledge of the requirements of the payors most frequently seen with the patient population.

3.10 Maintains a working knowledge of the resources available in the community for patient/family needs.

CRITERIA BASED JOB DESCRIPTION AND PERFORMANCE APPRAISAL

Please place the appropriate rating 0-4 in each of the boxes below.

4.0 Implements the appropriate plan (i.e., discharge for inpatient or other for outpatient) for the case managed population within the continuum focusing on maximum utilization and marketing of the Saint Francis Hospital System Network while respecting patient self-determination and choice.

| Weight |
| 30 Points |

4.1 Obtains necessary pre-certification for community care, documenting first and last name of managed care contact in the permanent medical record.

4.2 Refers patient to next level of care, by direct voice communication (telephone or in person) specifying the clinical indicators and services needed for the Plan of Care as documented in the patient's medical record (CARE system for inpatient) and the InterAgency Plan of Care (W-10) according to all accrediting standards and regulatory requirements.

4.3 Facilitates the transfer of necessary documents/data with the patient to the next level of care in compliance with accrediting standards and regulatory requirements.

4.4 Educates and mentors primary care staff in referring non-complex patients for community care according to Clinical Program specifics.

4.5 Maintains complete and disciplined documentation of case management activities to promote continuity of care via the care system, MedSWIS data base, PAS log, individual working folders, etc., according to needs of Clinical Program Lines and established guidelines.

CRITERIA BASED JOB DESCRIPTION AND PERFORMANCE APPRAISAL

Please place the appropriate rating 0-4 in each of the boxes below.

5.0 Establishes a system for coordinating the caseload patient's care throughout the entire continuum of care, spanning each geographical area in which care is provided.

Weight
30 Points

5.1 Establishes a means of communicating and collaborating with the patient/family, physicians, other team members, payors, and administrators.

5.2 Identifies the need for, arranges for, and attends or conducts health care team meetings when necessary to facilitate the coordination of complex services and resources.

5.3 Demonstrates a thorough understanding of patients' financial resources for meeting health care needs (insurance reimbursement, managed care plans, entitlement programs, and personal resources).

5.4 Seeks and provides interdisciplinary, peer consultation about cases that are presenting problems and/or experiencing significant deviations from the plan of care.

5.5 Participates in regular peer review regarding the management of the caseload.

5.6 Promotes the empowered functioning of the primary care staff.

5.7 Coordinates assessments and evaluations by professionals external to the organization, but legitimate to the individual case management process according to established guidelines.

5.8 Demonstrates the ability to manage a caseload effectively.

5.9 Manages each patient's transition through the system and transfers accountability to the appropriate person or agency upon discharge from the Case Management service according to established policies/guidelines.

CRITERIA BASED JOB DESCRIPTION AND PERFORMANCE APPRAISAL

Please place the appropriate rating 0-4 in each of the boxes below.

6.0 Monitors and evaluates the effects of case management on the targeted patient population.

Weight 30 Points

6.1 Establishes methods for tracking patient's progress through the health care systems within each episode of care along the continuum.

6.2 Explores strategies to reduce length of stay and resource consumption within the case-managed patient populations, implements them, and documents the results.

6.3 In conjunction with the patient and health care team, evaluates the effectiveness of the plan in meeting the established care goals.

6.4 In conjunction with the patient and health care team, revises the plan as needed to reflect changing needs, issues, and goals.

6.5 Participates in Quality Improvement and evaluation processes with particular emphasis on the JCAHO Continuum Care Function.

6.6 Concurrently analyzes variations (patient, system, and clinical) from expected pathway/outcomes to determine needed action for case managed patients. Actions may be consultation, referral, or direct intervention.

6.7 Assures utilization compliance with all managed care contracts/programs obtaining necessary authorizations as needed according to established guidelines.

6.8 Promotes outcomes management by interdisciplinary analysis of specific demographic, clinical, financial, and satisfaction data points for patient populations in clinical program lines.

6.9 Recommends improvement/changes in practice within Clinical Program Lines based on analysis of outcome data.

CRITERIA BASED JOB DESCRIPTION AND PERFORMANCE APPRAISAL

Please place the appropriate rating 0-4 in each of the boxes below.

7.0	Provides leadership by enhancing understanding of the integrated case management process throughout the Saint Francis Hospital System.	Weight 30 Points
7.1	Recognizes patient's rights by providing for confidentiality of patient information according to established policy and accepted professional standards.	
7.2	Engenders confidence of patients, families, staff and community through appearance and behavior, and by serving as a positive role model.	
7.3	Collaborates in establishing and maintaining Clinical Program goals, objectives, and evaluating progress toward their attainment.	
7.4	Serves as a liaison for the patient, physician, and health care team to implement processing of the patient throughout the system.	
7.5	Demonstrates a commitment to the Shared Leadership philosophy of the Saint Francis Hospital System by participation and leadership in the council structure.	
7.6	Attends all mandatory hospital-initiated training.	
7.7	Recognizes the value of continued professional growth in case management by demonstrated significant continuing education in this evolving specialty; documents same according to established policy.	
7.8	Reviews pertinent literature about case types managed and shares with peers and colleagues as needed.	
7.9	Contributes to the interdisciplinary process by sharing respective theoretical knowledge as it influences the case-managed populations.	
7.10	Demonstrates flexibility and creativity in identifying resources to meet patient/family needs.	
7.11	Demonstrates a commitment to the Case Management Team by a supportive and helping attitude and participating in coverage during long, short, and unexpected absences of self and other Case Managers.	
7.12	Assists patients and families to deal with the emotional issues of illness as they move within the continuum.	
7.13	Demonstrates the ethics of care, contact, and compassion in all patient and family interactions.	
7.14	Promotes professional image by adhering to the established dress code of the hospital system and wearing the name badge as evidenced by Manager's observation.	

2. Dekalb Memorial Hospital
Auburn, Indiana

JOB DESCRIPTION: Director, Patient Care Services
REPORTS TO: President
REVISED: March 7, 1996

The Director of Patient Care Services is responsible for overall coordination of Patient Care Services, direct management of nursing services division, including the clinical practice of nursing, the Social Services Department and Hospital-wide Quality Review Program activities; including state and federal Medicare/Medicaid regulatory programs and accreditation programs.

Through her leadership as senior Nursing Division Executive, she shall guide and direct the division toward the goal of meeting or exceeding the expectation of the patients utilizing the services of her division.

She shall likewise be accountable for upholding the hospital values of treating each person, patients, visitors, and other staff members with courtesy, dignity, and respect at all times.

The Director of Patient Care Services functions as a member of executive management, facilitating effective, efficient, and safe patient care services.

The Director of Patient Care Services provides leadership and direction to areas under her direction, ensuring the development, implementation, and evaluation of policies, programs, and services consistent with the mission, goals, and objectives of DeKalb Memorial Hospital.

The Director of Patient Care Services is delegated authority and is accountable for overseeing hospital attainment and adherence to Federal and State standards for hospital operations, with the exception of compliance with State and Federal laws as they relate to Financial matters.

She is also responsible for overseeing hospital compliance with standards as set forth by Joint Commission of Healthcare Organizations.

Executive Vice President of SNEI. Chief Operating Officer of the subsidiary corporation.

A. Responsibilities to the Patient

1. Define and maintain standards of nursing practice within the hospital.

2. Accountable for the clinical practice of nursing.

3. Make rounds of the nursing units routinely to maintain awareness of the appropriateness of the nursing care given, the general maintenance of each unit, and to strengthen rapport with the nursing staff.

4. Direct the formulation of nursing policies and procedures, obtaining medical approval where necessary, delegating this responsibility when appropriate.

5. Investigate complaints of staff and patients promptly.

6. Provide for monitoring and evaluation of the quality of patient care on a routine basis.

B. Responsibilities to the Nursing Staff:

1. Assure the employment of competent nursing personnel sufficient to provide safe, good, quality patient care in an efficient manner.

2. Assure that unit managers and supervisors evaluate each employee's work performance annually in order to develop their potential and strengthen their weak areas.

3. Evaluate the performance of unit managers, house supervisors, assistant nursing services administrators, the director of staff development, infection control nurse, and director of home health services.

C. Social Services

1. Direct and support department personnel.

2. Assure proper organization and direction of the hospital's discharge planning program.

3. Give direction regarding the Anatomical Gift Act.

4. Evaluate the performance of the social worker.

D. Quality Review Services

1. Direct and support the Quality Review Coordinator.

2. Coordinate the Hospital Quality Review program to ensure compliance.

3. Coordinate hospital-wide efforts to maintain compliance with state, federal, and accrediting agencies.

4. Evaluate the performance of the Quality Review Coordinator.

E. Responsibilities to Medical Staff

1. Attend medical staff meetings to act as liaison between nursing and the medical staff, having no voting power.

2. Consult with the chairman of appropriate committee when changes are proposed for medical staff review and approval.

3. Refer medical problems to the appropriate committee chairmen.

4. Coordinate the Surgical Review and Quality Review and Improvement Committees.

5. Refer medical staff policies to the appropriate physician committee chairman to review, and to obtain medical staff approval on a routine basis.

6. Monitor and coordinate medical staff activities ignored to maintain JCAHO standards compliance.

F. Responsibilities to Administration

1. Direct and participate in various committees.

2. Responsible for the development and maintenance of job descriptions for all Nursing division positions, and annual evaluations of Division personnel.

3. Direct and coordinate preparation of annual operating and capital budgets of those departments reporting to her. Prepare three year projections for funds needed for Capital Expenditures for her division.

4. Review hospital policies and procedures (as regards to Patient Services).

5. Develop and assume maintenance of productivity standards as appropriate.

6. Demonstrate responsibility to the consumer by directions, ongoing monitoring, and evaluations of the Quality Review and Improvement processes of the hospital.

7. Promote good public relations between hospital and communities served.

8. Coordinate and direct activities to keep the hospital in compliance with the regulations and requirements of state, federal, and accrediting agencies.

9. Advise the President and Medical Staff, including matters of patient care and nursing services.

10. Member of the Planning Committee. Leads development of Divisional and SNEI plans; recommends to Long-Range Planning Committee.

11. Ex-officio member of the Home Health Service Advisory Board reporting Home Health Service activities to the Hospital Board on a routine basis.

12. Act on behalf of the President in his absence in regards to Disaster Plan decision-making.

13. Attend Board meetings and provide regular reports as required.

14. Development of nursing department philosophy consistent with DeKalb Memorial Hospital's mission, goals and objectives.

15. Direct and coordinate Hospital Quality Review and Improvement activities and provide reports to the Hospital Board on a routine basis.

16. Represent Hospital Philosophy and Policy to various public agencies and consumers.

G. Qualifications

1. Licensed to practice nursing in the State of Indiana.

2. **Education**: A B.S.N. is required; A Master's degree is desirable but not mandatory.

3. **Experience**: Has had a minimum of five years of recent administrative/management experience in acute care general hospital (accredited by JCAHO is preferred, but not required).

4. Member of NEIONE and IONE.

<u>H. Other</u>

1. Equipment

   • Ensure that Divisional equipment and facilities are available as needed and approved.

   • Directs evaluation of new equipment and supplies for planning purposes.

   • Evaluate requests of Division for new equipment and major recommendations regarding the same.

2. Environment

   • Delegates to the unit managers the responsibility for maintaining the physical properties of each unit in regard to safety, cleanliness, and the promotion of a pleasant environment, regarding Human Resources staffing, management, and evaluation.

3. Reports and is accountable directly to the President.

3. GranCare
Novato, California

REGIONAL CASE MANAGER

JOB SUMMARY:

The role and responsibilities of this position will directly contribute to the creation of Patient Care Delivery Systems: a planned process which involves services coordination, monitoring, and management to achieve quality clinical outcomes, patient, physician, payor satisfaction, and the cost effective utilization of resources. Maintenance and enhancement of payor relationships.

Qualifications:

☐ Professional Licensure (R.N., L.V.N., M.S.W., L.C.S.W., Therapist) or related experience to assess clinical and psychosocial needs and interface with professional staff, both external and internal.

☐ Current certification in Case Management (or within 6 months of date of hire).

☐ Excellent clinical and assessment skills.

☐ Effective educator skills.

☐ Previous experience in marketing, presentation, or sales.

☐ Excellent written and oral communication skills.

☐ Effective crisis management skills.

☐ Effective team leadership skills.

☐ Knowledge of payment/reimbursement systems.

☐ Knowledge of patient rights and commitment to patient advocacy.

☐ Ability to collect and analyze data.

☐ Understanding of claims submission process.

☐ Word processing skills.

☐ Network access to community, state, and national resources and health services organizations.

☐ Knowledge of State and Federal regulations related to admissions and discharge planning for skilled nursing facilities and home health.

Duties:

- ☐ Provide training for the Director of Admissions.
- ☐ Monitor and manage Care Delivery Systems and clinical effectiveness from pre-admission to discharge.
- ☐ Maintain balance between cost effectiveness of care delivery systems and quality.
- ☐ Participate in strategic market cluster planning process and its implementation.
- ☐ On-site patient assessment training program.
- ☐ Development of reliable reporting systems to referral source, patient, family, physicians, payor sources, insurance/plan case manager, and corporate office.
- ☐ Monitor Interdisciplinary Care Team Conferences for the case managed patients.
- ☐ Liaison to community resources to facilitate access for the patient.
- ☐ Managed Care contract negotiations, development, and procurement.
- ☐ Development of in-services for presentations to Health Plans, Medical Groups/IPA, Employer Groups, Insurance Companies, Hospitals, etc.
- ☐ Negotiate and/or review all out-of-contact agreements.
- ☐ Assist in the recruitment, of Cluster Market and Facility Based Case Managers.
- ☐ Manage Cluster Market and Facility Based Case Managers.
- ☐ Facilitate the development of information/communications systems between facility departments (Nursing, Business Office, Admissions) to include inquiry traffic, screening evaluations, patient cost analysis, etc.
- ☐ Assist in the development and implementation of outcome measurement programs.

DIRECTOR OF CASE MANAGEMENT

Organizational Relationship:

❏ Matrix relationship to Director of Subacute Services, Pharmacy, Home Health.

❏ Provides support and resources to Directors of Operations.

JOB SUMMARY:

The Director of Case Management is responsible for overseeing the implementation of the Case Management Program throughout the GranCare regional markets. He/She works in conjunction with corporate staff to coordinate, monitor, and manage clinical, educational, and financial systems within the integrated services delivery model. The Director of Case Management maintains and enhances relationships with referral and payor sources.

Duties:

❏ The Director of Case Management will hire/appoint Regional Directors of Case Management

❏ Set up tracking systems for payor mix, census, and patient accounts.

❏ Participate with reimbursement and finance in the development of cost accounting systems for alternate payor sources.

❏ Orients, trains, and provides resources to regional Case Managers.

❏ Participates with Directors of Community Relations in census enhancement and maintenance.

❏ Develops working relationships with Directors of Operation, Directors of Finance, Directors of Reimbursement, Directors of Community Relations, Executive Directors, Director of Nursing, Director of Subacute Services, Medical staff, and other staff members to assure support systems essential to the success of managing and utilizing patient care in a cost effective manner while maintaining and promoting quality outcomes.

❏ Participates in local, regional, and national professional organizations, associations, and conferences for the purpose of establishing a network of educational opportunities.

❏ Participates in actualizing the continuum of care in conjunction with CompuPharm, GranCare, Home Health, and other lines of business.

❏ Implements Managed Care Contracts and provides education to regional staff on contract negotiations.

GOAL AND OBJECTIVES

Accountability Measures

☐   Recruitment and training of Regional Case Managers.

☐   Develop and implement contract education and utilization plan to include:
  - ■ Written instructions and transmittals for contract execution.
  - ■ Pairing of regional GranCare staff and payor designee as contract personnel.

☐   Multi-Level In-Service Education to include:
  - ■ DOs
  - ■ EDs/DONs
  - ■ Regional Case Managers
  - ■ Facility-Based Case Managers
  - ■ Business Office Managers
  - ■ Rehabilitation Personnel

☐   Develop tracking system to differentiate payor sources at the facility level.

☐   Develop tracking system to manage census, utilization of services, and profitability.

☐   Increase managed care census by 25%.

☐   Negotiate national contracts.

FACILITY-BASED CASE MANAGER

Organizational Relationship:

☐   Reports to facility Executive Director and Regional Director of Case Management.

☐   Coordinates the facility based rehabilitation and medical services team.

☐   Serves as the facility designee for interaction with the various referral and payor sources.

Duties:

☐   Manages the contract agreement and the specific criteria as they relate to levels of care and treatment.

☐   Works with payor source (case manager, claims representative, etc.) to verify and guarantee coverage and identify all items required to process the claims.

☐   Works creatively with payor source to help explore coverage solutions (flex benefits, out of contract, etc.).

☐   Assists with facility and community education.

☐   Monitors expense versus revenue for residents on a daily basis.

☐   Maintains case monitoring/tracking system to ensure appropriate allocation of benefits.

☐   Performs on-site assessments for all potential admissions unless geographically impossible or contract has set levels and competitive timing of admission will not allow. Should be the exception rather than the rule.

☐   Meets with patient, family, and rehab team to assist in "continuity of care."

☐   Coordinates the weekly interdisciplinary team meetings and plan of treatment for managed care patients.

☐   Acts as liaison with the payor source representative.

☐   Participates in plans for discharge with social services and rehab team.

☐   Develops and maintains relationships with referral sources and other case managers.

☐   Acts as a liaison between the health care team members and referring physician, acute hospital, discharge planner, social worker, utilization review nurses, rehab case manager, clergy, etc.

☐   Participates in annual goal planning with the rehabilitation department.

☐   Communicates effectively with community and facility staff regarding services available at GranCare healthcare centers.

Managed Care Marketplace:

An assessment of the managed care marketplace should be completed as a part of a facility strategic market plan to determine managed care growth potential, opportunities, penetration, service trends, relationships, networks, etc.

Financial Assessment:

Monthly Managed Care Profitability Worksheets will be reviewed by the ED, Regional Director of Case Management, and Director of Operation to assist in determining facility trends of managed care revenues and profits. The review will address the impact of hiring a facility Case Manager on facility financials (cost to benefit analysis).

Patient Acuity and Subacute Specialty Programs:

Severity and acuity of the managed care caseload must be considered as a factor influencing staffing needs for a Case Manager. Managed Care subacute patients will require greater demands of the Case Manager's time. (Facilities seeking subacute accreditation from JCAHO are required to have facility Case Manager.)

4. The Medstat Group
Nashville, TN

Director of Clinical Outcomes Support

Position Summary

The Director of Clinical Outcomes Support is responsible for providing support of the sales force in selling Disease Staging and Outcomes Analyst related products and services. This includes assistance in the development of client sales strategies, applications, proposals, RFP's, presentations, and seminars.

Duties and Responsibilities

- Stimulate the sales of $500,000 in 3 year Outcomes Analyst and Disease Staging revenue through direct sales and marketing support.

- Participate in the design and implementation of effective sales strategies for Outcomes Analyst, Disease Staging, and Ascent Quality Management System.

- Develop and maintain a consultative support relationship with MEDSTAT sales personnel.

- Understand and be able to effectively articulate Outcomes Analyst and Disease Staging applications in the market place.

- Document applications and their value related to MEDSTAT Outcomes Analyst and Disease Staging products and services.

- Insure all Outcomes Analyst related RFPs are accurately produced and delivered on time in an impressive format.

- Help develop successful implementation plans which insure value is received.

- Participate in at least 5 qualified contacts per month with prospective and existing clients.

- Aid sales personnel in the development of an average of 2 cost justified Outcomes Analyst proposals per month with an average value of $25,000.

- Continually develop product and market knowledge.

- Develop and administer training for sales and support personnel to further their Outcomes Analyst and Disease Staging client applications.

Credentials and Attributes Required

- Minimum of 5-10 years of clinically related experience in either patient care, clinical quality, or utilization management.

- Minimum of college or university educational preparation with health care professional licensure desirable.

- Must demonstrate effective interpersonal skills, innovation, tenacious, computer familiarity, and strong oral and written communication skills.

5. Children's Hospital
Birmingham, AL

ROLE OF THE CASE MANAGER/COORDINATOR

The Ward Team case manager coordinates treatment plans for each patient on the team. The case manager attends morning report and rounds to assist with case finding and problem identification, also works with team to assist in the following areas:

1.   Discharge Planning
      a) Case Finding
      b) Problem Identification
      c) Development of plan for discharge teaching
      d) EPSDT forms completion

2.   Coordination of Care
      a) Develop with the team a hospital and discharge plan
      b) Monitor delivery of care
      c) Effective use of resources (inpatient and outpatient)
      d) Facilitate the development of care maps
      e) Liaison between team and nursing staff
      f) Home follow-up after discharge

3.   Education
      a) Residents—discharge planning process and case management
      b) Staff—RN—discharge planing process and case management
      c) Patients/Family—home care—condition specific

4.   Continuing Quality Improvement
      a) Analyze and report data variances and trends
      b) Research
      c) Facilitate resolution of identified problems at both patient and system level

Venue Utilization by Federal Regulation

Utilization by Federal Regulation

ACUTE HOSPITAL   (42 U.S. Code Sec. 1395(x)(e))

The term "hospital" is defined as an institution that:
(1) is primarily engaged in providing, by or under the supervision of physicians, to inpatients (A) diagnostic services and therapeutic services for medical diagnosis, treatment, and care of injured, disabled, or sick persons, or (B) rehabilitation services for the rehabilitation in injured, disabled, or sick persons;

ADMISSION	CONTINUING TREATMENT	DISCHARGE	REIMBURSEMENT
Cite: Peer Review Organization Manual, HCFA Pub. 19, Transmittal No. 36, §4105 Medically Necessary and Appropriate: The patient must demonstrate signs and/or symptoms severe enough to warrant the need for medical care and must receive services of such intensity that they can be furnished safely and effectively only on an inpatient basis. Principal diagnosis must have occasioned the patient's admission to the hospital.	Cite: Hospital Manual (HCFA-Pub. 10) §275 Medically Necessary and Appropriate Must be an adequate written record of the reason for continued hospitalization of the patient for medical treatment or medically required inpatient diagnostic study; the estimated period of time the patient will need to remain in the hospital; and any plans for post hospital care. Reasons for continued stays should include medical necessity as well as availability of out-of-hospital facilities and services which will assure continuity of care.	Cite: Peer Review Organization Manual (HCFA-Pub. 19) §4140 Medical Stability Inpatient care rather than outpatient care is required only if the patient's medical condition, safety or health would be significantly and directly threatened if care was provided in a less intensive setting.	Medicare: DRG Payment Medicaid: Varies by state Managed Care: Varies by Payor Indemnity: Fee for Service

LONG TERM CARE HOSPITAL (42 U.S. Code Sec. 1395(x)(e) and 42 CFR 412.23(e))

An institution that:

(1) is primarily engaged in providing, by or under the supervision of physicians, to inpatients (A) diagnostic services and therapeutic services for medical diagnosis, treatment, and care of injured, disabled, or sick persons, or (B) rehabilitation services for the rehabilitation in injured, disabled, or sick persons; **Additionally,** It must have an average length of inpatient stay greater than 25 days.

ADMISSION	CONTINUING TREATMENT	DISCHARGE	REIMBURSEMENT
Cite: Peer Review Organization Manual, HCFA Pub. 19, Transmittal No. 36, §4105 Medically Necessary and Appropriate: The patient must demonstrate signs and/or symptoms severe enough to warrant the need for medical care and must receive services of such intensity that they can be furnished safely and effectively only on an inpatient basis. Principal diagnosis must have occasioned the patient's admission to the hospital. Must be an anticipation that based on patient's condition, length of stay will be greater than 25 days.	Cite: Hospital Manual (HCFA-Pub. 10) §275 Medically Necessary and Appropriate Must be an adequate written record of the reason for continued hospitalization of the patient for medical treatment or medically required inpatient diagnostic study; the estimated period of time the patient will need to remain in the hospital; and any plans for post hospital care. Reasons for continued stays should include medical necessity as well as availability of out-of-hospital facilities and services which will assure continuity of care.	Cite: Peer Review Organization Manual (HCFA-Pub. 19) §4140 Medical Stability Inpatient care rather than outpatient care is required only if the patient's medical condition, safety or health would be significantly and directly threatened if care was provided in a less intensive setting.	Medicare: PPS-exempt, Cost-based subject to TEFRA limit. Medicaid: Varies by state Managed Care: Varies by Payor Indemnity: Fee for Service

ACUTE REHABILITATION HOSPITAL or UNIT   (42 CFR 412.23(d) and 42 CFR   412.29)

A hospital or distinct-part unit which serves an inpatient population of whom at least 75 percent required intensive rehabilitation services for the treatment of one or more of the following conditions:

I.   stroke
II.   spinal cord injury
III. congenital deformity
IV.   amputation
V.   major multiple trauma
VI.   Fracture of femur (hip fracture)
VII. brain injury
VIII. polyarthritis, including rheumatoid arthritis
IX.   neurological disorders, including multiple sclerosis, motor neuron diseases, polyneuropathy, muscular dystrophy, and Parkinson's disease.
X.   burns

ADMISSION	CONTINUING TREATMENT	DISCHARGE	REIMBURSEMENT
Cite: Hospital Manual (HCFA-Pub. 10) §211. Must have pre-admission screening procedure under which each prospective patient's condition and medical history are reviewed to determine whether the patient is likely to benefit significantly from an intensive inpatient hospital program or assessment.	Cite: Hospital Manual (HCFA-Pub. 10) §211. Patient's condition must require the 24-hour availability of a physician with special training or experience in the field of rehabilitation. Patient requires the 24-hour availability of a registered nurse with specialized training or experience in rehabilitation. Patient must require and receive at least 3 hours a day of physical and/or occupational therapy.	Cite: Hospital Manual (HCFA-Pub. 10) §211. Discharge is appropriate when further progress toward the established rehabilitation goal is unlikely or it can be achieved in a less intensive setting.	Medicare: PPS-exempt, Cost-based subject to TEFRA limit. Medicaid: Varies by state Managed Care: Varies by Payor Indemnity: Fee for Service

PSYCHIATRIC HOSPITAL   (42 CFR §482.60)

A facility that meets all the requirements applicable to general hospitals, and is primarily engaged in providing by or under the supervision of a psychiatrist, psychiatric services for the diagnosis and treatment of mentally ill persons.

ADMISSION	CONTINUING TREATMENT	DISCHARGE	REIMBURSEMENT
Cite: State Operations Manual (HCFA-Pub. 7) §3106. The psychiatric principal diagnosis must be one contained in the Third Edition of the American Psychiatric Association Diagnostic and Statistical Manual, or in Chapter 5 (`Mental Disorders') of the International Classification of Diseases, Ninth Revision, Clinical Modification. There must be a need for active treatment, of an intensity that can be provided only in an inpatient hospital setting. A psychiatric evaluation must be completed within 60 hours of admission	Cite: State Operations Manual (HCFA-Pub. 7) §3106. Each patient must have a comprehensive treatment plan based on an inventory of his/her strengths and disabilities; and includes a substantiated diagnosis, short-term and long-term goals, specific treatment modalities, responsibilities of each member of the treatment team, and documentation which justifies the diagnosis and treatment and all active therapeutic efforts. Physician progress notes frequency are based on the condition of the patient, but they must be recorded at least weekly for the first 2 months, and at least monthly thereafter.	Cite: State Operations Manual (HCFA-Pub. 7) §3106. Patient no longer requires an inpatient level of care. The record of each discharged patient must have a discharge summary that must include a recapitulation of the patient's hospitalization in the unit, recommendations from appropriate services concerning follow-up or aftercare, and a brief summary of the patient's condition on discharge.	Medicare: PPS-exempt, Cost-based subject to TEFRA limit. Medicaid: Varies by state Managed Care: Varies by Payor Indemnity: Fee for Service

SKILLED NURSING FACILITY   (42 U.S.C. 1395x(j))

A freestanding facility or distinct part of an institution which has in effect a transfer agreement with one or more participating hospitals and that:
(1) is primarily engaged in providing to residents (A) skilled nursing care and related services for patients who require medical or nursing care, or (B) rehabilitation services for the rehabilitation of injured, disabled, or sick persons

ADMISSION	CONTINUING TREATMENT	DISCHARGE	REIMBURSEMENT.
Cite: Skilled Nursing Facility Manual (HCFA-Pub. 12) §212. Patient must have been an inpatient of a hospital for a medically necessary stay of at least 3 consecutive calendar days. In addition, the patient must have been transferred to a participating skilled nursing facility within 30 days after discharge from the hospital, unless there is a Medical Appropriateness Exception. Post hospital extended care services were required on an inpatient basis because of the patient's need on a daily basis, for skilled nursing or rehabilitation services, for either a condition for which he/she received inpatient hospital services prior to the transfer to the SNF. or for a condition which arose after transfer while he/she was still in the SNF for treatment of a condition for which he/she received inpatient hospital services.	Cite: Skilled Nursing Facility Manual (HCFA-Pub. 12) §220.3 Physician certification (of the conditions listed under admission) must be obtained at the time of admission, or as soon thereafter as is reasonable and practicable. Recertification must contain an adequate written record of the reasons for continued need for extended care services, the estimated period of time the patient will need to remain in the facility and any plans, where appropriate, for home care. Where the requirements for the second or subsequent recertification are satisfied by review of a stay of extended duration, pursuant to the utilization review (UR) plan, a separate recertification statement is not required.	Cite: Skilled Nursing Facility Manual (HCFA-Pub. 12) §220 Physician documents that the patient does not need, on a daily basis, skilled nursing or rehabilitation services for a condition for which he/she received inpatient hospital services.	Medicare: Routine service capped at published rate, with differential between hospital-based and freestanding. Ancillary services reimbursed on a reasonable cost basis. Medicaid: Varies by state. Managed Care: Varies by payor, typically on a per diem. Indemnity: Fee for service.

PARTIAL HOSPITILIZATION SERVICES (42 U.S.C. §1395(x)(ff)

Items and services described in (1) below, prescribed by a physician and provided under a program described in (2) below, under the supervision of a physician pursuant to an individualized, written plan of treatment established and periodically reviewed by a physician (in consultation with appropriate staff participating in such program), which plan sets forth the physician's diagnosis, the type, amount, frequency, and duration of the items and services provided under the plan, and the goals for treatment under the plan.

(1) The items and services described in this paragraph are—

- Individual and group therapy with physicians or psychologists (or other mental health professionals to the extent authorized under State law),
- occupational therapy requiring the skills of a qualified occupational therapist,
- services of social workers, trained psychiatric nurses, and other staff trained to work with psychiatric patients,
- drugs and biologicals furnished for therapeutic purposes (which cannot, as determined in accordance with regulation, be self administered),
- individualized activity therapies that are not primarily recreational or diversionary,
- family counseling (the primary purpose of which is treatment of the individual's condition,
- patient training and education (to the extent, that training and educational activities are closely and clearly related to the individual's care and treatment),
- diagnostic services, and
- such other items and services as the Secretary may provide (but in no event to include meals and transportation).

(2) A program described in this paragraph is a program which is furnished by a hospital to its outpatients or by a community mental health center, and which is a distinct and organized intensive ambulatory treatment service offering less than 24-hours-daily care.

ADMISSION	CONTINUING TREATMENT	DISCHARGE	REIMBURSEMENT
Cite: Partial Hospitalization Coverage., Program Memorandum (Intermediaries), June 01, 1995 Services must be reasonable and necessary for the diagnosis or active treatment of the individuals' condition. They must also be reasonably expected to improve or maintain the individual's condition and functional level and to prevent relapse or hospitalization. Partial Hospitalization may occur in lieu of either: Admission to an inpatient hospital; or A continued inpatient hospitalization. A partial hospitalization program is an appropriate level of active treatment intervention for individuals who: - Are likely to benefit from a coordinated program of services and require more than isolated sessions of outpatient treatment. Partial hospitalization is the level of intervention that falls between inpatient hospitalization and episodic treatment on the continuum of care for the mentally ill; - Do not require 24-hour care and have an adequate support system outside the hospital setting while not actively engaged in the program. - Have a diagnosis that falls within the range of ICD-9 codes for metal illness (i.e., 290 through 319). However, the diagnosis in itself is not the sole determining factor for coverage; and - Are not judged to be dangerous to self or others.	Cite: Partial Hospitalization Coverage., Program Memorandum (Intermediaries), June 01, 1995 Physician must certify that the conditions for admission to the program still exist, and that the treatment still remains reasonable and necessary.	Cite: Partial Hospitalization Coverage., Program Memorandum (Intermediaries), June 01, 1995 Treatment may continue until the patient has improved sufficiently to be maintained in the outpatient or office setting on a less intense and less frequent basis.	Medicare: Covered on a reasonable cost basis only if the individual would otherwise require inpatient psychiatric care. The 62 _ payment limitation does not apply to services that are not directly provided by a physician. Medicaid: Varies by state. Managed Care: Varies by payor Indemnity: Fee for service.

HOME HEALTH SERVICES (42 U.S.C. §1395X(M))

A public agency or private organization, or a subdivision of such an agency or organization, that:
(1) is primarily engaged in providing skilled nursing services and other therapeutic services;
(2) has polices established by a professional group associated with the agency or organization (including at least one physician and at least one registered professional nurse) to govern the services, and provide for supervision of such services by a physician or a registered professional nurse;

ADMISSION	CONTINUING TREATMENT	DISCHARGE	REIMBURSEMENT
Cite: Home Health Agency Manual (HCFA-Pub. 11) §204.1 Physician certification that patient is confined to the home, and that it is the patient's residence.	Cite: Home Health Agency Manual (HCFA-Pub. 11) §204.2 Treatment must be based on Plan of Care which specifies: Diagnoses, Patient's mental status, types of services, supplies and equipment required, frequency of visits to be made, prognosis, rehabilitation potential, functional limitations, activities permitted, nutritional requirements, all medications, safety measures to protect against injury, instructions for timely discharge or referral. Plan of care review required every 62 days.	Cite: Home Health Agency Manual (HCFA-Pub. 11) §204.2 Plan of care is considered to be terminated if the patient does not receive at least one covered skilled nursing, physical therapy, speech-language pathology service, or occupational therapy visit in a 62-day period, unless physician documents that the interval without such care is appropriate to the treatment of the patient's illness or injury.	Medicare: Reasonable costs subject to predetermined limits Medicaid: Varies by state Managed Care: Varies by payor Indemnity: Fee for service

COMPREHENSIVE OUTPATIENT REHABILITATION FACILITY (42 CFR 485.50)

A non-residential public or private facility that:

(1) is exclusively engaged in providing, under a physician's direction, diagnostic, therapeutic, and restorative services to outpatients for the rehabilitation of injured, disabled, or sick persons, at a single fixed location;

(2) provides, at least, the following services: (a) physician's services (rendered by physicians who are available at the facility on a full-time or part-time basis), (b) physical therapy, and (c) social or psychological services;

ADMISSION	CONTINUING TREATMENT	DISCHARGE	REIMBURSEMENT
Cite: Medicare Intermediary Manual, Part 3 (HCFA-Pub. 13-3) §3903 Patient is under the care of a physician, and was referred by the physician certifying that the individual needs skilled rehabilitation services. Written plan of treatment must be established and signed by a physician which prescribes the type, amount, frequency, and duration of the services to be furnished, and indicates the diagnosis and anticipated specific rehabilitation goals; and is reasonable and necessary in relation to the patient's rehabilitation potential and progress.	Cite: Medicare Intermediary Manual, Part 3 (HCFA-Pub. 13-3) §3903 Recertification every 60 days which includes treatment rendered, a description of the progress the patient is making toward attaining the rehabilitation goals, and the results of both subjective and objective tests and measures as compared to the initial or prior evaluation results, and a statement by the physician why treatment should be continued if progress is not being made.	Cite: Outpatient Physical Therapy Provider Manual (HCFA-Pub 9) §402 When the patient has reached a point where no further progress is being made toward one or more of the goals outlined in the plan of treatment, Medicare coverage ends with respect to that aspect of the plan of treatment.	Medicare: Reasonable Cost Basis - Lesser of Cost-to-Charge does not apply. Medicaid: Varies by state. Managed Care: Varies by payor. Indemnity: Fee for Service.

REHABILITATION AGENCY   (42 CFR §405.1702(i))

A "rehabilitation agency" (with respect to determining its qualifications as a provider of outpatient physical therapy and/or speech pathology services) is an agency that provides an integrated multidisciplinary program designed to upgrade the physical function of handicapped disabled individuals by bringing together as a team specialized rehabilitation personnel. At a minimum, a rehabilitation agency must provide physical therapy or speech pathology services and a rehabilitation program that, in addition to physical therapy or speech pathology services, includes social or vocational adjustment services

ADMISSION	CONTINUING TREATMENT	DISCHARGE	REIMBURSEMENT
Cite: Medicare Manual §3148.2 Patient must be under the care of a physician who certifies the need for the service. A plan of treatment must be established before treatment is begun. A plan must relate the type, amount, frequency, and duration of the physical therapy, occupational therapy, or speech pathology services that are to be furnished the patient and indicate the diagnosis and anticipated goals.	Cite: Medicare Manual §3148.2 The plan must be reviewed by the attending physician, in consultation with the physical therapist(s), occupational therapist(s), or speech pathologist(s) of the provider, at such intervals as the severity of the patient's condition requires, but at least every 30 days.	Cite: Peer Review Organization Manual (HCFA-Pub. 19) Exhibit 5.5 Goals have been met. Discharge plan should address discharge and follow-up care.	Medicare: Reasonable Costs Medicaid: Varies by state Managed Care: Varies by payor Indemnity: Fee for Service

CLINIC   (42 CFR §405.1702(b))

A "clinic" (with respect to determining its qualifications as a provider of outpatient physical therapy and/or speech pathology services) is a facility established primarily for the provision of outpatient physicians' services. To meet this definition, an organization must meet the following test of physician participation: (a) the medical services of the clinic are provided by a group of more than two physicians practicing medicine together, and (b) a physician is present in the clinic at all times during hours of operation to perform medical services (rather than administrative services only).

ADMISSION	CONTINUING TREATMENT	DISCHARGE	REIMBURSEMENT
Cite: Medicare Manual §3148.2 Patient must be under the care of a physician who certifies the need for the service. A plan of treatment must be established before treatment is begun. A plan must relate the type, amount, frequency, and duration of the physical therapy, occupational therapy, or speech pathology services that are to be furnished the patient and indicate the diagnosis and anticipated goals.	Cite: Medicare Manual §3148.2 The plan must be reviewed by the attending physician, in consultation with the physical therapist(s), occupational therapist(s), or speech pathologist(s) of the provider, at such intervals as the severity of the patient's condition requires, but at least every 30 days.	Cite: Peer Review Organization Manual (HCFA-Pub. 19) Exhibit 5.5 Goals have been met. Discharge plan should address discharge and follow-up care.	Medicare: Reasonable Costs Medicaid: Varies by state Managed Care: Varies by payor Indemnity: Fee for Service

PUBLIC HEALTH AGENCY   (42 CFR §405.1702(h))

A "public health agency" (with respect to determining its qualifications as a provider of outpatient therapy and/or speech pathology services) is an official agency established by a state or local government, the primary function of which is to maintain the health of the population served by performing environmental health services, preventive medical services, and, in certain cases, therapeutic services.

ADMISSION	CONTINUING TREATMENT	DISCHARGE	REIMBURSEMENT
Cite: Medicare Manual §3148.2 Patient must be under the care of a physician who certifies the need for the service. A plan of treatment must be established before treatment is begun. A plan must relate the type, amount, frequency, and duration of the physical therapy, occupational therapy, or speech pathology services that are to be furnished the patient and indicate the diagnosis and anticipated goals.	Cite: Medicare Manual §3148.2 The plan must be reviewed by the attending physician, in consultation with the physical therapist(s), occupational therapist(s), or speech pathologist(s) of the provider, at such intervals as the severity of the patient's condition requires, but at least every 30 days.	Cite: Peer Review Organization Manual (HCFA-Pub. 19) Exhibit 5.5 Goals have been met. Discharge plan should address discharge and follow-up care.	Medicare: Reasonable Costs Medicaid: Varies by state Managed Care: Varies by payor Indemnity: Fee for Service

MEDICAL DAY HOSPITAL
See Comprehensive Outpatient Rehabilitation Facility

ADMISSION	CONTINUING TREATMENT	DISCHARGE	REIMBURSEMENT
Cite: Medicare Intermediary Manual, Part 3 (HCFA-Pub. 13-3) §3903 Patient is under the care of a physician, and was referred by the physician certifying that the individual needs skilled rehabilitation services. Written plan of treatment must be established and signed by a physician which prescribes the type, amount, frequency, and duration of the services to be furnished, and indicates the diagnosis and anticipated specific rehabilitation goals; and is reasonable and necessary in relation to the patient's rehabilitation potential and progress.	Cite: Medicare Intermediary Manual, Part 3 (HCFA-Pub. 13-3) §3903 Recertification every 60 days which includes treatment rendered, a description of the progress the patient is making toward attaining the rehabilitation goals, and the results of both subjective and objective tests and measures as compared to the initial or prior evaluation results, and a statement by the physician why treatment should be continued if progress is not being made.	Cite: Outpatient Physical Therapy Provider Manual (HCFA-Pub 9) §402 When the patient has reached a point where no further progress is being made toward one or more of the goals outlined in the plan of treatment, Medicare coverage ends with respect to that aspect of the plan of treatment.	Medicare: Reasonable Cost Basis - Lesser of Cost-to-Charge does not apply. Medicaid: Varies by state. Managed Care: Varies by payor. Indemnity: Fee for Service.

AMBULATORY SURGERY (42 CFR §416.2)
The term "ambulatory surgical center" is a distinct entity that:

(1) operates exclusively for the purpose of providing surgical services to patients not requiring hospitalization;
(2) has an agreement with HCFA under Medicare to participate as an ASC; and
(3) meets the prescribed conditions for coverage.

ADMISSION	CONTINUING TREATMENT	DISCHARGE	REIMBURSEMENT
Cite: Peer Review Organization Manual, (HCFA Pub. 19, Transmittal No. 36) §4410 Medical Necessity and appropriateness Medicare: Only procedures which appear on the Ambulatory Surgery Case list may be performed in this setting.	Cite: Peer Review Organization Manual, (HCFA Pub. 19, Transmittal No. 36) §4410 Medical Necessity and Appropriateness Medicare: Ancillary services may be performed in conjunction with the ambulatory surgery procedure, where appropriate.	Cite: Peer Review Organization Manual (HCFA-Pub. 19) Exhibit 5-6 Post-operative care must be given prior to discharge. Discharge plan should reflect appropriate transition of care and plan including patient education and provision for follow-up care. Adequate patient education is defined as provision of appropriate teaching or transmission of pertinent information to meet the patient's needs, including any necessary postoperative instructions.	Medicare: Payment based on prospectively determined rate by procedure. Surgery procedure listings are grouped by body system, as follows: - Integumentary System - Musculoskeletal System - Respiratory System - Cardiovascular System - Hemic and Lymphatic Systems - Digestive System - Urinary System - Genital System - Endocrine System - Nervous System - Eye and Ocular Adnexa -Auditory System Medicaid: Varies by state Managed Care: Varies by payor Indemnity: Fee for Service

Venue Utilization by Federal Regulation

HOSPICE PROGRAMS (42 CFR §418.50)

A public agency, private organization, or a subdivision of either, that is primarily engaged in providing care to the terminally ill (individuals with a life expectancy of six months or less). The hospice must be primarily engaged in providing "core" services, including nursing services, medical social services, physician services, and counseling services.

ADMISSION	CONTINUING TREATMENT	DISCHARGE	REIMBURSEMENT
Cite: Medicare: Hospice Manual §201 Patient must be certified as being terminally ill, and make an election for Hospice Care. An individual is considered terminally ill if the individual has a medical prognosis that his/her life expectancy is 6 months or less if the terminal illness runs its normal course.	Cite: Medicare: Hospice Manual §201 After first 90 day period must procure written certification statement prepared by the medical director of the hospice or the physician member of the hospice's interdisciplinary group. Certification must include (1) the statement the individual's medical prognosis is that his/her life expectancy is 6 months or less if the terminal illness runs its normal course and (2) the signature of the physician.	Patient may elect not to continue Hospice care.	Medicare: Prospectively determined per diem limits, adjusted by region, grouped as follows: - Routine home care - Continuous home care - General inpatient care - Inpatient respite care Medicaid: Varies by state Managed Care: Varies by payor Indemnity: Fee for service

INDEX

ABOUT THE AUTHORS

Cherilyn G. Murer, J.D., C.R.A., is president and CEO of the Murer Group, a legal-based consulting firm that represents networks, multi-site health systems, and hospitals in 42 states, Canada, and Europe. She has been an advocate of a full continuum of care and a pioneer developer of alternative venues with an emphasis on postacute facilities. Ms. Murer received her Juris Doctorate degree with honors from Northern Illinois University and has coupled her background in law with her previous hands-on experience as director of rehabilitation medicine at Northwestern Memorial Hospital, Chicago, Illinois, and as administrator of one of the first CORFs in the United States. American Express recognized her leadership and outstanding accomplishments in its May 1994 "Preview" publication, in which they described Ms. Murer as "a healthcare pioneer who has been a leader in helping healthcare providers find cost-effective procedures without reducing the quality of care."

An innovator, she has written over one hundred articles; serves on the editorial advisory boards of Aspen Publishing and *Rehab Management, Case Review,* and *Continuing Care* magazines; and is a featured columnist for *Rehab Management.* A sought-after lecturer, she has keynoted national conventions, including the Case Management Convention in 1996, and lectured on American healthcare management techniques to audiences in Amsterdam, Budapest, Edmonton, Taipei, and Utrecht. A trusted advisor, she has received appointments from former Vice President Walter Mondale, Senator Robert Dole, and then–Vice President George Bush.

Lyndean Lenhoff Brick, J.D., is senior vice president with the Murer Group. She has been a driving force in the development of long term care hospitals and subacute care facilities throughout the United States. An innovator in her own right, she has authored numerous articles on systems, trends, and developmental issues. A frequent lecturer, she has addressed conventions and special interest groups, and has been a prime speaker for the McGraw-Hill Healthcare Education Group. Her operational experience has included administration of both inpatient and outpatient rehabilitation facilities in both the United States and Canada. Advocating corporate structuring integrity, regulatory compliance, and reimbursement optimizations, Ms. Brick often conducts due diligence investigations for venture capital firms.

Active in the international business of Murer Consultants, Ms. Brick has initiated and performed engagements with German and Swiss pharmaceutical companies and DME companies in Germany, Switzerland, France, and Spain. She has been instrumental in facilitating the entry of American companies into Europe and German companies into the United States.